Hog's Head Conversations

Essays on Harry Potter

Travis Prinzi
editor

Hog's Head Conversations
Copyright © 2009 Zossima Press
Allentown, PA

Zossima Press titles may be purchased for business or promotional use or special sales.

Cover artwork by Michael Politakis
Cover layout by Red Hen Productions

10-9-8-7-6-5-4-3-2-1

**Zossima
Press**

ISBN 0-9822385-8-4
ISBN-13 978-0-9822385-8-5

Table of Contents

Introduction

"You get a lot of funny folk in the Hog's Head."

~ Rubeus Hagrid

Two years after J.K. Rowling wrote about the boy wizard Harry Potter and his defeat of the evil Lord Voldemort, conversation about the stories has not died down in the slightest. All around the world, *Harry Potter* conferences are gathering hundreds of attendees. Academic papers, panel discussions, artwork, wizard rock, and all sorts of other creative endeavors are contributing to the ongoing discussion. Fan sites and weblogs continue to enjoy and analyze the series. *Harry Potter* courses are found on college and university campuses everywhere. Despite early predictions that this would just be a passing fad, Rowling's 7-book saga continues to delight and to fascinate.

Gathered together here are some of the best of the ongoing conversations on *Harry Potter*. While categorized into five different types of conversations there are, broadly speaking, two types of essays in this book: those explaining why this series is great literature, and those representative of the kinds of conversations happening in today's world of literature. The first three sections contain essays of the former kind, while the last two contain essays of the latter.

The two essays in "Conversations on Literary Value" defend *Harry Potter* as great literature. Colin Manlove, whose expert analysis on fantasy fiction has been published since 1975, lends a credible and seasoned voice to the chorus of critics who find great literary themes in Rowling's saga in his essay "The Literary Value of the *Harry Potter* Books." In "Repotting *Harry Potter*," James W. Thomas, a university literature professor for over 30 years, takes on the negative critics and argues that the "7-part book" is "legit lit," deserving a place in the Great Books canon.

The section titled "Conversations on Eternal Truth" examines how Rowling's stories interact with deeper matters of reality. John Granger's essay, "The *Deathly Hallows* Epigraphs," analyzes the two quotations that preface the final *Potter* book, *Deathly Hallows* -- quotations which Rowling said "sum up" the theme of her series. Danielle Tumminio, whose class on *Harry Potter* and Christian theology at Yale was featured at CNN.com, reflects in "God and *Harry Potter* at Yale" on how the *Potter* books have opened up conversations about God and faith.

"Conversations on Imagination" considers the appeal and power of imaginative fiction. Amy H. Sturgis, Tolkien expert, explores in "When Harry Met Faërie" how Tolkien's rejection of the false dichotomy of children's versus adult literature opens up the door for readers of all ages to enjoy the gifts of the true fairy tale. My own essay, "The Well-Ordered Mind," explores how Rowling's series embraces a moral imagination, making it literature that instructs in and inspires the striving toward right order in the soul and in society.

"Conversations on Literary Criticism" gives two examples of how different types of literary critics might approach the *Harry Potter* series. Ryan Kerr's essay, "Tom Riddle's Diary," explores the different ways we read books by looking at how characters interact with young Voldemort's journal. In "If J.K. Rowling Says Dumbledore is Gay, is He Gay?", Karen Kebarle explores how an intentionalist – one who believes an author's intentions are the key to a text's meaning – responds when Rowling's interpretation of her own text does not seem to fit the text itself.

"Conversations on Characters" explores the First Couple of the *Harry Potter* series – Harry and Ginny. Gwendolyn Limbach's essay, "Ginny Weasley – Girl Next Doormat?", takes a feminist approach to the youngest Weasley, arguing that a very strong female character was forced into a diminutive role because of Harry's need to be the male hero. Dave Jones's essay, "Interpret Your Findings Correctly," takes a look at the way Rowling wove together her key theme – choice – and three magical devices in the process of Harry's personal development.

A wide variety of conversations take place at The Hog's Head. These ten are not the final word on any of these subjects, nor does its editor agree with everything in them. The contributors may not always agree with each other, but that's the nature of conversation at The Hog's Head, where a variety of voices – "a lot of funny folk," as Hagrid would say – come together to enjoy

Rowling's saga. These are the kinds of conversations happening all around the world about the beloved *Potter* tales, and they are all essays which serve to further that discussion.

So pull up a barstool. Aberforth will pour you the drink of your choosing, and let's talk *Potter*.

~ Travis Prinzi, editor

www.thehogshead.org

Part I

Conversations on Literary Value

Chapter One

The Literary Value of the *Harry Potter* Books

Colin Manlove

Now that the world of the *Harry Potter* books has, with the appearance of *The Deathly Hallows,* been at once ended and finally brought into being, it seems right to speak not only of their plots but of their enduring characteristics – characteristics of their moral vision, of wizardry, of the invented world, of their various debts to books before them, and most of all of their style and their literary worth.

ANALYSIS OF EVIL: LORD VOLDEMORT

Let us start then, at the wrong end, with the evil wizard, Lord Voldemort. No simple villain he, though he would like to believe so. Child of the handsome Riddle and the downtrodden witch Merope, the former of whom repudiates him while the latter dies, poor Tom starts life in an orphanage. The likeness to the story of *Oliver Twist* is strong, and the contrasts no less striking. For like Oliver, Tom is rescued from his wretched life by a benign old gentleman who perceives his hidden worth. Unlike Mr. Brownlow, who is soon led to think ill of Oliver, Dumbledore's protégé seems at first all he could have hoped, becoming a star pupil and eventual head boy at Hogwarts School. Both stories involve the release of hidden powers – in the case of *Oliver Twist*, a power for good, in that of Tom Riddle a more intellectual gift for wizardry which can be turned to good or ill. Dumbledore perceives a nasty side of Riddle, but we are to suppose that he believes this to come from the frustration of his abilities. The headmaster, like all headmasters, admits many potentially evil people into his school, particularly the ambitious Slytherins, in the hope that growing knowledge will be married to developing citizenhood. But in Riddle this trust finds its limits, and the school takes a viper to its bosom. In effect, in schooling him, Dumbledore is the making of Riddle, whose sadistic talents would otherwise have been confined to the aimless torture of his little peers. Benign idealism is led to nurture evil, and in a sense Dumbledore is Lord Voldemort's true father. Indeed later we may ask what it was that led Dumbledore to this boy. Was it the fact that he felt drawn to an evil that was once his own, when he plotted with the ambitious Grindelwald to get hold of the immense power in the Deathly Hallows?

Thus the analysis of Riddle and his advancement is not quite of the flat, simplistic sort we often find in fantasy. He wants to learn, and he becomes a model scholar and head boy of the school. Yet under all this perfect behaviour, which fits with all that society commends, his spirit tends another way, despising love and all common things that make people happy. But here again he is not simply the standard ambitious and cold-hearted megalomaniac. He also harbours a weakness, a fear of death. Of course, everyone fears death to some degree, but only Voldemort makes it his leitmotif and his name. Something of the rejection of him by his father perhaps persists in his mind, and directs his murder of his parent in the hope of silencing his self-doubt. This may be speculation, but the book encourages us to speculate. The moral portrayal in the *Harry Potter* books is often subtler than may be supposed.

What then, of the transformation of Tom Riddle into Lord Voldemort? As we see him, Voldemort is the epitome of Gothic terror, the hideous bogey waiting to tear us to extinction and drink our blood. But he is also, somewhere, still Tom Riddle, the angry child of the orphanage. We learn that after a course of wickedness he started calling himself Lord Voldemort to awe his followers, but gradually he has become the evil he aped. C.S. Lewis once said that given enough of eternity, a grumbler will turn into a grumble, and maybe something of that is true also. But we may also suppose that the self as Lord Voldemort is there to hide the self that was Tom Riddle. Without parents, knowing that he was begotten out of fraud and later rejected by his father, his right to life is insecure. Without love, he is alone; without relations, he cannot relate, only inflict himself on others. If as Tom Riddle he is not fully alive, he must crush Tom Riddle and become another figure of terrifying energy. He seeks absolute power to give himself a mastery over life and death he does not feel. Maybe all people who seek absolute power do it, ultimately, to counter their fear of death and their sense of insubstantiality in the world. On the way they change their names: Timor the Lame becomes Tamburlaine, Schickelgrüber becomes Hitler, Dzhugashvili becomes Stalin. Riddle, though, Riddle who is a riddle to himself, becomes Lord Voldemort, which sounds wonderful until you consider that it means Lord Vol-de-Mort, Lord Fly-from-Death, which is hardly a description of ruthless potency. So Voldemort's most evident bogeydom is a front, a device; but at another less visible level, like a name on a stick of rock, it runs right through him.

Moreover the name Voldemort has another potential meaning, further from its owner's intention, and perhaps even more deeply true. For it can also be read as Lord Voule-de-Mort, or Lord Death-Wish. The strange thing about the people who fly from death is that they often surround themselves with all the paraphernalia of extinction, from dead bodies to Death-Eaters, and from gallows to gas chambers. Whenever we see Voldemort we see him in some disabled or diseased shape that makes him seem a living death. To fly from death, he must keep feeding it: told that his doom lies in the Potter family he attempts to slay them all; and were there no other reason he would keep on slaying till only he and the snake Nagini were left. At which point he might realize that he has only been killing himself in others all along. Those who fly from their extinction may really be in love with it, like the old story of the man of Aleppo, who, told by Death that he would come for him in a week, fled to far-off Damascus, only to find that it was there that Death was to meet him.

All this we know about Voldemort only from the smallest of his actual appearances, and from the memories of others put in Dumbledore's Pensieve. Of course, he is very vivid to others even in his absence, and almost all wizards scarcely dare mention his name through fear of invoking him. But for us, though over the seven books he has an increasing part to play in Harry's and others' lives, he is often absent. In *The Philosopher's Stone* he is only a face seen once on the back of someone's head; in *The Chamber of Secrets* it is only towards the end that we see him as the boy Tom Riddle; in *The Prisoner of Azkaban* he does not appear at all; and in *The Goblet of Fire* we meet him only in the first and last chapters. Only in *The Order of the Phoenix* and *The Half-Blood Prince* does he begin to move against Hogwarts through his servants. For quite a bit of the story, therefore, Voldemort is marginalized. Of course, the same could be said of Sauron in Tolkien's *The Lord of the Rings*: we hardly ever see him either. But the whole of Frodo's journey is directed towards Sauron; and throughout he draws closer and closer to him. Moreover Voldemort is repairing himself from a previous defeat, where Sauron has already accomplished this by the start of the story, and is an immediate threat to Middle-earth.

If J.K. Rowling was re-writing Tolkien's portrayal of evil here, this sidelining of Voldemort shows her subtlety. For if we consider what the *Harry Potter* books are *about*, they are just as much about Harry's life at school and all the things he finds there, as about any *story*. This is quite important. In the first book the business of finding the Philosopher's Stone is just one of many excitements; the plot of *The Chamber of Secrets* similarly only really gets going towards the end; and likewise with Sirius Black and the struggle to protect him in *The Prisoner of Azkaban*. Virtually all of *The Goblet of Fire* concerns school events and the Tri-Wizard Tournament. It is this sort of thing that gives the books all the fascination of a TV soap: we are as preoccupied with ordinary daily life as much as with any exciting events. J.K. Rowling will not focus everything in one direction in the way that Tolkien – and for that matter Voldemort – do. It may be that this is because she does not like life to be controlled by any one thing, or even to treat one thing as more important than another: and therefore she gives Voldemort no more actual space than, say, Quidditch, Care of Magical Creatures or Dobby the house-elf. She also gives unexpected significance to things and people we might pass by, such as Moaning Myrtle of the girls' lavatories, Quirrell, an old schoolboy's diary or Ron's pet rat Scabbers. Harry is at a school that is a kind of wild compendium of different things – indeed one reason why the setting is a school is that one's mind is constantly being changed as one moves from subject to subject. It is the people who want life to be just one thing, and hate variety, and things relating or contrasting, that J. K. Rowling seems to dislike: and she sums them up in Voldemort and his followers. Draco Malfoy and his father insist on blood and racial purity: they sneer at Hermione, who has Muggle parents; and of course Harry's mother was also a muggle-born. They spend their lives excluding others, rejecting and purifying to the point of nothingness. The school, however, by its very nature is all-inclusive.

Thus in J.K. Rowling's books we are not just following a story about a school increasingly brought up against a megalomaniac, but we are looking at a human community founded on love, in opposition to a fragmentary and fearful herd who live only by the exclusions of pride and self-protective hatred. And that in the end is why Lord Voldemort, as Lord Voldemort, has so little space: there is really very little to say about him; he has just gone the way of evil, losing his humanity over the years until he has made himself the black-clothed, red-eyed, snarling cliché of every cheap romance. But the school is quite another matter. It has so many different experiences, relations and approaches to life to offer that we can never have enough of it: and so we do not, for it fills and fills all of the first six books. This variety implicitly mocks the self-simplification of Voldemort.

The Presentation of Evil

So much for the analysis of evil. What about its presentation? Reading the books sequentially, the terrible Voldemort is almost all we know for the first five books, and it is only in the sixth that his life as a human child is presented via Dumbledore's Pensieve. This has the effect of deflating the earlier terrors: when all is said and done, what Voldemort has become is ultimately the result of bad parenting. But it is also a way of reflecting back on Harry Potter. Across all the books he has refused Voldemort's mystery by continually naming him, as a mere individual: now he is old enough to see just how sad evil really is. The revelation of Voldemort's true nature measures the growth of Harry's perception.

What then of the Dementors, the Nazgûl of these books? What is a place like Azkaban doing in the same world as Hogwarts, with warders who annihilate the souls of their charges, leaving them mere zombies? For the jailed followers of Voldemort this may just be acceptable, but what, say, of the decent Hagrid, who might have been given into their care on a trumped-up charge? Here, however, we must take into account the third center of power in the books, the wizard Ministry, dedicated to the regulation and conduct of magic, eventually to the point of taking over the school to ensure it. It is the Ministry that is responsible for Azkaban, and for the hiring of the Dementors while Voldemort and his followers are in eclipse. Moreover the Ministry's chief officials can often be on the road to evil themselves – Fudge, Crouch, Umbridge and Percy Weasley are variously ruthless, ambitious and inhuman. Concerned as they are with their own power within their islanded world, such people are able without unease to ensure wizard conformity to Ministry edicts by the harshest of means. They share with Voldemort's followers and even with Harry's guardian Vernon Dursley an obsession with purity that leads to cruelty. Because of the Ministry the world is not a safer, but a much more dangerous place.

Evil in the _Harry Potter_ books might at first appear the alien, something entirely outside the good characters. However, Harry Potter himself is more involved with evil than he cares to know. Harry's boggart, the thing he most fears, is a Dementor; and Dementors keep threatening him – one of them comes for him on the Hogwarts train, two appear near the Dursley's home, a sinister protective guard of them is thrown round Hogwarts, Harry thinks they will freeze him while he is playing Quidditch, he dreams of them night by night. Then, too, Harry's life is bound up with Lord Voldemort's. His scar, sign of Voldemort's failed attempt to kill him in babyhood, lets him increasingly into Voldemort's mind, so that he can see what the evil wizard is about to do and try to prevent it. Eventually it is to be the sign of a much closer bond between Harry and Voldemort than either of them would have wished. And in the seventh book it turns out that the two are cousins, if in a three-figure degree: they are descended from the brothers Peverell.

Harry's life is in many ways parallel to Voldemort's, as Voldemort himself remarks (*Chamber* 233). Like Voldemort, Harry is an orphan brought up in a hostile world and rescued by Dumbledore who admits him to Hogwarts. Both Harry and Voldemort are by nature Slytherin, though Harry refuses that house when the Sorting Hat offers it to him. Both are developing their powers and expanding their sphere of operations throughout the story. Whenever Harry meets Voldemort he is alone, as though he alone can meet him. He leaves the others behind and goes on to do final battle himself in both *The Philosopher's Stone* and *The Chamber of Secrets*. Though accompanied by Cedric Diggory when Voldemort captures them at the end of *The Goblet of Fire*, he is soon alone, for Cedric is immediately killed on Voldemort's orders. Harry's return alone puts him under suspicion throughout *The Order of the Phoenix*. Meanwhile Voldemort himself is increasingly obsessed with Harry as a possible threat to him, and tries variously to kill him or to find out the prophecy concerning him. That prophecy seals the relation of the two, for it says one will kill the other.

None of this is to say that Harry is in any way contaminated by evil, only that he and it are very close and have unique access to one another. [As the poet says, 'Evil into the mind of God or Man/ May come and go, so unapprov'd, and leave/ No spot or blame behind.'] But why do we have this situation? One possibility, which involves a bit of a shift in the thinking here, is that the *Harry Potter* books may be considered as dreams by Harry himself. Every one of them involves a journey inwards, suggestive of a movement into the mind – first, through several underground rooms to the Philosopher's Stone; then through tunnels beneath Hogwarts's plumbing to the secret lair of the serpent; inwards to Hogwarts from Azkaban past a ring of Dementors; inwards through a maze to a goblet at its center; through a series of rooms to the secret center of the Ministry; and through a rock wall into an underground cavern with a deadly lake surrounding an island that holds a Horcrux. Each dream-story starts and ends with 'real life' with the Dursleys, as Harry travels away from them each term to Hogwarts and must return to them in the holidays: this parallels the process of waking, dreaming, and waking again. It is often hard to understand why Harry must return from the joys of Hogwarts to the unpleasant Dursleys every holiday, and it is not until the very end of the fifth book that we learn that by being with them he was protected from Voldemort by his family blood.

The first book lends itself readily to consideration as a dream. For on one level, what else is it but fantasy as wish-fulfilment? Harry is an orphan being wretchedly treated by his relatives, living utterly alone and with only miserable prospects. Such a child would be ready to invent a happier fictional world, one where from being alone he acquires perfect friends, where from being rejected he becomes a cynosure, where from a life of endless monotony he enters one of continual variety, where from being confined his spirit and power may expand in the vastness of Hogwarts and the exercise of magic. (There is a dream-like quality from the start in the gathering of the owls outside no. 4 Privet Drive, and in their postal assault on the house.) But such dreams of delight are frail, and always under threat from the darker real life of the self. The darkness of spirit that is banished to impotence in the first book, gradually grows in strength and menace through the rest, until it threatens Hogwarts and the whole fantasy of delight. When Harry realizes that he must kill Voldemort or Voldemort him, he is seeing that the fantasy can only go on if he can finally destroy the darkness in his own life.

This idea can only be speculation: but it is worth pointing out that many other children's fantasies around the time of the first *Harry Potter* books are in the form of dreams or mental projections, and involve cruel relatives, paranoia, demonic figures, and people turned to zombies. In Pauline Fisk's *Midnight Blue* (1990) the girl Bonnie flees from her bullying grandmother to find a new and better version of her family on the other side of the sky. Helen Cresswell's *The Watchers* (1993) centers on two children both failed by their mothers, who find their way to a sinister magical fairground where they are pursued by a demonic figure. The same author's *Stonestruck* (1995) describes young Jessica's evacuation to Wales from her parents during the war, and how she finds there a band of terrible ghost-children under a Green Lady who turn other children into zombies. In Annie Dalton's *Demon Spawn* (1991) the bowl of demon-spawn is the expression of Nina's angry feelings towards her domineering friend Carly; and in Dalton's *The Dream Snatcher* (1998) a wizard steals children's dreams because his father cut him off from his own when he was a child. In Gillian Cross's *Pictures in the Dark* (1996) young Peter is so badly treated by his family that he is driven to turning into an animal. Elinor in Ann Halam's *Crying in the Dark* (1998) has lost her parents, and lives with her bullying aunt and uncle, at the mercy of her fears, which involve her mind being taken over by the spirit of an even worse treated girl from the past. Darkness, death, insecurity, supernatural terrors are the emotional landscape of these books. And all of them are written, for the first time in English children's fantasy, direct from the viewpoint of a child, without adult irony or instructional distance – just in the way that Rowling gives us Harry Potter's viewpoint without any criticism save occasionally through his friends. And it is in this medium that the first *Harry Potter* books are written.

Harry Potter – Good Literature?

I want to move now to a question that follows from the relative moral and perceptual subtlety of J.K.Rowling's books. This is, are they good literature? It is at least remarkable that they have won none of the main British children's literature awards apart from the Smarties. One has no wish to push them upstairs into the land of snobs, but it makes one unhappier to see them so thrust down to the cultural cellars. So far what we have seen of their moral sophistication and their ambiguity of being might suggest that they have a good deal more to offer than is so readily supposed. Here we have no simplistic moral divisions, no ready separation of heroes and villains; and here too we have books that operate on several levels at once, not least in their being both literal stories and potential dreams. Might there not be other ways in which they repudiate their detractors?

Consider, for instance, the frequent accusation that the *Harry Potter* books are derivative. The reply to this is that of course they are. They have debts stretching from Ovid to Diana Wynne Jones. But in this dependency they are no different from say, Chaucer, Spenser, Shakespeare, Milton and Pope, accepted giants of the English literary canon. Chaucer rewrites Boccaccio, and Shakespeare steals whole passages direct from Holinshed's *Histories* or North's *Plutarch*. Of course, these writers recreate what they use: but then so does J. K.Rowling. From Ursula Le Guin's *A Wizard of Earthsea* she may take the idea of a wizard school with its own peculiar curriculum, and also the hostile relationship between Harry and Draco Malfoy, but she modifies both, the one into a school at once serious in intent and often comic in execution, and the other into an exercise in patience for Harry. Rowling rejoices in her literary debts: she is glad to be part of a community, and she is writing about a community, a school, where everyone learns from past knowledge and experience, and each headmaster both follows those who have gone before him and adds his own personal contribution. Her debts are indeed wider than is often supposed: has anyone for instance ever considered how much she may owe to James Joyce's method in *The Portrait of the Artist as a Young Man*? Or that C.S.Lewis's *That Hideous Strength* (1945) may be behind parts of *The Order of the Phoenix*? Or that the transformation of the old lady Bathilda Bagshot to a snake in *The Deathly Hallows* may well come from the description of the metamorphosis of the poison-pen letter writer Dora Wilmot to a serpent in chapter twelve of Charles Williams's *The Place of the Lion* (1931)?

What then of the way the books are put together? Are they just stories, if very good ones? Or are they, hideous term, ART? By which I mean do they have any idea or underlying motif that makes them not only narratives, but meaningful narratives? There are those who have argued for a Christian meaning behind all of them, but I feel that this rings true with them only in patches – mostly from the climactic battles with Voldemort, in which all sorts of potentially Christian symbols – phoenixes, stags, unicorns, cups – are deployed. But the books are filled with so many other strange images suggestive of other ideas. There are Hagrid, Diagon Alley, Gringotts, Platform 9¾, the Hogwarts Express, Dumbledore, the Sorting Hat, the movable stairs, the talking portraits, Nearly Headless Nick... the list is almost endless. But somehow they are not just random: somehow they all ring the same bell.

They are in fact all forms of pleasure for Harry. The whole of his first year at Hogwarts is especially a cornucopia of delights, a granting of almost everything he never had, and of much more that he never dreamt of. The theme even becomes explicit in the account of the Mirror of Erised, or desire backwards. Even the climax at the end is adventure as a sort of terrifying pleasure – singing the ludicrous Fluffy to sleep, escaping the devil's snare, choosing the right key, the right chess move, the right potion; though I grant the discovery of Voldemort on the back of Quirrell's head is a shade horrid. And the Philosopher's Stone itself represents the ultimate desire, the desire to transcend death. But the point is made that while almost every desire may be gratified, no desire is to be sought, or if gained, clung to. That is the Blakeian lesson of the Mirror of Erised: desire is part of time, and one must move on. But the mirror also teaches a far deeper lesson: that nothing outside ourselves, whether gold, diamonds or dead parents, is inherently desirable; we only make them so through our lack of them. What Harry sees in the Mirror of Erised is only his own projected picture of his lost parents, and he daily seeks it out and clings to it. But when he looks for the Philosopher's Stone, Harry does so not out of desire for it but to prevent its misuse; and when he comes to the chamber where it is, he alone can lay hands on it because he unlike Voldemort is now the master and not the slave of appearances.

The idea of desire in *The Philosopher's Stone* works like a recurrent theme in music, which reappears through all the most diverse passages. It serves in fact to make the book art, an arrangement of impressions producing a sense both of harmony and of revelation. This sounds like a high claim for the book, and it is: for what we see here is no less than the sort of architectonic skill and subtle unity we trace in say Chaucer, Spenser or Shakespeare. While not adhering to the current view of literature that puts Pope on a level with Pop, it is interesting to find in humble children's books as much skill and depth as we readily grant to the more mainstream novels taught at universities.

Having found a single motif like this so deployed within the first book, it is natural to ask whether the same sort of thing is to be found in others. At first sight however *The Chamber of Secrets* does not seem to be so different from *The Philosopher's Stone*: it begins with such 'desirable' adventures as the visit to the Weasleys' home, flight to Hogwarts in Mr. Weasley's car, and victory again at Quidditch. However, looking back from having read the whole book, one has quite a different feeling about its recurrent mood, which seems not at all one of gratified wishes. If one thinks about it, in the first pages we have a situation in which Harry's wish to escape the Dursleys is obstructed by the appearance and loud behaviour of the house-elf Dobby, who destroys the dinner-party downstairs. And not long afterwards, Harry and Ron find the access to Platform 9¾ blocked, so that he and Ron miss the train to Hogwarts. Then, when Ron has the idea of taking his father's flying car to get them to school he crashes it into the Whomping Willow in the school grounds. Not very desirable at all.

In fact, quite frustrating: and if, by now alerted, we consider the rest of the book, we soon find that it is packed with frustration. Ron's wand backfires, Harry is constantly dragged into the vanity-hunting of Professor Lockhart, lessons are badly taught, Filch cannot find who hung up Mrs. Norris by her tail, and later the Quidditch Final is cancelled on the point of starting. Meanwhile Harry is suspected of being Slytherin's heir, and his elaborate scheme to prove that it is Malfoy comes to nothing; and a mistake with the Polyjuice Potion hospitalizes Hermione for weeks, after which she is petrified during her researches in the library. People keep pursuing Harry - not only Lockhart but the admiring new boy Colin Creevey, and an importunate Dwarf is sent to read out an embarrassing Valentine to him in front of Malfoy and many others. Tom Riddle puts Harry off the scent for some time by tricking him into accepting that Hagrid may be the real enemy; and meanwhile Hagrid is arrested and Dumbledore suspended, so that they cannot give help. It is only Harry's deductions from the fragments of knowledge that have been gleaned from these many frustrations that lead him to the truth and Moaning Myrtle. The plot has indeed been serpentine, or Slytherin.

If we now actively start looking for recurrent ideas and images in the books, we may see that in the next one, *The Prisoner of Azkaban*, the dominant motif is multiple realities. Hermione takes two subjects per hour by living the same time twice over; and the same happens at the end of the book when she and Harry save both Buckbeak and Sirius Black by adjusting events. Harry goes to Hogsmeade while pretending to be at Hogwarts. Black and

Lupin have other lives as dog and wolf, and Pettigrew lives as Ron's pet rat Scabbers. Harry's Patronus is a stag. Wizards create Boggarts and Patronuses out of their heads. Harry agrees with Aunt Marge that he goes to a school for the incurably criminal, and has to think of another reality while she taunts him. The Marauder's Map shows people moving about in their separate realities within Hogwarts. There are numerous false realities which in the end do not work: Malfoy's lies about Hagrid are exposed, Harry is found out coming back from Hogsmeade, Lupin's concealments fail, the deceptions of Pettigrew are revealed, Harry's false view of Black is overthrown. The book seems to say that the world is much more complex and ambiguous than we previously supposed. This has particular relation to Harry's view of his parents. In this book he begins to let go of them as the frozen paragons of his lonely childhood, and to see them as they really were – and in the case of his father this is to be an unpleasant shock.

In the following book, *The Goblet of Fire*, the leitmotif is interruption. Think of how closed circles of friends are broken into, of how the Death Eaters interrupt the initial wizard games, how the three selected for the Tri-Wizard Tournament have to accept a fourth, how Rita Skeeter continually forces Harry into distorted publicity, or how at the moment of winning the Goblet Harry and Cedric are transported to Voldemort – think of these and you have some of the main 'interruptions' of *The Goblet of Fire*. In addition there is a motif of helping others – Harry's kindnesses to Cedric, Dobby and Moaning Myrtle are returned, helping him win the Tournament; he rescues Ron and Gabrielle underwater even though it will lose him first place, and at the moment he could win the Goblet for himself he lets Cedric share the victory with him. Together these motifs suggest an ethic of going out of the self.

The Order of the Phoenix centers on motifs of communication and invasion. It starts with Harry listening to the radio news, but receiving none from Hogwarts. He cannot persuade the wizard authorities that Voldemort has returned, and his fellows cannot trust him after Cedric's disappearance; further, Dumbledore will not talk to Harry because he thinks Voldemort has invaded his mind. The whole story is directed to finding a communication – the prophecy concerning Harry and Voldemort: this is futile, for the prophecy is already known to Dumbledore. Harry frequently dreams of approaching a door he must open, when he is inside the mind of the snake Nagini. Different contexts become joined: Dementors invade Little Whinging and Harry does magic in Muggledom to remove them, Sirius speaks to Harry in Hogwarts via a fire in his London house and comes as a dog to see Harry off at the station. The Ministry takes over the school and is reputed to be about to take over Gringotts Bank. People take one another's places: Grubbly-Plank replaces Hagrid, 'the nag' partners Trelawney, and eventually Umbridge usurps Dumbledore. Kreacher is forced to obey a 'Mudblood'; Harry forms Dumbledore's Army at fifteen; Sturgis Podmore is arrested while breaking into the Ministry. The lines Harry has continually to write for Umbridge simultaneously etch their message into his flesh. Almost all these communications and invasions are negated or reversed by the end of the book. The Sorting Hat says that instead of the different houses of the school warring against one another, they must come together.

The motif of invasion persists into the sixth book, *Harry Potter and the Half-Blood Prince*, with Dumbledore entering the Dursleys' house, and the Death Eaters penetrating into Hogwarts. Even an old Potions textbook Harry is given has been 'invaded' by its previous owner with continual annotations. Here too there is the idea of mind on its own being able to control the world, as in the non-verbal spells Harry is taught by Snape. And there is entry into one's own or others' minds via the Pensieve, to find out about Voldemort's origins or, via the Half-Blood Prince's book, to learn how to make better potions. Harry knows in his mind that Malfoy and Snape are plotting something, but he cannot find proof, and his insistence begins to look to his friends like irrational obsession. In a way the book is dualistic, mind and body separated – exemplified by the occasion when Harry is invisible in the luggage rack of Malfoy's train compartment, trying to learn his plans, and his body gives him away. But this book also has a motif of growing togetherness. Dumbledore takes over Harry's education personally, and they go together in search of the Horcrux at the end. Harry and Ginny grow close, as do Ron and Hermione; even in the Pensieve we see the desperate Merope led to trick her way into intimacy with the noble Riddle. In the end however, intimacy gives way to separation, as Dumbledore is killed and Harry parts from Ginny as he leaves Hogwarts to follow his destiny.

The presence of such underlying motifs in each of these books makes them not just stories but meaningful narratives. And if we put all six of the stories together, this becomes true of them as a whole. From desire to frustration, from multiple realities to widening society, and from communication to intimacy, these motifs map a journey out from the self that we must all make from childhood if we are to become true citizens of a complex world. And what adds a darker note to this theme is that it is both paralleled and parodied in the development outwards of Voldemort himself from houseless malignity, to dilated power. The final book will involve that last journey out of the self that we call death.

The broad pattern across all the books is a movement from innocence to experience, and from a protected to an unprotected world. *The Philosopher's Stone* is close to being an idyll of magic, in which Harry discovers a new world with a child's wonder. (It is actually not far from our infant response to the initial strangeness of our own world.) This idiom continues in the first part of *The Chamber of Secrets*, with the flying car, the Whomping Willow and the mandrakes, but thereafter we have to do more with sinister threats and monsters in the lavatories. Death increasingly makes itself felt within the life of Hogwarts: there is a Deathday party, we meet Professor Binns still teaching long after he has died, a hissing voice in the walls wants to tear Harry to pieces, Filch's cat Mrs. Norris is found hung, Justin Finch-Fletchley and Nearly Headless Nick are found seemingly dead in a passage, Harry and Ron are nearly killed and eaten by spiders in the forest, and in the last book Harry himself has to die at Voldemort's hand in order to destroy him.

Increasingly, people are not what they seem. Voldemort's face under Quirrell's turban in the first book is relatively incidental beside the uncertainties regarding Tom Riddle and Hagrid in *The Chamber*, the continuing ambiguity of Sirius Black in *The Prisoner*, or the impersonation of Mad-Eye Moody in *The Goblet*. At the same time people become more morally mixed: Harry's idealized notion of his father becomes qualified when via the Pensieve he sees him bullying Snape at school; and we have characters of whom we are increasingly uncertain such as Ludo Bagman, Barty Crouch, Cornelius Fudge, Percy Weasley and even Horace Slughorn. The world becomes more complex and ambiguous. In the last book we even find that Harry has a piece of Voldemort's soul in him.

Meanwhile Harry has developed outwards, as it were; by the second book he is visiting Ron's family home in the country; by the third he is finding his way from the school to Hogsmeade, and his fortunes become bound to Sirius Black, a person from outside; by the fourth book his school is opened up to the wider wizard world through sport and the Tri-Wizard Tournament; in the fifth, *The Order of the Phoenix*, Harry spends part of his time in London, either with the Order at Sirius Black's house or fighting Voldemort's followers in the Ministry; and *The Half-Blood Prince* sees Harry travel far outside Hogwarts with Dumbledore, after whose death he quits Hogwarts for good in pursuit of Voldemort. Appropriately, as he leaves the school, he leaves the ring of his friends around Dumbledore's grave: he is outside the charmed circle now, moving off into unknown territory. That territory we traverse in the seventh book, *The Deathly Hallows*, where Harry scours the country looking for Horcruxes, before eventually returning to Hogwarts to find them.

The Deathly Hallows is more complex than the others, in that it involves drawing together the threads of the whole series and giving a satisfying account of all the issues that have been implicit in earlier books. At its heart are three closely linked motifs, one concerning ignorance versus knowledge, one the disclosure of secrets, and one the relation of chance, free will and design. These help to deepen the meaning not only of this book but also of the whole series.

The pattern of a journey from ignorance to knowledge has been behind every one of the *Harry Potter* books. They have all involved finding out something – the meaning of the Philosopher's Stone and who is trying to steal it, who or what is the Heir of Slytherin, the true nature and history of Sirius Black, the source of Harry's selection for the Triwizard Tournament, the prophecy regarding Harry and Voldemort, the identity of the Half-blood Prince and the existence of Horcruxes. And across all six of them he has moved some way from relative innocence to experience. But in the last book his journey involves increasing knowledge of himself and his limitations. In a sense he recapitulates the journey of the first six books at a deeper level, as a youth on the threshold of adulthood.

In this last book Harry is on his own, without a given structure to his life. He is starting all over again in a new and much less ordered world than the school, literally without a clue; symbolically he is for much of the time wandering the wild country, searching likely spots for the remaining Horcruxes. None of them are to be found wherever he goes, and he wastes time and nearly brings about his capture trying to find them in the wrong places, such as the orphanage of Voldemort's childhood or Godric's Hollow where Harry and his parents once lived. Lacking Dumbledore's guidance, and without a plan or direction he is lost and enfeebled: Ron leaves him and Hermione after an argument, and Harry's wand is symbolically broken and he is 'fatally weakened' (286). Now he becomes drawn to a search for the Deathly Hallows, three ancient objects used in the past to defy death. He has left the track for a by-path, and he is now thinking defensively about how to preserve himself, rather than how to kill Voldemort. After a futile visit to Xenophilus Lovegood which almost has them captured, the friends are taken by Death Eaters when Harry forgets and speaks Voldemort's name. The whole story of their time in the country has been a series of blunders in the dark.

But now things start to come right, as though Harry has served his time in the wasteland of his spirit. Knowledge starts to pour in on him, and ignorance diminishes. Now Harry's insights into Voldemort's thoughts start to help him. When Voldemort realizes that the Horcrux in the bank has gone, Harry sees him thinking that one of those remaining is lodged in Hogwarts. Harry still has no plan or direction (*Hallows*, 445-6, 459), but when he asks for help from other pupils at the school, he is given a lead. Thereafter, thinking and remembering under pressure leads him eventually to the diadem-Horcrux in the Room of Requirement.

Then, led again by another insight into Voldemort's thoughts, Harry is in time to receive from the dying Snape a piece of his memory, which reveals that he, Harry, unknown to Voldemort, is himself a Horcrux. For when Voldemort was destroyed in trying to kill him as a baby, a fragment of his soul flew off to become part of Harry. In other words, while Harry lives, Voldemort cannot be killed. Harry must give himself to Voldemort for slaughter if the latter is to die.

'Finally, the truth' (554). So thinks Harry when Snape's memory is done. He thinks he has been trapped into being a sacrifice. But this is not the whole story, and Harry is still acting in relative ignorance when he goes to his death. Still this is now a necessary ignorance, and one that is a good. One of the most vivid moments of the book is Harry's lonely decision to give himself to a death which he believes is annihilation, and his walk under the Invisibilty Cloak through the battle in the school and the grounds outside, silently bidding farewell to his friends and the daylight. He dies what he believes is a final death for him, to save others. In fact, however, he is to be told that this ensured his survival. He had to give himself away completely in order to get himself back.

If Harry's survival comes as a surprise, or 'too much of a happy ending to take', we have to remember that resurrection itself is inherently a surprise. We are dealing here with something of Tolkien's idea of 'eucatastrophe' at the end of fairy tales, which

> is a sudden and miraculous grace – never to be counted on to recur. It does not deny the existence of *dyscatastrophe*, of sorrow and failure: the possibility of these is necessary to the joy of deliverance; it denies (in the face of much evidence, if you will) universal final defeat and insofar is *evangelium*, giving a fleeting glimpse of Joy, Joy beyond the walls of the world, poignant as grief.   (Tolkien, 'On Fairy Stories' 1964)

'Eucatastrophe' is of its very nature a surprise, jutting out from the previous material like a fountain from a desert. And so with Harry's surprising survival here.

The 'deeper magic' involved here is close to the story of Aslan's sacrifice of himself to the White Witch in C.S.Lewis's *The Lion, the Witch and the Wardrobe*, a story well-known to J.K. Rowling. Like Harry, Aslan dies for another's sake; like Harry he feels all the misery and fear of being about to die; like Harry he gives himself into his enemy's hands amid the jeering of his followers. And like Harry, Aslan comes back to life through a more potent magic than the Witch could ever know, namely, that if one gave his life for another, death would be defeated. Here the story of Harry Potter begins to take on Christian overtones. But Harry is not Christ, he is not dying like Aslan for Edmund's sins: he only partakes in the nature of Christ, like all people who sacrifice themselves for another, in actions large or small – like Neville for instance, at the end of the first book, trying vainly to stop his friends from putting themselves in danger. Nevertheless, the deeper Christian pattern or 'plan' lies at the root of Harry's sacrifice in *The Deathly Hallows*. And in participating in it, Harry learns in his very soul the point where magic becomes metaphysics.

This learning is continued when after his 'death' Harry meets Dumbledore in King's Cross between the worlds. There he is told another truth that leaves magical for mystical explanations. Voldemort thought only magical power mattered, but here we find again that in the wizard world, self-sacrificing love has a power beyond any wand; and that a mother who gives her life for her child makes that child impossible to kill. Dumbledore has always known that love is more powerful than any magic. This answer brings us full circle, from the time Harry first unknowingly destroyed Voldemort as a baby, to the time when he himself must give his own life to save Hogwarts, and so again remove Voldemort, this time for good. Sacrifice, and the hallowing of blood: this is far beyond the Deathly Hallows; this is nearer the sacramental idea of our being saved through the blood of Christ.

Throughout the story till now, Harry has been 'Ignotus' not only in the sense of being unknown, but also in that of being ignorant. His story has for him been a continual expansion of awareness, to the point where Dumbledore can tell him, '"I have no secrets from you any more"' (571). For us too the book has worked as a series of widening circles of knowledge, until at last when it is done no mystery remains, save that of love itself, which must always be mysterious. Ignorant or not so far as his understanding goes, Harry has always done as his mother did for him in the beginning, given himself away for others to the very end. Whether, in love, there is ever an end, the book leaves us to consider as it ends this story.

So far we have discussed ignorance in terms of its steady removal through increasing knowledge, as though it is something to be abolished. But in *The Deathly Hallows*, finding out is not quite everything. Harry is also the descendant of Ignotus Peverell, and 'Ignotus' means 'ignorant of' as well as 'unknown'. And Harry's ignorance of the true facts is imposed upon him, because Dumbledore could have enlightened him at any time, directly or by proxy, that he is a Horcrux, and that he is protected by his mother's sacrifice. It seems to be considered better that Harry should remain ignorant than that he should be informed straight away.

Or, to put it another way, this knowledge is something that he must grow into rather than simply be given. While ignorance is something to be removed, from another point of view it is a condition that saves one from the folly of too-early knowledge. Knowledge should be arrived at over time, through experience, not given at once lest it provoke the arrogance of unearned power in the still juvenile spirit. And that that would be the danger with Harry is shown in his growing obsession with obtaining the Hallows. Further, what is involved in this story is not Harry finding out someone else's true identity, as with Professor Quirrell, Tom Riddle, Sirius Black or Mad-Eye Moody in earlier books, but Harry coming to knowledge of himself. And this he finds to be a self that can be just as tempted by power as once was Dumbledore, whom he blames for it. In one sense, when Harry is told near the end that he is himself a Horcrux, with a fragment of Voldemort's evil soul in him, this is only a magical gloss on a moral condition that has been partly his own. Only now can he get rid of it.

The growing process Harry undergoes in the wilderness is partly carried through by the ancient myth of the romance hero that underlies the story. The hero – good instances are *The Odyssey* and the medieval story *Sir Gawain and the Green Knight* (c.1450) – goes into wild nature or a wasteland to endure a maturation process that will fit him for the final battle against his adversaries. He is disarmed (the broken wand), naked and exposed (the freezing pool in the forest), subjected to temptations (the Hallows) and wandering: this archetypal pattern underwrites Harry's own journey here. Having endured and passed through these things, the hero may be returned to society to overthrow his enemies. This happens when Harry returns to the school.

As part of the theme of increasing knowledge, the book is full of secrets that are eventually revealed. Of these secrets Harry himself is the first. He is for most of the story hidden, unknown, 'Ignotus'. From the start we see him being elaborately concealed from Voldemort and his followers in the escape from Little Whinging; and at the marriage of Fleur and Bill he is disguised as a Weasley relative. When he is captured by the Death Eaters they cannot be sure they have him because Hermione has magically disfigured him. For half of the story he is hidden in the countryside, and even when Voldemort almost catches him, the form he sees eluding him is not Harry's (279).

It is not inappropriate for Harry to have 'gone to ground', because this book is much concerned with the earthy, the old and the past and the hidden things they turn up. Central here is Godric's Hollow, with the ruined cottage of Harry's parents, the corrupt hovel of Bathilda Bagshot, the burial ground where the various dead are brought together, and the pool in the forest where the Sword of Gryffindor is found. It is in the graveyard that Harry finds once more the strange triangular symbol that intrigued him at the wedding of Bill and Fleur, on the chest of Luna Lovegood's father Xenophilus. This leads him on an irrelevant-seeming quest to find out the symbol's meaning, and with it the ancestry of his family and that of Dumbledore and Voldemort in three brothers called Peverell. In Bathilda Bagshot Harry hopes for some revelation of the past, but what he is given instead is the eruption of the evil snake Nagini from her body. Meanwhile, a book by Rita Skeeter based on Bathilda's memories has exposed the evildoing of Dumbledore when he was a young magician. But these revelations, unpleasant though they are, tell Harry truths he needs to know. They reveal much about Voldemort's mind, and will in the end help turn his love for Dumbledore from a boy's to an adult's.

The Deathly Hallows is also of course about the discovery of the various hiding places of the Horcruxes. Persuasion makes Mundungus reveal that Dolores Umbridge has the locket, a mistake by the Death Eater Bellatrix points them towards the cup in her vault in Gringott's Bank, Harry's asking for help from his school friends suggests the lost diadem of Ravenclaw, and a memory of Snape's reveals to Harry that he is himself a Horcrux. The last also implies that Nagini the snake is the last unknown Horcrux. Only Voldemort himself seems to remain after that.

As the end approaches with all its revelations of the truth, it is symbolic that the fire that destroys the Room of Requirement when Harry secures the diadem Horcrux also destroys 'the secrets of the countless souls who had sought refuge in the room' (508). For a moment we touch on a larger revelation, an ending of all secrets and a fire that will purify the world. This is caught up again in Dumbledore's declaration to Harry when they meet, '"I have no secrets from you any more. You know"' (571).

The third of the motifs underlying this final book is that of the contingent versus the planned. Much is made towards the end of Dumbledore's plans and arrangements before his death to ensure that everything would be brought to the best conclusion. But in fact Dumbledore's plans involve only occasional moments in the story: the successful escape from Little Whinging, putting the Sword of Gryffindor in the forest and leading Harry to it, trying to remove the power of the Elder Wand by dying with it, and telling Harry through Snape that Voldemort can only be overthrown if Harry is killed by him. All these arrangements Harry learns only by last-minute chance, when he is just in time to receive the dying Snape's memory.

Two other determinants of Harry's life are also discussed by Dumbledore: the fact that since Harry himself is one of Voldemort's Horcruxes, he cannot die while Voldemort is still alive, and the effect of his mother's sacrifice on his blood – and then on Voldemort's blood also. These feel much more like constraints on Harry's will, but they were never plans. The one was apparent chance, a fragment of Voldemort's exploding soul lodging itself like original sin in the baby Harry. And the sacrifice by Harry's mother to save him was no plan, but an instinctive act. However these events then limit, or extend, the kinds of free choice one has, and knowledge of them begets plans either to destroy or to utilize them. But we should remember that they also constrain Voldemort.

Certainly as the book proceeds, Harry seems to become part of larger identities and stories. He realizes that he is in a sense the third brother of the story of the Three Brothers and Death. He finds that he is a Horcrux. And he is saved from being finally killed by Voldemort through the fact that his blood is under a sacramental law that restores him to life. As he proceeds, and more and more knowledge comes in, everything seems to be beginning to interlock into a pattern, a much larger plan that is like box within box. It seems more and more as though Harry is enacting a preordained story, and as though every step opens up some new and deeper pattern that has led him to make it. But in truth nothing forces Harry: he is given the facts, and then has to choose whether to further the pattern by sacrificing himself. The Harry who sought to protect himself with the Hallows, must in the end choose whether to give himself away as a Horcrux. Perhaps the most vivid part of the book is Harry's lonely decision to give himself to a death which he believes is personal annihilation, and his walk under the Invisibilty Cloak through the battle in the school and the grounds outside, silently bidding farewell to his friends and the daylight. But on the way, it is an essential part of the plan as he now knows it, to tell Neville Longbottom to destroy the

remaining Horcrux that is Voldemort's snake Nagini. And that is part of a
still larger plan that lay waiting all these years – that Neville, born on the
same day as Harry, is in a sense another self, and can now take his place. The
activation of things that have been long buried or forgotten is recurrent in
the book.

The plan is not so much a plan, as a series of patterns and constraints on
the future set up by past actions of free choice. It becomes a plan only to those
who have the knowledge to envisage the possible sequence of events. There
was no certainty that Harry would consent to die, only that his character
would lead one to suppose so. Acts of free choice, from Harry's mother dying
to protect him to Harry's dying to protect others from Voldemort, make a
magic that then produces predictable outcomes. In freely choosing to go
back to Hogwarts and kill Voldemort, Harry will complete the magical
pattern and the plan. But this was never an action imposed on him, more the
foresight of what could happen. And there are many things in the story that
happen outside any foreknowledge of Dumbledore's, such as the capture of
Harry, Ron and Hermione by Death Eaters, or the revelation by Bellatrix that
there is a Horcrux in her vault in Gringotts. When Dumbledore attempts a
more direct manipulation of events his scheme does not work: his plan that
the Elder Wand should lose its power through his death fails – though it then
succeeds in a way he never intended. Voldemort's doom is ultimately brought
about not by a plan but by the limitations of his evil. He simply could not see
what he was up against. But then, as Dumbledore says, if he had, he could
not have been Voldemort (569).

What in the end we have, as theologically we must have, is a broad sense
of Harry's following a larger pattern or plan, with only qualified evidence
of it. Right up in front of us is Harry making choices that could go in any
direction, but which in the end are shown to bring the larger patterns into
being. At the same time his story as he sees it partakes in the tale of the Deathly
Hallows; and for us his apparently random wanderings in the country follow
the pattern of the hero monomyth described by Joseph Campbell. But in the
end much of this depends on perspective: if you are close to the action you
do not see the larger patterns it is fitting into, and if you are at a distance
from it, you tend to see patterns in it. When Harry has leisure, as he all too
often does when camping, the excited connections his mind makes between
himself and the old myth of the Hallows may not be so close as he thinks.
The issue of fate versus free will is certainly however raised by the book, as it
raises the other issues of knowledge and ignorance, secrets and revelation. It
is the most philosophical book of the seven, and this is not least because it is
dealing with last things.

What then, finally, of the peculiar form of the book? For structurally it is made up of a series of different settings. We start in Little Whinging, move to the wedding at the Weasleys' house, then to a Tottenham Court Road café, No. 12 Grimmauld Place, the Ministry, a tent in the country, Godric's Hollow, the house of Xenophilus Lovegood, the Forest of Dean, Malfoy Manor, Shell Cottage, Gringott's Bank, Hogwarts, the Forbidden Forest, King's Cross between the worlds, and King's Cross back in this world. Meanwhile we have followed accounts of Voldemort's Europe-wide searches for the Elder Wand, and of Dumbledore's past doings with Gellert Grindelwald and his own family. None of the other six books has been quite as fragmentary as this. At the narrative level, this is because Harry has to be continually on the move, either in escaping Voldemort or in trying to find the Horcruxes. But this does not quite explain it.

However if we consider each of these scenes a piece of a jigsaw puzzle, then we may find a reason. The book is as we have said partly about a journey from ignorance to knowledge. If we see its fragmentary character in terms of pieces of information that are progressively brought together, then the form and content of the book will be married. And this is what is happening: each item adds a piece to the next until the whole picture is made. It is just like the way islanded acts of free choice are later shown to have fitted a plan. Each place and action is a mere fragment until we see how each fits in the developing pattern of the book, the education of a hero. The book as a whole also gives form to the six that preceded it, in that like the first of them it involves finding out what one really is: but whereas Harry Potter of the first book was given his new identity as a wizard, in the last he earns his new self as a man. We have gone in a spiral, returning while advancing. It is somehow typical of the series that it should contain and harmonize such a dual vision.

The epilogue to the book, where we see Harry and Ginny, and Ron and Hermione bidding their own children farewell as they set off for Hogwarts from Platform 9¾ at King's Cross nineteen years later, has often been disliked by readers. But it tells us that life goes on, while at the same time returning to the station from which Harry first set out for Hogwarts himself. It brings us full circle, while letting the line of the future draw itself out with the train along the tracks. It is somehow the last piece of the puzzle, taking us far away from the heat of this story to give us quietening perspective, as we see the beginnings of other stories waving from every window of the train.

Chapter Two

Repotting *Harry Potter*
Popular Lit Made Legit

James W. Thomas

In the late Kurt Vonnegut's 1987 novel *Bluebeard* a woman asks an artist how you can tell a good painting from a bad painting. The artist's answer is, "All you have to do . . . is look at a million paintings, and then you can never be mistaken." So, how do you tell good literature from bad, or great literature from good? My answer is, "All you have to do is read a million books, and then you can never be mistaken." For my entire adult life, I've studied serious literature and read great books, legitimate classics. I've also read a lot of books about those great books. I *feel* like I've read a *million* books, so I ought to know when I come across a great one – which brings me to J. K. Rowling and the *Harry Potter* books.

With the exception of Book 7, and the possible exception of Book 6, I'm not sure the rest are great books, when taken individually. I wouldn't want to argue that *Sorcerer's Stone*, alone, is a great book, or *Chamber of Secrets* or *Prisoner of Azkaban* or *Goblet of Fire* or even *Order of the Phoenix*. But I see no reason to take them alone, for Harry's story is a seven-part saga which, collectively, in my view, *is* a great book. It's a book that took the author seventeen years to write and a book that took all of us ten years to read for the first time (we were forced to pace our reading, weren't we?). Now, though, consider Harry's story as a 4100-page book we can reread any time, and as many times as we like. And it's doing just that, I believe, that convinces us that Rowling's Potter story is a great book, is legitimate literature, legit lit.

We re-readers of the *Potter* books can easily think of them as a unified whole for the simplest of reasons. The plots are continuations and are interlinked – You-Know-Who has split his soul thousands of pages before we even know what a Horcrux is. The theme is consistent – and has it ever been described more succinctly and accurately than when John Granger wrote in 2004: "Love's victory over death in story form"? And the characters evolve naturally over time. This latter point is obvious not only as we consider how

Harry and the other *young* characters evolve and mature; but also how many of the older characters are not nearly so static or one-dimensional as we first thought them to be – as in the cases of Dumbledore and Snape.

PRUBONIC PLAGUE

Yet all of what I've just said is predicated on having read every page of all seven books, whether you conceive of them individually or as a unit with seven parts. Ah, but there's the rub: reading Rowling's books before judging them. What makes assessing the *Potter* novels as legit lit or as canonical literature for some people problematic and difficult is that they, incredibly, *haven't read the books.* And some of them (and some of my friends are in this group) judge negatively without having read a word. They suffer from a malady I call Presumptive Reader Unworthiness Based on Non-Reading, or PRUBON. You and I know there's still a virtual PRUBONic plague out there among Harry haters who've never read the Potter books, but may have seen one or two of the film adaptations before concluding that Rowling's books are, like TRIX, for kids.

Famous early adverse critics of the *Potter* books are William Safire, A. S. Byatt, and Professor Harold Bloom of Yale. Professor Bloom, who had read only *Sorcerer's Stone* before condemning the books in a July 2000 *Wall Street Journal* article, is my poster boy for PRUBON. He has later called the books "rubbish," and seems to me to be a reminder of the frustration that comes not so much from *Potter* readers trying to convince non-readers of the worth and wonder of the books, but from nonreaders trying to convince readers of their worthlessness. It's hard to imagine judging the entire *Potter* series on *Sorcerer's Stone* alone. Suppose you ask someone if they've read *Hamlet*; and they answer, "Yes . . . well, I read part of the first act, and I didn't think *Hamlet* was so great – just a bunch of palace guards and a ghost."

Call me a Pottersnob if you like, but I'm really not interested in hearing how bad the books are, or how unworthy as classic lit they are, or how inferior they are to those of Lewis or Tolkien by people who've read fewer than all 4100 pages of Rowling. Again, would a lover of *Hamlet* want to sit down to the taking of toast and tea and talk about the play with people who didn't quite make it to the "to be or not to be" part, or who don't know their Fortinbras from their Guildenstern?

How can you explain a Horcrux to a reader who thinks Fluffy is as menacing as it's going to get? How, except by reading the whole, could you possibly explain how Harry's saga progresses from a fear of being hit by a Bludger to a fear of being bludgeoned to death by a killing curse; from a dread of detentions to a dread of dementors; and from dying of embarrassment in Potions class in a dungeon to a decision to die for those dearly loved in the depth of the Forbidden Forest?

Forty-one hundred pages is a big novelistic mountain to climb, a lot of negative inertia to overcome, I admit. So is a book the size of *War and Peace* or a novel as difficult as *Ulysses* or *Finnegan's Wake* or a play as complex as *Hamlet*. But in the cases of Tolstoy and Joyce and Shakespeare, we have academics who've read those literary texts thoroughly and encourage (or require for a grade) you and me to read them as well. With Rowling, we have some academics *not* reading literary texts that they then discourage *us* from reading and taking seriously. They suffer from PRUBON and know not what they do. So the first problem in curing someone of PRUBON is getting them to read the book, the whole book, and nothing but the book.

The next possible reason for some people's resistance to the idea that the Potter books are legit lit has to do who wrote them. Indeed, *who has* written them? People were asking this question by the hundreds of thousands ten or eleven years ago. These wildly successful "children's books" were written by She-Who-Could-Not-Be-Named, an unknown, a first-time author, a woman hiding behind a man's initials. And She-Who-Could-Not-Be-Named had a name we didn't even know how to pronounce; did it rhyme with *howling* or *bowling*? The early stories that circulated about Rowling were that she was a single mother, living on the government dole, writing these books on napkins in a café, and living in her car (I think maybe here in America that last rumor was borrowed from the Hilary Swank and Jim Carrey rags-to-riches stories). So, maybe, in some of the more narrow academic minds, a composite picture of the author and of these books was taking shape: Rowling is "not Oxford, not Cambridge, not intellectual, not sophisticated, maybe not respectable, not male" (once the J.K. was solved) – alas, she's a poor, pale imitation of Tolkien and Lewis, a female Inkling wanna-be. And *that's* a lot of negative inertia to overcome too, isn't it?

THE THREE DEATHLY HALLOWS FOR ACADEMICS

Let's now consider another problem some academics might have with the notion that Rowling's books are serious and enduring literary works. Conventional wisdom in academe would be that the Potter books, or any books for that matter, should surely not be considered "legit lit" for one or more of these three reasons: they're too juvenile, they're too recent, and they're too popular. In the *TIME* magazine article on Rowling as a "Person of the Year" runner up, I am quoted as calling these condemnations of the books "the three Deathly Hallows for academics." Let's consider the first Deathly Hallow: too juvenile. Academics in traditional adult literary fields tend to hallow "serious" literature written for adult readers, not juvenile fiction; they write articles and books about Moby Dick, not Flipper. Yet, as C. S. Lewis said long ago, a children's book that is not enjoyable to adults is not a very good children's book. Is it inconceivable that a book for both children and adults is a really good, if not a great book for both? What does reader reaction suggest? Do a significant number of adults find Rowling's "juvenile" books worthwhile? Apparently so; this would appear to be a safe assumption from the hard evidence of millions and millions of adult sales statistics, to the soft evidence of simply looking around in a public place a day or so after a new volume has come out and noticing who's reading *Harry*.

The *New York Times* best seller list would have continued to be dominated by Rowling's books for years to come, I'm sure, until the separate "juvenile" category was created (in her honor, or to her dishonor?) in the summer of 2000 – so that Rowling became the woman who parted the "read" sea at *The New York Times*. That renowned newspaper or any publication or person can label the *Potter* books as "juvenile" all they want, but we know those hundreds of millions of "juvenile" readers from their late teens to, perhaps, their nineties are smiling and turning the pages constantly.

Now, let's think about the second academics' Deathly Hallow, the assumption that the *Potter* books are too recent to be considered serious literature. Academics hallow books that have "stood the test of time." It would seem that the world has to wait until the author has been long and safely dead before the work is fully appreciated and praised. By this scenario, the phrase "starving artist" becomes redundant, since the artist will *always* be starving during his lifetime; such has been the case from time immemorial, from Poe to Van Gogh. Time, much time, must pass before greatness is recognized. Don't think I haven't been struck by the irony of driving to teach my *Harry Potter* classes at Pepperdine University in a car considerably older than the books I'm going to teach (my car is a 1992 Acura and is a serious candidate for *Pimp My Ride*). However, I would argue that – whether old or recent, whether a centuries-old "classic" or an oxymoronic "instant classic" – a good book is a good book. Relevant to this point may be what Robert Frost once said about how a great poem affects us, that readers of such poems don't have to wait a long time to see if they remember the poem; they know at first reading that they'll never forget it. After all, I know how I felt about *Othello* the moment I first read it when I was about sixteen years old. The play just happened to have been written a few centuries before I first discovered it, but I would have felt the same about it if it had been written a week ago last Tuesday.

Thirdly, let's think about the academic Deathly Hallow that a book really popular with unwashed masses of readers (like you and me) could not possibly be great literature. After all, literary history seems to teach us that the masses will always be wrong, will always prefer Nathaniel Parker Willis to Edgar Allan Poe, Richard Henry Dana to Herman Melville, and John Neal to Nathaniel Hawthorne (Willis, Dana, and Neal are real authors who were once more widely read and appreciated than those other guys). To some in the academy, a popular book is the antithesis of "serious" literature. Historically, best-selling authors are not Pulitzer- or Nobel-prize winning authors (Hemingway would disprove this point, but Faulkner and a few hundred others would prove it). Popular lit is usually not literature that rewards with rereading. Once we know "who done it," we don't revisit the book to see if he/she "done it" again.

Yet, the facts that Rowling's popular books are being taught in universities, that they are the subjects of a growing number of scholarly studies, and that they are reread continuously by millions of readers indicate to me that she has done the more than improbable: she has written immensely "popular classics" – which richly reward "ordinary" re-readers and scholarly researchers alike. Her works exemplify and yet defy the characteristics of popular lit. Like all classic lit, a *Potter* book remains a thing of beauty that is a joy even after we know that Harry lives, that Dumbledore dies, and that Snape is not pure evil – which is precisely like still loving and still rereading other classics even though we know that Dimmesdale is the father, that Mr. Darcy is really good, and that Daisy was driving the car. I *would* say, "Sorry for the spoilers," but for the serious student of serious literature there *are* no spoilers, and nothing can really be spoiled.

Now, if some in academe feel strongly that Rowling's popularity, her contemporaneousness, and her "kiddy books" forever disqualify her from entrance into the coveted literary canon, let's think for a few moments about that literary canon. The *Webster's Collegiate* dictionary meaning that applies here is that a canon is "a sanctioned or accepted group or body of related works [such as] (the [canon] of great literature)." How this plays out in reality is that the canon of, say American literature, would be works that are taught in colleges and universities, are published in anthologies, and serve as the subjects of book-length studies, articles, theses, and dissertations by professors and those studying to become professors in colleges and universities. Notice in my previous description, we're back to where we started, colleges and universities.

When I was an undergraduate the canon in American and in British literature was DWEM dominated (Dead White European Males); today it is far more diverse, far more of a loose canon. Yet, still, for some in academe, I strongly suspect that the idea of Rowling's *Potter* books being within the established canon of great books is unthinkable. The fact is that Rowling's books are being taught in a significant number of colleges and universities throughout the world now; and, in the U.S., they're being taught at my own university, Georgetown, Swarthmore, Frostburg State, Kent State, James Madison, Vanderbilt, Harvard, Kansas State, at the Universities of Oklahoma, Alabama, and Washington, *and* at Professor Bloom's university, Yale, to name just a few. In many cases, like my own classes, the books are being taught as if they are *bona fide* literary works worth serious study and attention to the text, as if they are main-line, canonical, legit lit. And so far, to my knowledge, neither my fellow *Potter* professors nor I have been arrested by any guardians of the conservative canon - Life Eaters, let's call them: canon crusaders who would ferret out teachers, like me, who put Billy Collins on their syllabi and force them to substitute Hart Crane.

HARRY POTTER IN THE UNIVERSITY CLASSROOM

In my classes, I put Rowling in the best of company, past and present. If an amazingly deft handling of narrative misdirection or ironic foreshadowing comes up in class, we talk about some earlier master of the techniques, like Jane Austen. When the Rowling wit is wicked, the humor is working, and the air is as thick with puns as with flying gnomes, we talk about Mark Twain or Swift. When we come to Dumbledore's "Remember Cedric Diggory" speech, we read A. E. Housman's beautiful "To An Athlete Dying Young." Great literature reminds you of great literature.

I'd like to discuss what my classes in the *Potter* books have consisted of, what they've required of the students, what kinds of things we've talked about, and what kinds of subjects the students have researched and reported on. To give it away right at the start (here's a spoiler), we didn't do anything different from what we'd have done if we'd been studying a famous, time-honored literary work by one securely in the canon, like Tennessee Williams' *The Glass Menagerie* or Faulkner's *The Sound and the Fury*. I've taught first-year seminars in the *Potter* books (100-level classes) the past two fall terms, and this past January semester I taught a 300-level upper-division class on Rowling's books. In each case, the class was open only to students who had

already read all of the *Potter* books. Rereading any text as richly encoded as
Rowling's yields uncountable rewards and surprises, and the fun starts early
– as when the name Sirius Black and the reference to his motorbike surprise
unsuspecting re-readers a mere fourteen pages into the 4100.

My classes, both the first-year and the upper-division courses, have
been open to students of all majors, not just English. The variety here has
been quite interesting; I've had students majoring in virtually everything my
university offers a major in, including that most popular of all majors for
beginning students, undeclared. One thing the students in all of these classes
had in common, in addition to being Harry-lovers, is that they were always
prepared, almost all were enthusiastic, and most were quite talkative. I don't
recall a single class meeting when students didn't seem fresh from the assigned
rereading. I'll have to confess that as a long-time teacher of upper-division
literature classes *for literature majors,* I have all too often gotten a distinctly
different impression about students having done the assigned reading for that
day. There have been times when *The Glass Menagerie* was assigned, but some
of my students hadn't been called on by the gentleman caller yet, some days
when we're starting *The Sound and the Fury* and my students have not yet
arrived on Mississippi soil.

All four classes I've taught thus far in the *Potter* books have been
fully enrolled, and at one point last fall during pre-registration, I had more
students on the waiting list than were already registered for the full class. Just
in case you think I think I had anything to do with that student demand, by
the way, none of the first-year students had met me or (I'm sure) even heard
of me in advance; and, of the upper-division students, I had had only one in
a previous class. So if it wasn't the professor, I wonder why student demand
for those *Potter* courses was so high? I'll bet it was the easy work load; after
all, only a little research, two essays, an oral presentation, and reading 4100
pages was involved.

Subjects related to the *Potter* books were our focus in the classes
during the second part of the term – after we'd all re-read and discussed
the seven books one more time through together. These discussions and
student presentations were on the following topics: (1) literary analogues and
antecedents of the *Potter* series; (2) comparisons and contrasts of the *Potter*
series with those of Tolkien and Lewis; (3) *Harry* haters and *Harry* lovers,
critical and popular support of and opposition to Rowling's books; (4) Harry's
lies and rule-breaking, some ethical considerations; (5) S.P.E.W. and beyond
– race, racism, discrimination, and prejudice in the *Potter* books; (6) women
in Harry's world, feminist views on the *Potter* books; (7) the wise, the boring,

the mundane, and the mean – the Hogwarts professors and their pedagogy; (8) Harry goes to the movies – an overview of the *Potter* film adaptations; (9) Christian symbols and themes in the *Potter* books – WWHD; and (10) the metaphorical possibilities of being magic or Muggle.

Both for me and my students, secondary sources proved invaluable - not only those established and respected web sites we all know and love, but print sources as well, like the collections of essays edited by Giselle Anatol, David Baggett and Shawn Klein, Lana Whited, and Elizabeth Heilman. Books by David Colbert, John Granger, Tom Morris, John Killinger, Philip Nel, Connie Neal, and many other writers were wonderful secondary source material for all my classes to learn from. These are books published by the likes of Tyndale and by university presses, books that are written by current university professors and by former Vanderbilt and Notre Dame professors of theology and philosophy. Taken together, they represent a small but growing number of academics who are devoting time and energy to the study of Rowling's work.

So talking about some of the ideas these scholars present in their articles, books, and web sites, along with using these secondary sources for our class discussions and presentations occupied the second half of the term. But now that I've put the cart before the thestral, let me return to our rereading of the seven books together – our class meetings during the first half of the term. With each of the *Potter* books, just as with each book I come to with my students in literature classes dealing with established canonical writers, we talked about impressive and noteworthy fictional elements. We were least interested in plot, intricately plotted though the books may be. We were, after all, re-readers, not just readers. So, as I've already said, once we know that Harry lives, that Dumbledore is really dead, that Snape loved Lily his whole life long, and other such matters, we go elsewhere, beyond plot, to satisfy our curiosity and find our surprises. This is why I didn't lose any sleep before Book 7 appeared over whether Harry would live or die. Of course I wanted him to live (and, of course, I predicted precisely that to my friends; didn't we all?); but if plot Harry were to die, literary Harry would live on. Plot Hamlet dies, but literary Hamlet is going on 408 and counting.

It is instructive, by the way, still on the subject of plot, to consider how Book 1 leads to the titular adventure in a conventional, formulaic way: boy confronts evil in a turban; boy wins, and boy gets stone. Things become a little more complex, and less predictable, with each book until, by the end of Book 7, "all" Rowling is doing is keeping us up with the status of a few dozen characters whom we care very dearly about, advancing the plot toward the final confrontation between good and evil, reporting on the casualties in the Battle of Hogwarts, and taking Harry *Agonistes* through his Gethsemane and to his Golgotha. With regard to the Battle, Rowling uses the proverbial cast of thousands involved in waging "botanical warfare" (Sprout and Neville and their plants that do nasty things to the enemy), "pedagogical warfare" (McGonagall sends desks on the march), "divinational warfare" (Trelawney launches her crystal balls and makes them good for something), and "giant warfare" (as Grawp does his part) – while the other side employs arachnidian weapons and dementoric warfare. Shades of *Götterdämmerung*. You might say the plots of the seven books range from the simplicity of a sitcom to the complexity of a Wagnerian opera.

REREADING POTTER

Literary studies thrive on close and repeated re-readings for matters quite beyond plot, no matter how complex and impressive the plot may be; let's call these meta-plot readings of a text. So, beyond plot, here are some of the things we talk about in my classes – the parts of the novels that make the whole so impressive, the innuendoes, the implications and applications, the richness of the books. Consider first wit, humor, puns, and wordplay – which, arguably, some might consider the least significant literary feature of a great work of literature.

Humor

Rowling's full range as a gifted humorist is evident upon rereading. Humor is there in many forms, from slapstick and sight gags – Fred and George's pyrotechnic exit from Hogwarts – to the subtle humor of Arthur Weasley's interest in how the Anglia flew overriding his chiding of his sons the car thieves. Rowling is a wordsmith and a neologist (that is, she creates neologisms, coins words – and, technically, I coined neologist, so it's a neologism). She does this over and over with Latin and quasi-Latin-English mixtures for so many of her named items in the *Potter* books. If you need to move a Christmas tree, it's *Mobiliarbus* (making the arbus mobile); if you want to raise a body, it's *Levicorpus* (levitate the corpse). I might say here it helps me a bit that I did make it to Latin III in high school (notice my preposition, made it *to* not *through* Latin III); but Rowling knows Latin, Greek, and French very well. John Granger has called Latin her second language. But bilingual word humor or punning aside, check out how often she's punning on "grim" and "serious" and "seriously" in Book 3 – the book that is essentially about the serious matter of Sirius Black – like when McGonagall tells Harry he can have his Firebolt back, and he says "Seriously?" Sirius-ly he received the

Firebolt, and seriously he gets it back.

You might notice the gradual introduction of semi-bawdy humor in the *Potter* books too. Is it accidental that Rowling has Harry see, in Book 3, a book on a table display at Flourish and Blotts called *Broken Balls: When Fortunes Turn Foul?* Surely it's not accidental in Book 4 that Myrtle seems to be recalling with pleasure watching Cedric in the bathtub for "ages and ages" until "nearly all the bubbles had gone" (464). Notice too that we get "he swore" or "Lee Jordan swore" and similar comments in the early books, but Rowling treats us to a few oaths of the magic world by Book 7, with Ron's swearing in the name of "Merlin's saggy left – " (92). The sentence is unfinished; was that going to be left *arm*? I don't mean to belabor the point. You know the books are very effectively comedic, and in my classes we get serious about Rowling's humor and wordplay, right down to the individual words, seriously.

Narrative Misdirection

The predominant narrative technique used throughout the Potter books is a third-person limited point of view, limited to what Harry knows at any given time, which is, more often than not, not much or not correct. Here are three quotes from the first three books: "Harry didn't have a clue what was going on (*Stone* 258); "Harry didn't have a clue what was going on . . ." (*Chamber* 195), and "Harry didn't have a clue what was going on" (*Prisoner* 393). Of course, so often when Harry thinks he knows *exactly* what's going on, he's just as clueless – as are we. This is the beauty of narrative misdirection, so often used by Jane Austen in the novels Rowling has mentioned as her favorites. We're just as clueless about Snape until near the end of the final book, as we were when we, along with Harry, first sized him up with his greasy hair and cruel stare. First-time readers of Book 3 have told me, in fact, that they are convinced Crookshanks is the animal with the magical powers and a heart of evil, not "poor Scabbers." Many scenes with cat and rat lead us in that direction; Rowling is capable of animal narrative misdirection, as well as human.

Foreshadowing

As we went through each book together in class, we talked of Rowling's deftness with another literary device, foreshadowing. It starts with the first chapter of the first book with the mention of that motorbike. Foreshadows involving Peter the Rat in the descriptions and comments about Scabbers, or the reaction of Neville when he sees the Cruciatus Curse demonstrated in class are examples of straightforward foreshadowing, literary hinting at what will come to pass. Yet there are ironies upon ironies sometimes, as when Hermione is worried that, horrible thought, Harry's Firebolt might have been sent to him by Sirius Black – which it was, but not by Sirius the evil killer escaped from prison, but by Sirius, Harry's godfather wanting to make up for thirteen years of birthday gifts not given. The Russian playwright Anton Chekhov observed that if play goers see a gun in Act I, it had better go off by the final act. An incredible number of the guns we have seen in the *Potter* books seem to go off by, or in, Book 7 – whole arsenals of them in fact.

    I'd like to cite one last example of foreshadowing for you to appreciate more fully Rowling's accomplished technique in this area. Colin Creevey's death in Book 7 is, it seems to me, strongly foreshadowed in Book 2. In *Chamber of Secrets*, just after Harry talks with Dobby in the hospital wing, Dumbledore and McGonagall bring in the petrified body of Colin. McGonagall has found him "trying to sneak up here to visit Potter" (180). When Harry overhears this, his "stomach gave a horrible lurch." The description of Colin's *death* in Book 7 is strikingly similar. Harry sees the body of Colin, again borne by two people, Neville and Oliver Wood, being taken to the Great Hall with the others killed in the Battle of Hogwarts. Harry "felt another dull blow to his stomach": Colin Creevey, though underage, "must have sneaked back" to fight in the battle (694). The parallels are indeed close; taken together, they show not only the care Rowling takes in her narrative voice, but also the consistency of Colin's character. He is under-aged and undersized for what his heart tells him to do, and he twice pays a price for his considerable courage. The crucial difference in the two very similar scenes is simple and profound. In Book 2, in the end, when the Mandrakes are ready, Colin, Hermione, and all the others who've been petrified are returned to normal; but in Book 7 no Mandragora, no magic of any kind, can bring Colin back. "He was tiny in death."

    I suspect that Rowling structures even another passage, many pages earlier in *Chamber of Secrets*, at least in part, as a foreshadowing of tiny Colin's eventual fate. The scene takes place in a crowded hallway after classes are over and students are rushing to dinner. Harry, with Ron and Hermione, walks along, preoccupied about another matter, and as they pass Colin, he, predictably, says an enthusiastic, "Hiya, Harry!" (153). Harry says hello back "automatically," but before Colin can finish a sentence, he's lost in the crowd. Since Colin "was so small he couldn't fight against the tide of people bearing him toward the Great Hall; they heard him squeak, 'See you, Harry!' and he was gone."

Character

Even a minor character like Colin, first seen as the shutterbug, following Harry around like a puppy, in the end has enough depth and character that we care about him. Over 4100 pages think how rounded and dynamic and three-dimensional so many characters become. You could almost pick a name out of a hat and find plenty to say by way of character analysis; hopefully you wouldn't get Mundungus Fletcher, but think, for example, about Molly Weasley: stereotypically maternal; sometimes nagging, but always loving mother and wife; fearing above all what her Boggart turns into; realizing those worst fears when she loses Fred; loving Harry and eventually Fleur unconditionally; and using the "b" word on just the right occasion. Molly's use of *bitch* is as right as Rhett Butler's famous *damn*, isn't it?

I can't leave the subject of character without asking you, what if you'd pulled Snape's name out of the hat and had to write a character analysis of him? Would you need to read past Book 1 to write a good and true report? Scene after scene, twenty glimpses into who Snape really is, each more revealing than the last, finally, come three chapters from the end of the last book. In the amazing "The Prince's Tale" chapter, we begin to understand this magnificent literary character. Even Dumbledore is moved to tears, as he sees the silver doe, asking "After all this time?" followed by Snape's one word, "Always." (687) And Snape's final whispered words to Harry, "Look . . . at . . . me" (658), speak volumes now that we know what we know. Seeing Lily's eyes in Harry's as he dies, Severus Snape, hated by Harry for seven years, called "coward," a traitor, is, Harry will tell his son, "probably the bravest men I ever knew." Snape's death scene holds its own very well among a whole host of literary deaths on the pages of many of those books in the canon; and it's even more impressive when we reread it knowing what we find out about his life from the Pensieve scenes.

Magical Devices

Since I just mentioned the Pensieve, just think of all the devices and inventions these Rowling books have given us. From the Put-Outer, to the Pensieve, the Remembrall, Howlers, the craziness of Quidditch, and, though only the name is her invention, Muggles. I like to think of them not as people without magic, but people without imagination (or people who don't read Rowling). I always enjoy a little Muggle-related humor in the books. You might not have noticed one little barb directed at Muggles buried in a passage describing Hermione's homework load in Book 3. Each night in the common room, she has her notes and books spread out, poring over such things as "Arithmancy charts, rune dictionaries, diagrams of Muggles lifting heavy objects . . ." (244). Surely these diagrams are in her text for the Muggle Studies course. And what a curiosity and even a wonder it would be to depict for magical people all the things that non-magical people have to do to move a sofa or pick up slab of marble without being able to say *Mobilisofa* or *Accio marble*.

Pathos

In addition to all these inventions and devices, Rowling gives us a number of unforgettable scenes of great pathos in the books. Near the end of Book 4, Molly's bending down to embrace Harry, who had no memory of ever feeling a mother's embrace before; Harry's efforts in Book 5 following Sirius' death to communicate with Sirius through the mirror and by his frantic questioning of Nick about contacting one who has passed through the veil; the night the Weasleys await news of whether Arthur will live or die from the snake attack; Christmas on the closed ward at St. Mungo's when Neville, gum wrapper in hand, defies Harry or anyone else to laugh at the actions of his afflicted mother; Dumbledore's funeral; the return of Percy in Book 7 and the death of Fred – these scenes, like Frost's example of poems we read, are scenes we know at first sight we'll never forget. In fact, the palpable, undeniably emotional responses my students felt from these and many other passages came from still young readers with uncountable life experiences awaiting them that will surely cause them to react more emotionally over time. I surely feel these scenes more keenly as a result of life experiences. My parents passed through the veil years ago. I spent a long night in a hospital once waiting to see if my father would live or die, and I have been to more than my share of funerals and memorial services for some as good and wise as the headmaster himself.

Style

Still another matter, so often obvious in how such scenes as these are described to us, is the author's changing style. As Harry and his friends mature, so does the narrative voice. Somewhat poetic passages begin to appear in Book 3, passages with cadences, even rhyme, and rhetorical elegance and eloquence. One such passage is Hermione's return of the broken parts of Harry's whomped Nimbus: Hermione turns the bag upside down on Harry's bed "and tipped a dozen bits of splintered wood and twig onto the bed, the only remains of Harry's faithful, finally beaten broomstick" (*Prisoner* 182). Later, in a description of Harry's dilemma of the dementors enabling him to hear his mother's voice, but hearing that voice in agony, Rowling writes:

"Harry dozed fitfully, sinking into dreams full of clammy, rotted hands and petrified pleading, jerking awake to dwell again on his mother's voice" (184). Readers of the *Potter* books are hearing a narrative voice more poignant and poetic than before as well.

Consider the style in which Rowling writes of the death of Fred in Book 7. First we have Fred's laughter over the prodigal Percy's having made a joke, then the explosion, and then, like lines out of John's Apocalypse, Rowling writes: "the world was rent apart . . . And then the world resolved itself into pain and semidarkness . . ." (636). Then she takes our hands, as Harry takes Hermione's, and leads us to the grieving others at whom "Fred's eyes stared without seeing, the ghost of his last laugh still etched upon his face" (637). Rowling's next sentence is reminiscent and worthy of many a lament from antiquity, from Homer or the Old Testament or Shakespeare; they sound the same. She writes: "The world had ended, so why had the battle not ceased, the castle fallen silent in horror, and every combatant laid down their arms?" (638). The old, pain-filled hyperbole – a loved warrior has fallen, how can the war go on, a brother has been killed, how can the world continue? – is achieved beautifully here by Rowling.

Magical Creatures

A couple of Rowling inventions that take on quite an effective and natural symbolism about them as well are the dementors and thestrals. Most who have written on the dementors generally take the creatures to be embodiments of depression. Giving a form, an existence, to depression – something which, when and where I grew up, was often left untreated and unacknowledged – is noteworthy. Another literary creation somewhat like the dementors would be the Garp family's understanding of the Undertoad in John Irving's *The World According to Garp*.

In addition to dementors, Rowling invents thestrals. You might recall that when Hagrid explains to the class about thestrals, Parvati, among the many students who cannot see thestrals, repeats the conventional wisdom about them: they're unlucky, and all sorts of horrible misfortune will come to those who see them. Hagrid, laughing, says that's just superstition and that thestrals are clever and useful. We later learn too that they have a great sense of direction to take us wherever we need to be. Being able to see thestrals, witnessing someone passing from life, forever affects how one views life; this seems to be Rowling's implication in the whole matter of "seeing thestrals." As with the dementors, Rowling makes the intangible and inexpressible more accessible by embodying it in a created thing, in this case a beautiful animal not to be feared, dreaded, or avoided, once we know how to look at it, once we can see it. These veiled observations about death, that next great adventure for the organized mind, and about those who have seen death are quite unforgettable – especially to those of us, and I am one, who can see thestrals.

THEMES: FEAR AND LOVE

How about still another category by which we might assess the greatness of Rowling's series: themes that grow out of the books that might have real-life meaning and application for millions of readers. I would argue that Rowling's dominant themes are that we should fear what fear can do to us, and that we should love unconditionally. Forty-one hundred pages, and I come up with "against fear" and "for love" by way of analysis. Yes, just that.

First a word about fear. In Book 3, not only will Lupin pick up on Harry's worst fear being fear during the dementor lessons; we also have an anticipatory scene about being afraid to the point of ruining your life back at good old Flourish and Blotts. The bookstore manager sees Harry looking at the cover of a book entitled *Death Omens: What to Do When You Know the Worst Is Coming* (54). What the manager tells Harry is priceless advice and widens the scene in the bookstore considerably by its implications for a very frightened contemporary culture, it seems to me. The manager tells Harry that he shouldn't read *Death Omens* because Harry will "start seeing death omens everywhere. It's enough to frighten anyone to death" (54). How many death omens are out there for us to see if we're looking for them? Here's a partial list: terror alerts and terror attacks, WMDs, West Nile virus, bird flu, mad cow disease, anthrax-laced packages, e coli on lettuce leaves, tainted tomatoes, lead paint in toys, and poisoned dog food. Rowling's brief scene involving a discussion of fears of death seems all the more extraordinary since it was written two years before 9/11, as well as before fears growing out of most of the other "death omens" on my list. I know more than a few people personally (and I see others on television) who seem to see death omens everywhere and seem frightened to death of death. The bookstore manager's right, and so is Lupin: look away from that book, Harry, and you're wise to fear fear.

From fear to love we go in this profoundly simple view of two of the books' most pervasive themes. Fear and love come together in both the graveyard scene in Book 4 and in the forest scene in Book 7, for in both cases the presence of the essences of Harry's loved ones are a source of courage for Harry. In *Goblet of Fire*, James and Lily tell him to "hold on," assure him that "it will be all right," and enable him to escape Voldemort by the Portkey (667-68). In "The Forest Again" in Book 7, James, Sirius, Lupin, and Lily emerge "neither ghost nor truly flesh" and "on each face, there was the same loving smile" (698-99). As Harry walks into the forest toward what he thinks is his sure death, "Beside him, making scarcely a sound, walked James, Sirius, Lupin, and Lily, and their presence was his courage, and the reason he was able to keep putting one foot in front of the other" (700). How's that for love triumphing over fear, even fear of death?

Of course, if we're going to talk about love, we're going to talk about Dumbledore. Because it is in the headmaster's words that Rowling has written most about love – just love. The professor has taught (or reminded) us that sacrificial love is a very great source of power, that it's in our very skin, that the dead whom we love never really leave us, that when we have been and are loved we are protected by an ancient magic, and that, in the Prophecy, "the power the Dark Lord knows not" just means love – "Yes, just love." One of the last things Dumbledore says in the "King's Cross" chapter of Book 7 brings together these twin themes of fear and love. He's telling Harry that Voldemort would probably not have been interested in the Resurrection Stone even if he knew its powers, for "whom would he want to bring back from the dead? He fears the dead. He does not love" (721). The great professor is still professing after death, isn't he?

CONCLUSION: IS HARRY POTTER GREAT LITERATURE?

Now, by way of summary and review, we've been appropriately critical of those who condemn but don't read Rowling, we've tried to give an overview of scholarly activity and of Harry on college campuses, where, after all, literary canons are established, and we've just gone through what I think are very impressive intrinsic reasons to take Harry's story as seriously as we take the *Narnia* chronicles or *The Lord of the Rings* trilogy. We've looked at just a very few examples of effective humor, wit, and wordplay; Rowling's narrative technique; her uses of foreshadowing; her memorable characterizations; the devices and inventions; her many scenes of genuine pathos; her evolving style; her symbols; and the themes permeating her work.

Every time I look back at these impressive aspects of the novels, I am struck too by how much better the books get. We re-readers know this and, in frustration, know that partial readers don't and can't possibly know this. Forgetting for the moment that Rowling conceived and planned so much, much more than even the most sophisticated first readers realized, there is, too, a natural authorial phenomenon often observed – the maturing of the writer on the pages of the books, right before our eyes. So it's useful and accurate to think not only of the difference in sophistication, complexity, deftness, and style between *Sorcerer's Stone* and *Deathly Hallows* as comparable to the differences between an eleven-year-old child and a seventeen-year-old young man. But it's also instructive to think, by way of comparison, of the differences between Faulkner's early novel *Mosquitoes* and *The Sound and the Fury* or Melville's first novel *Typee* and *Moby-Dick*.

I have had countless wonderful conversations about the *Potter* books both in and out of the classroom, and I have also had a number of awkward and sometimes confrontational conversations with fellow academics who, at best, are worried about me and my new literary passion and who, at worst, are maybe worried about a tarnishing of the sacred British literary canon. These unpleasant conversations, in my case, have always, ALWAYS, been with a non-reader or a partial reader (the PRUBONic plague strikes yet again).

In fact, since Book 7 was published and Rowling's story was complete, I have yet to find a single reader of all 4100 pages who thinks the books are worthless *or* who thinks that they are vastly inferior to the works of those famous fantasy worthies, J. R. R. Tolkien and C. S. Lewis, august members of the Inklings. Many readers of Rowling, though, have an inkling (sorry) that she is equal to or better than Tolkien and Lewis, but many non-readers remain so convinced that this is impossible, outrageous, and a sacrilege that they will remain Rowling non-readers forever, chronically impaired by PRUBON. As I've said in public several time before, as a *bona fide* academic, a professor, a thirty-plus year teacher and reader of literature, reader and re-reader of more than a few books (maybe not a million, but a lot), I will tell you that I prefer the *Potter* books over those by Tolkien and Lewis *and* that I consider them superior literary works. In my view, Tolkien's trilogy seems to be more for adults than for children; Lewis's chronicles seem to be more for children than adults. Tolkien seems to me to be more for the head than the heart; Lewis more for the heart than the head.

Rowling's seven-part story, in my view, is one that is so rare as perhaps to be unprecedented in contemporary literature in that it is equally for child and adult, equally touching the heart and challenging the mind. It is solid gold; and, like the porridge, the chair, and the bed in *Goldylocks*; it is "just right." Carl Jung once wrote: "In every adult, there lurks a child – an eternal child, something that is always becoming, is never completed . . . " (98). The *Potter* story seems to speak uniquely to the child in the adult and the adult in the child, which might explain the eighty-year age range of those who read the books.

This is all a matter of taste and opinion, of course, but I do have my own personal ratings scale. This scale is a totally unscientific way I have of evaluating a literary work not for its relative greatness for all readers for all time (I'm a professor, not a pontificator), but just for the establishment of my own personal hierarchy of the books I read and teach. I consider if the work is *intellectually challenging*, and I rate it from 1 to 10 (10 being high). Then I ask myself if it is *emotionally rewarding*? Again, 1 to 10.

Now, for me, Tolkien's trilogy, for intellectually challenging gets a 10, for emotionally rewarding a 5. Lewis, on intellectually challenging, gets a 5, and emotionally rewarding a 10. The *Potter* books I give an 8 and an 8, for a total of 16, just narrowly beating out the Inklings on the Thomas scale. As you see, this is all very scientific and precise and not a bit arbitrary, is it? This is a bit like when Poe writes that the most sonorous sound in all of poetry is the long *o*, followed by the consonant *r*. I wonder why Poe would come up with *that*? (Lenore, floor, door, shore, nevermore, etc.) So, similarly arbitrarily, I make up a quantitative looking scale for a qualitative personal judgment since I prefer J.K. to J.R.R. or C.S.

The relative worth of these three writers aside, though, every time I look back at the *Potter* saga – the seven books or, as I prefer, the seven-part book – I see all kinds of reasons to assess these immensely popular books as serious literature well worth rereading and very likely to endure so long that my grandchildren will be reading them to their grandchildren. To vary the old saying, if these *Potter* books look like literature, smell like literature, taste like literature, feel like literature, and sound like literature, they must *be* literature. Despite the spiteful things some people say to the contrary and against all odds, they surely *must be* legit lit.

I'll close with a quotation from Lewis and one from Tolkien, which I'll apply to Rowling. Near the end of the last *Narnia* book, Lucy says, "This garden is like the stable. It is far bigger inside than it was outside" (224). Reminiscent of Rowling's tents and beaded purses and the Ford Anglia's trunk, these big books she's written, large as they are, *are* bigger on the inside than they are on the outside. And how much larger they *are*, re-readers find out with each rereading. So it is with great books.

In his forward to *The Fellowship of the Ring*, Tolkien writes about his goals in the trilogy: "The prime motive was the desire of a tale-teller to try his hand at a really long story that would hold the attention of readers, amuse them, delight them, and at times maybe excite them or deeply move them." Isn't Harry's "really long" story precisely that – a long story that holds attention, amuses, delights, excites, and deeply moves? So it is with great books; and so it is with Rowling's story of Harry, which, I must conclude, simply and sincerely, is a great book.

Bibliography

Jung, Carl. *The Wisdom of Carl Jung.* Ed. by Edward Hoffman. New York: Citadel Press, 2003.

Lewis, C.S. *The Last Battle.* New York: HarperTrophy, 1956.

Rowling, JK. *Harry Potter and the Chamber of Secrets.* New York: Scholastic,
1999.

___. *Harry Potter and the Deathly Hallows.* New York: Scholastic, 2007.

___. *Harry Potter and the Goblet of Fire.* New York: Scholastic, 2002.

___. *Harry Potter and the Half-Blood Prince.* New York: Scholastic, 2005

___. *Harry Potter and the Order of the Phoenix.* New York: Scholastic, 2004.

___. *Harry Potter and the Prisoner of Azkaban.* New York: Scholastic, 2001.

___. *Harry Potter and the Sorcerer's Stone.* New York: Scholastic, 1997.

Part II

Conversations on Eternal Truth

Chapter Three

The *Deathly Hallows* Epigraphs
Aeschylus and Penn Point to the Meaning of Harry Potter

John Granger

It seems borderline undeniable to me that the best writing is *inspired*, which is to say, not fully a product of the author's or poet's understanding. All those poets, playwrights, and wordsmiths who cry to their muse for inspiration – hacks like Homer, Virgil, Dante, Shakespeare, and Keats – and those critics who note the evident gap between the artist's conception and understanding of their work and the reality of it – know-nothings like Socrates, Aquinas, and Ruskin – back me up.

As important, I don't think Ms. Rowling believes she is the final authority for interpreting her work. She just doesn't play the part. For instance:

She doesn't answer questions about the meaning of even small details of her work, say, the reason she chose "Harry Potter" as the name of her lead character, except with the most nebulous and evasive answers. For this example, it has to be noted in a work in which most characters have names with layered meanings and referents, "I've always liked the name 'Harry'" and "there was a family on the street where I grew up named 'Potter'" are not substantive responses. She has also never given an interview to an adult literature maven to discuss her artistry, her intentions as a writer, or the influences of other writers on her work.

In this close-to-the-vest posture, Ms. Rowling is not being cagey or reclusive. This is in perfect conformity with the tradition of English letters, in which poets and writers leave the interpretation of their books to their readers. As George MacDonald once said in declining to parse the meaning and symbolism of one of his fantasy novels, "So long as I think my dog can bark, I will not sit up to bark for him" ("The Fantastic Imagination"). The work speaks for itself; failing that, it doesn't get a post-publication gloss from the author.

My bet is that this traditional "no comment" position is acknowledgement that, beyond the deliberate and pain-staking artistry of writing, much of the meaning is extra-personal, inspired, or, not to put too fine an edge on it, spiritual. Better writers are self-aware enough to know this and not posture as if they are their own muse; lesser writers are smart enough to act like better writers.

While Ms. Rowling balks at discussing the meaning of her works, she is quite generous in suggesting on her website and in interviews the lines of sight along which she thinks her meaning is best discerned. We have no less than *four* seemingly unrelated passages that the author shared with her readers as "the key" for understanding "all the books."

Ms. Rowling's Epigraph Comments: "They say it all to me. They really do"

We'll start with Ms. Rowling's interviews and her pointing to specific parts and passages of *Deathly Hallows* as important. In brief, the "key" bits are to be found in chapter 34, "The Forest Again," the scripture engraved on the Godric's Hollow gravestones Harry and Hermione read on Christmas Eve, Dumbledore's farewell to Harry at the non-local place he thinks of as King's Cross, and the epigraphs that start the book.

Deathly Hallows itself begins with two religiously themed epigraphs, one from *The Libation Bearers* by Aeschylus, which calls on the gods to "bless the children"; and one from William Penn's *More Fruits of Solitude*, which speaks of death as but "crossing the world, as friends do the seas." No other book in the series begins with epigraphs – a curious fact, perhaps, but one that Rowling insists served as a guiding light.

"I really enjoyed choosing those two quotations because one is pagan, of course, and one is from a Christian tradition," Rowling said of their inclusion. "I'd known it was going to be those two passages since *Chamber* was published. I always knew [that] if I could use them at the beginning of book seven then I'd cued up the ending perfectly. If they were relevant, then I went where I needed to go.

"They just say it all to me, they really do," she added (Adler).

In the same interview, she said the scriptural passages (Matthew 6:19, 1 Corinthians 15:26) on the headstones in *Deathly Hallows* (Chapter 16) "sum up – they almost epitomize the whole series." She told *TIME* magazine, too, that the First Corinthians quotation, "the last enemy to be destroyed is death," is "the theme for the entire series" (Gibbs).

Ms. Rowling wants her readers to think long and hard, too, about *Deathly Hallows* Chapter 34, "The Forest Again." She told Meredith Viera on *The Today Show* that her "favorite passage" and "favorite scene to write" are in that chapter (Viera). In her remarkable interview with Spanish reporter Juan Cruz, she explained, "That chapter is the key of all the books:"

> Everything, everything I have written, was thought of for that precise moment when Harry goes into the forest. That is the chapter that I had planned for 17 years. That moment is the heart of all of the books. And for me it is the last truth of the story.

When he walks into the forest, "it all came down to conscience," she said (Cruz).

In that same interview, she says the chapter *after* "The Forest Again" contains another "key" she waited seventeen years to write:

> Q: There's this dialogue between Harry and Professor Dumbledore: "Is this real? Or has this been happening inside my head?"

> A: And Dumbledore says: "Of course it is happening inside your head, but why on earth would that mean that is not real?" That dialogue is the key; I've waited seventeen years to use those lines. Yes, that's right. All this time I've worked to be able to write those two phrases; writing Harry entering the forest and Harry having that dialog.

Please note that Ms. Rowling hasn't told her readers *anything* in these interviews about what the books mean. She is explicit, though, about where to look to find this meaning. The "destruction of death" is somehow the "theme of the entire series," Harry's exercise of "conscience" in walking into the Forbidden Forest is "the heart of all the books," and Harry's final question to Dumbledore at King's Cross is "the key" to opening up the books. The *Deathly Hallows* epigraphs "cue up" this meaningful ending and "say it all."

Without conceding that she is the sole or even the best authority on what *Harry Potter* means, we can assume that her recommendations to serious readers looking for that meaning are excellent places to begin the search.

THE MEANING OF HARRY POTTER

In *The Deathly Hallows Lectures* and my other books I explore the four layers of meaning and ten genres "rowled" together seamlessly in the Hogwarts Saga. The core meaning of the books is intertwined with the story-line but well out of sight, beneath the surface story, the postmodern morality trumpeting the virtues of tolerance and loving sacrifice, and beneath both the alchemical scaffolding and explicit Christian symbolism. The "heart" of the books, if you will, is found by reading Harry's adventures as the story of the heart's purification and enlightenment.

There are several ways of "seeing" Harry as a story stand-in or symbol for the eye of the heart. You can review the alchemical symbolism and realize that Harry is the lead being changed into gold, which "hard darkness" to "solid light" transformation reflects the enlightenment of the alchemist's heart. You might look at Ron-Hermione-Harry trio and be struck how they are a body-mind-spirit triptych straight out of stories as diverse as *The Brothers Karamazov* and *Star Trek* (Harry being 'spirit' or the heart). You may even "see" this "eye of the heart" symbolism in Harry's use of the Invisibility Cloak, under which he can see all but cannot be seen.

The fast way or short cut, though, is in the *Deathly Hallows* King's Cross dialogue that Ms. Rowling has told us is so important:

> "Tell me one last thing," said Harry. "Is this real? Or has this been happening inside my head?"
>
> Dumbledore beamed at him, and his voice sounded loud and strong in Harry's ears even though the bright mist was descending again, obscuring his figure.
>
> "Of course it is happening inside your head, Harry, but why on earth should that mean it is not real?"

There is a chapter in *The Deathly Hallows Lectures* that explores this exchange in light of the eye and mirror symbolism of *Deathly Hallows* and the fascinating terrain and activity of what Harry thinks of as King's Cross but describes repeatedly as a "palace." My conclusion there is that Dumbledore's "reality inside your head" comment is consistent with a reading of the books as a story-symbol of Harry the *Logos* conscience or eye of the heart being purified – and 'King's Cross' as his experience of the Kingdom of Heaven within him. Call it "*Logos* land."

In brief, Ms. Rowling is writing within the symbolist tradition of English fantasy writers beginning with Samuel Taylor Coleridge and peaking, perhaps, in the works of the Inkling writers of the mid 20th century. One of the signature beliefs of these writers is that "the inside is bigger than the outside" (think about the Weasley car, Hermione's bag, and the Wizarding World's tents), which reflects in turn the belief that, as C. S. Lewis put it (citing Owen Barfield, the Coleridge maven), the "whole universe [is], in the last resort, mental" (Lewis, *Surprised* 209).

Not "mental" in the way Ron asks Harry, "Are you *mental?*" but in the sense that "mind" or conscience is continuous with if not identical to the

Logos, the Divine Principle which brings everything into existence. Lewis said Barfield taught him that "our logic [mental life] was participation in a cosmic *Logos*" (209). Our thinking and our ability to know anything, in other words, is the *Logos* within us, what Coleridge called the "primary imagination," Lewis "conscience," and Christ with the Hebrew prophets the "heart," recognizing the *Logos* beneath, behind, and within all created things.

Dumbledore's comment to Harry is "key" to understanding the series because it points to Harry as the story symbol of this *Logos* faculty within every human being (John 1:9). The dialogue between Harry and Dumbledore at what Harry calls "King's Cross" takes place within this non-local *Logos* in Harry's head and heart – where Harry quite uncharacteristically knows everything and is able to think things like robes into existence.

This *Logos* reality is "inside" his head but, instead of that meaning Harry's experience is subjective or delusional, it indicates that it is *more* real than anything "on the outside." The *Logos* is the fabric of reality itself.

As I explain in *Harry Potter's Bookshelf,* this is not Ms. Rowling's invention but her spectacular conformity to the Romantic tradition in which she writes, which tradition's *Logos* cosmology and epistemology in story form is a Christian counter-attack on materialists and scientism. It is the explanation of the King's Cross dialogue being a "key" to the series and why Harry's exercise of "conscience" in walking into the Forbidden Forest is "the heart of all the books." As we'll see, the *Logos* inside our hearts being "bigger" than anything "outside" also reveals the meaning of the Scriptural passages and the *Deathly Hallows* epigraphs.

Let's start with the "Greek chappie," as Hagrid might say, and look at Aeschylus' epigraph for hints of this *Logos* key that unlocks Harry's meaning.

The Libation Bearers Epigraph: Aeschylus in a Nutshell

I first wrote about Aeschylus at HogwartsProfessor.com in 2005, well before any of us could have imagined *Deathly Hallows*. I posted a thread about Aeschylus and Greek Drama way back then because it seemed to me that Ms. Rowling was rather obviously modeling Harry on Orestes, the hero of three plays by Aeschylus usually called *The Oresteia*. There are simply no other "young man coming into his own stories" which feature a boy with scar on forehead prophesied and determined to avenge the murder of his father. Not to mention that Orestes in one form of his legend marries Hermione, his cousin, the daughter of Menelaus and Helen.

Aeschylus is a giant in world literature and the scar-revenge-Hermione links between Harry and Orestes are fascinating, but, let's face it, most of us couldn't name three things Aeschylus wrote or place him in the right century on a timeline. I'm not going to turn this into an Aeschylus immersion course, though. My plan here is to lay out the passage Ms. Rowling chose as her opening for *Deathly Hallows* as it is in the context of *The Libation Bearers* and the *Oresteia* as a whole. That will allow us to move on to a discussion of what it means in relation to the Penn passage she selected as a complementary epigraph and ultimately how it was meant to work in relation to the events of Harry's final confrontation with the Dark Lord.

The first thing to say is that the epigraph she chose acts as a pointer to the actual events and qualities of the *Deathly Hallows* finish. Insomuch as Harry's victory is cathartic and conclusive if relatively comic compared to Orestes' finish, the epigraph is the foreshadowing bit of genius. Its greater value, though, is in its communicating the traditional worldview and understanding of the relationship of living and dead succinctly and mysteriously. These ideas are the power and point of the *Potter* epic – of *Hallows* especially – and the presentation of these profundities in the opening epigraph is one of Ms. Rowling's best touches.

Let's look at the Aeschylus epigraph (translation from the Greek by Robert Fagles):

> Oh, the torment bred in the race,
> the grinding scream of death
> and the stroke that hits the vein,
> the hemorrhage none can staunch, the grief,
> the curse no man can bear.
> But there is a cure in the house,
> and not outside it, no,
> not from others but from *them*,
> their bloody strife. We sing to you,
> dark gods beneath the earth.
> Now hear, you blissful powers underground –
> answer the call, send help,
> Bless the children, give them triumph now.
> (emphasis on 'them' in original translation)

The context of the passage in the play in which it is found, *The Libation Bearers*, helps in understanding its meaning. Orestes' sister Electra has been sent by their mother Clytemnestra to their father Agamemnon's tomb to pour a libation or gift offering. Clytemnestra murdered Agamemnon on his return from Troy and isn't sleeping well. She has had a dream about being murdered by a serpent she has birthed and fed at her breast. At the tomb, Electra prays with the Chorus of slavewomen for her brother Orestes to return from exile and avenge their father's murder and her family's disgrace.

But Orestes is already there, and, through a series of signs – locks of hair he has left at the tomb, foot prints she recognizes – she figures out he is nearby. The remaining part of the first act in this two act play is a series of invocations to father and mother by Orestes, Electra, and Chorus at the tomb to prepare and inspire Orestes for the vengeance he is to exact in the next act at his mother's place. The Chorus passage that Ms. Rowling chose as an epigraph, short of the brother-sister song between acts, is the most important piece of this lengthy peroration to the murder of Clytemnestra.

In the context of the three play *Oresteia* as a whole, this choral song is the middle point of the middle play (a fourth play, something of a masque not introducing new story points per se or reordering the facts of the drama – think of it as an epilogue? – has been lost). In *Agamemnon*, the first play, the father is murdered by the mother. In *The Libation Bearers*, the father's murder is avenged by his children. In the *Eumenides*, the Furies attack Orestes for his matricide and he seeks relief in court (!). The *Hallows* epigraph, literally and figuratively, is the turning point or pivot of the Oresteian Trilogy in which the drama of the first play reaches its end, the cause of the end play has its beginning, and the action of the center piece crystallizes.

So what?

Well, three things come to mind.

First, the passage is an invocation of "the dark gods beneath the earth" to "bless the children" and "bring them victory now." The Chorus believes only the players on stage, the three "children" Orestes, Electra, and Pylades, Prince of Phocis and Orestes' *de facto* brother in spirit, can avenge Agamemnon and restore something like justice and order to the world. The fate of the world falls on this young trio, two guys and a gal, believe it or not, and they will need all the otherworldly help and inspiration they can get. Hold that thought for a second; we'll come back to the *Potter* parallel in a moment.

Next, Electra's first invocation for help, her prayer for Orestes to return, had already been answered unknown to her as she speaks. She was sent to offer libations to sooth the spirit of Agamemnon but prays instead for an *Avenger*; Orestes and Electra and Chorus then pray together with the Chorus for Agamemnon's spirit to rise and bless them. Orestes, who will announce his death in a bit of ironic play-acting before his mother in the next act, essentially dies to himself here and becomes the serpent of his mother's dream as well as the vehicle of justice and of his father's spirit. To avenge the regicide and murder of his father, he must become a matricide himself and someone as accursed and haunted by the Furies. Hold on to that thought, too.

Third and last, the event around which the first act of *The Libation Bearers* turns is Electra's prayer and recognition of her brother Orestes. Euripides makes a point of mocking Aeschylus' unlikely story points (locks of hair? foot prints recognized from child hood runs in the sand? right…) in his retelling of the *Oresteia*; Euripides gives Orestes a forehead scar instead in an allusion to Odysseus meant to be demeaning to Orestes and Aeschylus. However silly (or meaningful) the Aeschylean references to head and feet as Electra's points of recognition, however, the central event of this pivotal act is prayer and a revelation that is cast as a *recognizing*. That's the third thing to remember.

The first point you're holding on to is the surface reading of the epigraph from Aeschylus. Orestes, Electra, and Pylades are Harry, Hermione, and Ron story parallels about to undertake a sacrificial mission to avenge the murder of a parent (or two), fulfill the destiny prophesied for the boy who lived, who knowingly embraces his almost certain death. For the action of *Deathly Hallows*, this scene and prayer is a great lead in. The defeat of the Dark Lord and restoration of order and justice all come down to the Terrible Trio and their acting their parts. And we get a boost from the shades of Harry's parents in the Forbidden Forest.

The second point is the moral reading of the epigraph which points to the alchemical drama and resolutions at hand. To avenge a murder, Orestes/Harry must both die to themselves and commit a murder on top of this death-to-persona. In order to slay the Heir of Slytherin, Harry must acknowledge that soul part in himself that is serpentine and Voldemort's, if only to die with it. It is this acknowledgment and death to self in which he transcends death and the murder he will commit.

Just as Harry's soul is not rent by the death of Voldemort in the Great Hall, a death for which he is, of course, responsible even if Voldemort essentially self-destructs in his inability to feel remorse, Orestes is ultimately freed from the Furies' pursuing him after Clytemnestra's murder. An Avenger's destiny involves contradictions – murdering murderers because of the evil of murder being only the most obvious – but contradictions that can be lived with or transcended if the Avenger acts impersonally or dispassionately. [Note especially Orestes' identification with the serpent of Clytemnestra's dream and the story parallel of Harry's learning he is a Horcrux; his scar is the serpent within him.]

The third and last point, Electra's prayer followed by revelation as recognition, all of which precedes and substantiates the Chorus passage used as epigraph, brings us to the second epigraph, William Penn, and the ideas of spiritual vision in both *More Fruits of Solitude* and *Deathly Hallows*. "Recognition," it turns out, is the key to understanding why Ms. Rowling thinks Harry's walk into the Forest and conversation with Dumbledore "is all about conscience."

FRUITS OF SOLITUDE:
HARRY AS 'THE INNER LIGHT' OF THE SOCIETY OF FRIENDS

Here is the Penn epigraph as it appears in *Hallows*:

> Death is but crossing the world, as friends do the seas; they live in one another still. For they must needs be present, that love and live in that which is omnipresent. In this divine glass, they see face to face; and their converse is free, as well as pure. This is the comfort of friends, that though they may be said to die, yet their friendship and society are, in the best sense, ever present, because immortal.

William Penn's *More Fruits of Solitude*, the book from which this passage is taken, couldn't be more different than Aeschylus' *Libation Bearers* in form or subject. Penn's small tome is a treasure in several respects, especially if read as it was written. The 3" by 5" copy I have, unlike much of what can be found online or in print, has **not** been expanded with commentary and historical glosses, translated into contemporary English, or included with other works as part of a collection. This book is both *Some Fruits of Solitude* (1693) and the harder to find *More Fruits of Solitude* (1702) as they were written, and, I suspect, in a spirit much like they were published. The diminutive format, what is quite literally a "pocket book," is fit for reading in secret as its first readers in Restoration England almost certainly did.

From what I can piece together from biographies, Penn wrote *Some Fruits of Solitude* while in hiding. He was under indictment for treason, his Irish estates had been confiscated by Parliament, and his Pennsylvania holdings were at risk because of his fall from favor after the Restoration.

The four years he was obliged to live in secret, moving from place to place, however, were among Penn's most productive as a writer; in addition to *Fruits*, he also wrote *Essay on the Peace of Europe*, which, as an essay in favor of something like the EU, was not meant to win him many friends at court.

Penn rises Mandela-like eventually, though, from his Rushdie existence and his rights to property are restored. He retires to Pennsylvania but is compelled to return to England in 1701, when he again finds himself in trouble, this time more financial than political. He does a brief spell in debtor's prison and dies penniless years later.

What is perhaps most striking, consequently, while reading *Some Fruits of Solitude* and *More Fruits*, written during his later troubles, is their equanimity and absence of bitterness, partisanship, or any hint of martyrdom. Written by one of the great lights of the Quaker non-conformist movement, they are valuable Society of Friends statements of how human life is to be understood and lived in the nimbus of the "inner light," regardless of external circumstances and trials.

The passage that Ms. Rowling chose as one of the epigraphs opening *Deathly Hallows* is from *More Fruits of Solitude*. Before getting to how the epigraph presented differs in presentation from the original, let me say a few words about the style of Penn's writing. As noted, we're a long way from Greek tragedy here.

There's no way of knowing this from the epigraph in *Deathly Hallows*, but *Some Fruits* and *More Fruits of Solitude* are collections of numbered one-liners and aphorisms; the numbers run 1-566 in *Some Fruits*, 1-299 in *More Fruits*. The one-liners aren't stray shots; the pithy and pointed, often profound pieces are collected in small bunches something like Bible verses have chapters and line Stephanus numbers (e.g., 'Matthew 6:19'), albeit with a title for the aphorisms collected under each heading. To give you a flavor of these titles, the first five in *Some Fruits* are "Ignorance," "Education," "Pride," "Luxury," and "Inconsideration." The heading for the sentences in Rowling's epigraph is "Union of Friends."

The subject matter of these aphorisms, namely, virtue, vice, and spiritual mindedness, have long passed from the short list of popular topics in our public square, but their format is as jarring to the modern reader as their "moralistic" content. To 17th century readers, though, the proverb or "trenchant sentence" made popular in La Rochefoucauld's *Maximes* (properly, *Reflexions ou Sentences et Maximes Morales*, 1655) were an art form and literary genre of great value.

And the *Maximes* are a delight; who can argue with the pithy observations that "Hypocrisy is the homage vice pays to virtue," "There is no disguise which can hide love for long where it exists, or simulate it where it does not," and "We are so accustomed to disguise ourselves to others, that in the end we become disguised to ourselves"?

Pascal's *Pensees* (1670) and Penn's *Fruits of Solitude* (1693, 1702) are perhaps the best of this sort of writing, and if you acquire the taste for it, a collection of aphorisms is simultaneously challenging, edifying, and entertaining. Imagine writers of this type as genetic crosses of Plato, John Henry Newman, and Henny Youngman, and you'll have an idea of the single and joined effect of these one-liners aimed at heart and head simultaneously. Coleridge begins his *Aids to Reflection* (1825) with aphorism sets, which speaks both to their poetic and philosophical power, not to mention the longevity of the genre.

Having set the context of the work, we can look at the specific epigrams Ms. Rowling chose as one of her *Hallows* epigraphs. The first thing to note is that the sentences chosen are only *half* of the sentences under Penn's heading "Union of Friends" and that they are not presented as they are in the original, either with respect to being numbered thought-arrows or in their appearance, most notably with respect to capitalization.

Here is the original "Union of Friends" section from *More Fruits of Solitude*:

127. They that love beyond the World, cannot be separated by it.

128. Death cannot kill, what never dies.

129. Nor can Spirits ever be divided that love and live in the same Divine Principle; the Root and Record of their Friendship.

130. If Absence be not Death, neither is theirs.

131. Death is but Crossing the World, as Friends do the Seas; They live in one another still.

132. For they must needs be present, that love and live in that which is Omnipresent.

133. In this Divine Glass, they see Face to Face; and their Converse is Free, as well as Pure.

134. This is the Comfort of Friends, that though they may be said to Die, yet their Friendship and Society are, in the best Sense, ever present, because Immortal.

Before jumping into the meaning of these Quaker *Pensees* in themselves or in the context of *Deathly Hallows*, it may be useful to observe some differences in this version and Ms. Rowling's epigraph and explain whence they may have come and why they're worth noting. The differences:

(1) Ms. Rowling's epigraph is sentences 131-134 of *More Fruits*, which four *bon mots* are half of the eight aphorisms under the heading "Union of Friends;"

(2) The second epigraph in *Deathly Hallows* is presented as a paragraph rather than numbered individual sentences; and

(3) The capitalization of the original work has been replaced in all words that don't begin sentences with lower case letters.

So what? Well, the changes may have been just because these sentences are frequently quoted as examples of Penn's best writing (the editor of the books I have cites and quotes "Union of Friends" as 1 of 2 examples to illustrate Penn's genius – and he leaves out the sentence numbers).

But eliminating the capitalization, for one, obscures to modern readers what was almost certainly Penn's reference in writing about "Friends" crossing the Seas (131) and the Immortality of their "Society" (134). William Penn is a Quaker, which Christian sect is more formally known as "The Society of *Friends*." Penn is writing a book as a *Friend* for other *Friends* in an age of religious persecution and penal transportation. "Penn's Woods" was born as something of a Friends' Utopia and an escape from the hardships of life in Commonwealth and Restoration England (Catholics and Protestants both thought Quakers fair game for persecution).

Making "Friends" a lower case noun obscures not only the reference of the people about whom Penn is writing but the nature of their fraternity. These aren't friends like your drinking buddies or sorority sisters; the bond of these Friends is well beyond casual brother-homeboy acquaintances or even partisan political or denominational religious association.

Collapsing the numbered sentences into a single paragraph diminishes the impact and singularity of each aphorism, too, and cutting out the one-liners numbered 127-130 further occludes our understanding of what exactly constitutes the "Union of Friends." We get that Friends are those "that love and live in that which is Omnipresent" (132), but we miss that these are the Friends indivisible in spirit "that love and live in the same Divine Principle; the Root and Record of their Friendship" (129), the parallel sentence that precedes it.

Which brings us to the meat of Penn's meaning in the original. The "Divine Principle," "that which is Omnipresent," that joins the Friends, and what makes them immortal and forever joined, is the "inner light" and Word of God (*Logos*). William Penn described the beliefs of the Society of Friends first and foremost as believers in the *Divine Principle* God put in men as *conscience*:

§ 1. That which the people called Quakers lay down as a main fundamental in religion is this– *That God, through Christ, hath placed a principle in every man, to inform him of his duty, and to enable him to do it*; and that those that live up to this principle are the people of God, and those that live in disobedience to it, are not God's people, whatever name they may bear, or profession they may make of religion. This is their ancient, first, and standing testimony: with this they began, and this they bore, and do bear to the world....

§ 4. *It is to this principle of Light, Life, and Grace, that this People refer all*: for they say it is the great Agent in Religion; that, without which, there is no Conviction, so no Conversion, or Regeneration; and consequently no entering into the Kingdom of God. That is to say, there can be no true sight of sin, nor sorrow for it, and therefore no forsaking or overcoming of it, or Remission or Justification from it. A necessary and powerful Principle indeed, when either Sanctification nor Justification can be had without it. In short, there is no becoming virtuous, holy and good, without this Principle; no acceptance with God, nor peace of soul, but through it. But on the contrary, that *the reason of so much irreligion among Christians, so much superstition, instead of Devotion, and so much profession without enjoyment, and so little Heart-reformation, is, because people in religion, overlook this Principle, and leave it behind them.* (Penn, "Primitive")

Penn and the Quakers believe – and were persecuted by Protestant and Catholic church and state authorities for this belief – that conscience is much more than an ethical sense; it is the voice of God and the divine light within us. He writes in *A Key* that men and women only become Christian, which is to say, fully human, when they "receive and obey the manifestation of His Divine Light and grace in their conscience." Conscience, the Light of God in us, is all.

This bedrock Friends belief is the context of the *More Fruits of Solitude* "Union of Friends" passage. Let's read those eight sentences again in *the light* of the Quaker idea about the Divine Principle within man as conscience:

Quakers "love beyond the World" (127) in living in obedience to the Divine Principle that is the love (1 John 4:16) that creates all things (John 1:3) and which "gives light to every man" (John 1:9) and is "the light of the world" (John 8:12). "Death cannot kill what never dies" (128) because this

Principle in which Quakers live is Life itself (John 14:6). "Nor can Spirits ever be divided that love and live in the same Divine Principle; the Root and Record of their Friendship" (129); if you are indeed a "Friend," you are one because you "live and love in the Divine Principle." "If Absence be not Death, neither is theirs" (130); having been joined in the Christ within them, Friends cannot be separated by death.

"Death is but Crossing the World, as Friends do the Seas; They live in one another still" (131); the shared identity of Friends in the transpersonal self of *Logos*-conscience means that they live in one another despite distances of space and time or the appearance of separation at death. "For they must needs be present, that love and live in that which is Omnipresent" (132); an echo in phrasing and meaning of sentences 128 and 129, the Divine creative principle or *Logos* in all human beings and the stuff and substance, the reality of existence, is omnipresent and those who live in it deliberately and without compromise are necessarily always close.

"In this Divine Glass, they see Face to Face; and their Converse is Free, as well as Pure" (133); a reference to St. Paul's mirror comment in 1 Corinthians 13:12 ("For now we see through a glass, darkly; but then face to face: now I know in part; but then shall I know even as also I am known"), Penn is referring to the *Logos*-reflection Friends see in one another of the Divine Principle, and, in repose, of the Principle Himself. "This is the Comfort of Friends, that though they may be said to Die, yet their Friendship and Society are, in the best Sense, ever present, because Immortal" (134); the Society of Friends, a conscious incarnation of the *Logos* Principle with many individual members joined in conscience, believes itself as ever present and immortal as the Word in God *en arche* (as Principle, *in principio*, "in the beginning," John 1:1).

This was one radical Christian sect. The Quakers who followed George Fox and William Penn out of conventional Protestant and Catholic churches in the 17th century were known as "non-conformists" because they were, to use C. S. Lewis' language, determined to pursue "the conformity of soul to Reality" above everything else. Obedience to traditions and religious practice and ritual divorced from communion with the inner light of conscience was risible nonsense to them. They identified themselves and their inner light instead with the Creative and Rational Principle that became incarnate as Jesus of Nazareth rather than with any church building or beliefs.

What, then, do the four sentences from Penn's set of eight that Ms. Rowling chose as one of the *Deathly Hallows* epigraphs mean in the context of the *Potter* finale? *Mirabile dictu*, I'm almost certain it means there much the same thing as Penn did in *More Fruits of Solitude*, if obviously Ms. Rowling wasn't writing as a Society of Friends sectarian. I'd go so far as to say that this Quaker "seeing eye" of conscience as we encounter it in Ms. Rowling's magical sub-creation is what Dumbledore calls the "power beyond any magic."

I have three arguments for this position:

• *Logos* cosmology and conscience clears up the jumble of *Deathly Hallows* items Ms. Rowling has identified in interviews as "key" to understanding her novels,

• *Logos* reflection as the means to God (Penn's and Paul's "seeing face to face" mirror imagery) is a *topos* or commonplace of symbolist writing, the stream of English literature in which Ms. Rowling writes, and

• The text of *Deathly Hallows*, especially the eye and mirror symbolism and chapters 34 and 35, support a *Logos*-focused interpretation of what present day beliefs and assumptions the book is trying to subvert. *Deathly Hallows* is as subversive a book as *More Fruits of Solitude* and for much the same reason.

HARRY IN *LOGOS*-LAND

We'll start with Ms. Rowling's interviews and her pointing to specific parts and passages of *Deathly Hallows* as important. As you recall, the "key" bits are to be found in chapter 34, "The Forest Again," the scripture engraved on the Godric's Hollow gravestones Harry and Hermione read on Christmas Eve, Dumbledore's farewell to Harry at the non-local place he thinks of as King's Cross already explained above, and, of course, the epigraphs that start the book.

Looking at the Penn epigraph – we'll have to come back to Aeschylus – the Dumbledore farewell, Harry walking into "The Forest Again," and the scripture quotations, one interpretation that joins them all requires Penn's radical vision of the conscience or *Logos*-mind as the human means to divinization and immortality. The epigraph itself I parsed above. Let's move on, then, to the scripture quotations that "epitomize the whole series" and see if the epigraph key is a match with the scripture keys.

On Ariana Dumbledore's tombstone we read, "For Where Your Treasure Is, There Your Heart Will Be Also" (Matthew 6:21). This passage and the verses that follow it would be favorites of Penn. It is about, after all, non-conformity, the eye of the heart, and the light that is in all men. Here is the Sermon on the Mount context of the "treasure" line:

> 19 Lay not up for yourselves treasures upon earth, where moth and rust doth corrupt, and where thieves break through and steal:
>
> 20 But lay up for yourselves treasures in heaven, where neither moth nor rust doth corrupt, and where thieves do not break through nor steal:
>
> 21 *For where your treasure is, there will your heart be also.*
>
> 22 The light of the body is the eye: if therefore thine eye be single, thy whole body shall be full of light.
>
> 23 But if thine eye be evil, thy whole body shall be full of darkness. If therefore the light that is in thee be darkness, how great is that darkness!
>
> 33 But seek ye first the kingdom of God, and his righteousness...

If you see the light, eye, treasure, heart, and kingdom of the Sermon on the Mount from Penn's *Logos*-conscience perspective, which is to say, that the eye is the *Logos* conscience that is the light of all men and the kingdom of heaven within us, we can proceed to the scripture carved into Harry's parents' tombstone: "The last enemy that shall be destroyed is death" (1 Corinthians 15:26). To risk repeating myself (by repeating myself and Penn), "Death cannot kill what never dies" (*More Fruits of Solitude*, 128) because this Principle in which Quakers live is Life itself (John 14:6). "Nor can Spirits ever be divided that love and live in the same Divine Principle; the Root and Record of their Friendship" (129); if you are indeed a "Friend," you are one because you "love and live in the Divine Principle." "If Absence be not Death, neither is theirs" (130); having been joined in the Christ within them, Friends cannot be separated by death.

The scripture passages are reconcilable with the Penn epigraph, then; how about Chapter 34, Harry's walk into "The Forest Again," the part of *Deathly Hallows* Ms. Rowling says is "the key to all the books"?

The main events of "The Forest Again" are Harry's acceptance of his task, his walk from the castle and brief exchange with Neville about Nagini, his opening of the Snitch and use of the Resurrection Stone, the walk and talk with James and Lily and Sirius and Remus to Aragog's grove in the Forest, and Harry's sacrifice of himself in obedience to Dumbledore's plan. My favorite part of the author's most important chapter is its beginning and

Harry's sudden awareness of his heart, the "funeral drum" (*Deathly* 692):

> He felt his heart pounding fiercely in his chest. How strange that in his
> dread of death, it pumped all the harder, valiantly keeping him alive.
> But it would have to stop, and soon. Its beats were numbered. How
> many would there be time for, as he rose and walked through the castle
> for the last time, out into the grounds and into the forest? (691)

Even Hogwarts is likened to a giant heart, "all its remaining lifeblood...
concentrated in the Great Hall" (694). He almost gives Neville "heart failure"
(695). A "chilly breeze" that interrupts Harry's brief consoling talk with the
spiritual bodies (1 Corinthians 15:44-55) of his parents, Godfather, and
mentor "seemed to emanate from the heart of the forest" (700). Before Harry
reveals himself to Voldemort, his "heart was now throwing itself against his
ribs as though determined to escape the body he was about to cast aside"
(703).

Why the stacked heart imagery? It is because Harry is the story symbol
of the "eye of the heart," the noetic faculty of soul in the Harry-Hermione-
Ron body-mind-spirit soul triptych. Which is the *Logos* conscience or inner
Divine Principle and light that unites the Friends and is their "Comfort;"
because, "though they may be said to Die, yet their Friendship and Society
are, in the best Sense, ever present, because Immortal." Harry's comforting
experience of the "cloud of witnesses" that allow him to walk "with patience
the race set before" him (Hebrews 12:1) is his consoling transition to the
world of *Logos* that is outside, beyond, within, and behind the appearances
of time and space.

As Rowling says, Harry's decision "all came down to conscience"
(Cruz).

In brief, the *Logos* conscience in our heads, because it is at least some
aspect or reflection of the Divine Principle that creates all things and is the
cause of their existence and "reality," is the most real thing-not-a-thing or
place-not-a-place that Harry has ever known or experienced. "King's Cross"
is in Harry's head *and* more real than "anything made that was made."

Rolling through Ms. Rowling's four highlighted passages, then, the
parts of her last book she has said "epitomize" or are "the most important"
for understanding her work, they all can be understood in terms of the Penn
epigraph and the peculiar *Logos* cosmology, epistemology, and soteriology
specific to Penn's Christian sect, the Society of Friends. I suppose that might
have been expected, both because most things take on the qualities of the

lens you look through to see them and because Rowling told us as much about the Penn and Aeschylus selections: "I always knew [that] if I could use [the epigraphs] at the beginning of book seven then I'd cued up the ending perfectly. If they were relevant, then I went where I needed to go."

SUBVERTING THE MATERIALIST MENTALITY

How surprised should we be that chapter 34, the end of 35, and the scripture quotations resonate with Penn's epigraph when the author says the epigraphs were selected near the story's conception to "cue up" the ending, and the test of her having arrived where she "needed to go" with the story was the relevance of these epigraphs?

Not very surprised. The tradition in which Rowling writes, after all, depends on a *Logos* epistemology and symbolism, in large part. As I argue in *Lectures* and *Harry Potter's Bookshelf,* she is writing in the same imaginative vein as Lewis, Tolkien, Sayers, Goudge, MacDonald, and Carroll, to much the same purpose, and that these symbolists are all working ultimately from the esoteric natural theology of Samuel Taylor Coleridge – which has an awful lot in common with George Fox, William Penn, and the Inner Light theology of the Society of Friends.

In chapter 5 of *Lectures,* 'The Seeing Eye,' I make the Coleridge-to-C. S. Lewis-to-Rowling connection in terms of the *Logos* as creative rational principle and Lewis' idea (via Barfield, MacDonald, and Coleridge) that "the universe is mental." Again, not mental as Ron thinks things are "mental" (though Ron's asking Harry if he "is mental" is meaningful…), but in terms of everything, including most especially thinking and conscience, being a "participation in the cosmic *Logos.*"

And from C. S. Lewis' "The Seeing Eye," these surprising thoughts about religious conformity and those who listen to conscience, the power of mind "continuous with" the unity of existence:

> …To some God is discoverable everywhere; to others, nowhere. Those who do not find Him on earth are unlikely to find Him in space. (Hang it all, we're in space already; every year we go a huge circular tour in space.) ['The Seeing Eye' was written in response to Soviet atheist cosmonauts remarking on re-entry that they had not seen God out in space either.] But send a saint up in a spaceship and he'll find God in space as he found God on earth. Much depends on the seeing eye.

... Indeed the expectation of finding God by astronautics would be very like trying to verify or falsify the divinity of Christ by taking specimens of His blood or dissecting Him. And in their own way they did both. But they were no wiser than before. What is required is a certain faculty of recognition.

If you do not at all know God, of course you will not recognize Him, either in Jesus or in outer space (61-62, emphasis added).

This "faculty of recognition," the means by which something seen corresponds with something in our heads, be it a mental image, a memory, or an idea, when mentioned as a means to know God in Jesus is the *Logos* conscience of Penn and the Quakers, the light of the body in the eye from the Sermon of the Mount, and Paul's "glass" in 1 Corinthians in which the *Logos* is reflected "darkly," but still recognized by the *Logos* within looking at itself in the mirror of the world. This *Logos* foundation of reality (the "mental universe") and of mind or conscience is an idea found at the base of Lewis' apologetics, his philosophical work contra naturalism, his *Narnia* novels (e.g., it is the "inside bigger than the outside" of the stable in *The Last Battle*, Chapter 13, and of Rowling's many "inside bigger than outside" magical objects), and his social criticism (e.g., the universal moral law or Tao of *The Abolition of Man*). This isn't just a "Quaker thing."

More to the point, these esoteric and, to the devotional Christian at least, metaphysical conceptions of "the life in Christ," non-conformist as they are, may explain Ms. Rowling's two minds about C. S. Lewis and her frequently asserted disdain for "fundamentalism" of any kind. Lewis is a symbolist whose *Logos* orientation Ms. Rowling seems to share, but he also presents himself to the postmodern reader as a bedrock "conservative" who is as determined to save Narnia from the Calormenes as Tolkien was in defense of the Shire.

Rowling, in contrast, is from the "subversive" bank of the symbolist stream of writers; she wants Harry to defeat Voldemort and save Hogwarts, true, but, that battle being won, the hostility of the Order and Dumbledore's Army for the Ministry suggest big changes are on the horizon. Colin Manlove described the subversive symbolists as those writers, unlike the Inklings, who aim "to undermine [their] reader's assumptions and ways of seeing the world" either "for the sake of broadening our perspective on life" or "for the purpose of leading us towards God" (235).

And what beliefs or assumptions is Ms. Rowling attempting to subvert?

The seven texts of the *Harry Potter* saga that we have suggest the core beliefs under attack are the empiricist assumptions of our age. Harry's final question to Dumbledore in "King's Cross" is a neat statement of the dichotomy between objective reality and subjective opinion ("real or in my head?") that is the postmodern "way of seeing the world." Dumbledore's answer and the allegorical and anagogical meaning of Harry's alchemical adventures as the "Seeing Eye" beneath the Invisibility Cloak both tell us that the "real" is in our heads, that the objective/subjective materialist mental dichotomy is a false dilemma, and that we make our closest contact with the "unity of existence" and God when we listen to the Word between our ears and in our hearts.

Which I'm betting is a non-conformist message William Penn would have liked.

Was Aeschylus a Quaker, too? What does the epigraph from *The Libation Bearers* tell us about our "inner light" of conscience?

The heart of *The Libation Bearers* is Electra's recognition of Orestes and the *Logos* mind of her conscience, prayers, and, ultimately, her vengeance. The play is meaningful for *Potter* readers not only because it has two friends, one with a forehead scar, and a girl fighting evil to revenge a murdered parent. It is the *Logos* cosmology and epistemology shared by Greek "pagans" (Rowling's word) and Christians like Penn, a *Logos* or Word in everyman (John 1:9) that prays, that speaks to us as conscience, and that understands and knows through recognition of itself and its absence in other people, things, and ideas.

Penn speaks to the bond of this "inward light" being the eternal life together of Friends, meaning those who know themselves as vehicles of the Light of the World (John 8:12); Rowling represents this noetic faculty of soul and its purification symbolically through Harry Potter and his seven adventures. Harry as *Logos* is the "inside of the head" that is more real than the outside. And, in *Libation Bearers*, it is this divine mind from and to which the children and Chorus cry out for help.

Ms. Rowling reports the epigraphs "just say it all to me. They really do." If by "all" she means the surface, moral, and mythic or spiritual meanings of the series, I am obliged to agree.

BIBLIOGRAPHY

Aeschylus, *The Oresteia.* Translated by Robert Fagles. Penguin Classics, 1984.

Adler, Shawn. 'Harry Potter' Author J.K. Rowling Opens Up About Books' Christian Imagery, *MTV,* Oct 17 2007;   http://www.mtv.com/news/articles/1572107/20071017/index.jhtml

Cruz, Juan. "Ser invisible... eso sería lo más," El Pais, 8 February 2008 http://www.elpais.com/articulo/cultura/Ser/invisible/seria/elpepicul/20080208elpepicul_1/Tes http://www.the-leaky-cauldron.org/2008/2/9/jkr-discusses-dursley-family-religion-us-presidential-election-and-more-in-new-interview

Gibbs, Nancy. "J. K. Rowling: Person of the Year Runner-Up 2007," *Time.* December 2007 http://www.time.com/time/specials/2007/personoftheyear/article/0,28804,1690753_1695388_1695436,00.html

Lewis. C. S. *Essay Collection* (HarperCollins, 2002), chapter 8, 'The Seeing Eye.'

Lewis, C. S. *Surprised by Joy.* Harcourt, Brace & Co., New York, 1955.

Manlove, Colin. "Parent or Associate?: George MacDonald and the Inklings," in *George MacDonald: Literary Heritage and Heirs.* ed. Roderick Gillis. Zossima Press, 2008.

Penn, William. *A Key: Opening the Way to Every Capacity; How to Distinguish the Religion Professed by the People Called Quakers, from the Perversions and Misrepresentations of their Adversaries; With a Brief Exhortation to All Sorts of People to Examine Their Ways, and Their Hearts, and Turn Speedily to the Lord,* 1692, emphasis added; http://www.tractassociation.org/AKey.html

Penn, William. *Primitive Christianity Revived: In the Faith and Practice of the People called Quakers,* 1696, emphasis added; http://www.strecorsoc.org/penn/title.html

Rowling, J. K. *Harry Potter and the Deathly Hallows.* Scholastic, 2007.

Vieira, Meredith. "J.K. Rowling One-On-One: Part One." *Today Show* (NBC), 26 July 2007 http://www.accio-quote.org/articles/2007/0726-today-vieira1.html

Chapter Four

God and *Harry Potter* at Yale
Faith and Fiction in the Classroom

Dannielle Tumminio

Not many people get to say that studying *Harry Potter* is part of their job, but I am one of the lucky few. In the spring of 2008, I offered a seminar at Yale University entitled "Christian Theology and *Harry Potter*," which sought to assess whether and to what extent the series espoused a Christian worldview.

Seventy-nine students showed up on the first day. They crammed into the classroom, and when it was filled beyond capacity, they spilled into a courtyard chill with the Connecticut winter wind. I left that afternoon with a pile of applications, some of which had typed requests and photographs of teenagers dressed in Hogwarts robes. Two said they wrote their college admission essays on the series; several founded *Harry Potter* organizations at their schools; one created the Quidditch Club at Yale, and another won a Scholastic book award and got to meet J. K. Rowling. I was allowed to choose 18 of them.

In the end, I emerged with a talented and diverse group of students: a Kenyan Anglican and a Southern Baptist, a Chinese atheist, a Hindu who went to Catholic school and a Mormon karate enthusiast, to name just a few. They had very little in common – they were freshman and seniors, majoring in everything from biology to French. They came from different corners of the globe, and hailed from a variety of residential colleges at Yale (the residential college system is much like the House system at Hogwarts). But what the students did share was this: a love of learning and a loyalty to the *Harry Potter* series.

I recognized at the beginning that there was the possibility for intolerance or even bigotry in a group that diverse – after all, the worldview of a secular Jew certainly differs from those of a South Baptist. Yet what amazed me from the start was how thoughtful and interactive my students were. Each was willing to learn from the next, and they embraced the fact that there were as many different theological viewpoints as there were students in the course. It was the kind of group that I imagined might have walked the hall of Hogwarts, the kind of group of which J.K. Rowling would have been proud.

Our group convened for two hours every Wednesday afternoon to discuss various theological topics, ranging from love and death to Christ's identity and the nature of atonement. The semester's reading included all seven *Harry Potter* books, which were assigned along with a hefty compilation of theological essays. We read from historic voices like Augustine and Blaise Pascal as well as more contemporary theologians and biblical scholars. I also made a point of pairing each *Harry Potter* book with a relevant theological counterpart: the second half of the fourth book was paired with readings on Eucharistic theology to contrast the relationship between biblical depictions of the Last Supper and the Voldemort's rising; *The Prizoner of Azkaban* was paired with readings on salvation (soteriology is the technical word), to raise questions of whether or how Snape sins at the end of the book; while reading *The Order of the Pheonix*, we discussed eschatology and prophecy, and at the end of the series, we read theological perspectives on death, love, and grace. It was therefore my hope to expose students to a wide variety of theological topics during the semester, showing them various trends of thought and asking them to probe whether and how these ideas appeared in the series.

RESPONSES TO OPPOSITION

The "Christian Theology and Harry Potter" seminar went through a rigorous approval process at Yale that lasted four months. My proposal was submitted to all twelve residential colleges and reviewed by a panel of faculty and students. I then went through an interview process with individual colleges that were interested in sponsoring the class. Following the interviews, students from each college convened to debate who would sponsor the seminar (or if they would sponsor it at all). Competition for sponsorship can be intense because if a college sponsors a seminar, it guarantees that a certain number of their students are guaranteed admission to the course. So, if you imagine that Gryffindor sponsored a seminar at Hogwarts, it would mean that, say, six of the eighteen students in the class would have to come from Gryffindor. That means Gryffindor students have an advantage when it comes to admission.

Not all classes at Yale go through a process like this to be approved. The College Seminar program, of which my course was a part, is designed to allow upper level graduate students and non-Yale affiliated professionals opportunities to teach courses at the university that otherwise would not be offered. It is a unique forum that draws experts from outside the Academy – such as lawyers, journalists, filmmakers, and writers – and gives them an opportunity to bring their passions to the classroom.

As a theologian myself, I decided to propose the class because I wanted to find new ways to teach Christian theology. The way theology is usually taught involves asking students to memorize historical thinkers' take on various doctrines to see how their theories differ. So, one might reason, "Augustine says that evil exists because Adam and Eve were willfully disobedient in the Garden of Eden, whereas John Hick says that evil exists to help us grow in the likeness of God. The difference between the two thinkers is that for Hick, humans benefit in some way from the existence of evil; they learn and grow because of their experiences with it. For Augustine, there is no such benefit to evil." Now, there is much to say for this method; it is rigorous and forces the student to use the logical side of their brain to the max. I myself was taught in this way, and I am a stronger thinker for it. But what teaching in this manner lacks is an opportunity for students to apply what they've learned, leading many to think that theology is abstract or irrelevant, food for thought but not food for life. It's the difference between making students learn percents without giving them an opportunity to put that knowledge to use – by figuring out the tip on a bill, for instance. Using literature as theologically intriguing as the *Harry Potter* series provided a vehicle to move through the problems I saw in theological teaching, because it created an environment in which students not only had to reason through concepts in Christianity, they also had to assess how they were relevant. Instead of only asking my students to memorize concepts, I wanted them to apply them, to see how they interrelated, and to discover the consequences of thinking one way or another about a theological concept.

By teaching theology in a new way, I was also hoping to respond to an ever-rising group of critics who call theology irrelevant. Theology may be dense; it may be mind-boggling and existentially challenging. It may cause individuals to question their place in the cosmic order and the ethics of their relationships. It may do any one of these things, but it is not irrelevant. Yet the reason that many of these charges of opposition exist is because the entire discipline of theology is understood as merely an abstract logic problem. Such critics are not seeing the positive ways theology is at work in the world – how it affects our worldview and shapes our perspectives. To that end, I wanted to create a class that gave students an introduction to the discipline while encouraging them to see theology at work in the world. And what better way to do that than with *Harry Potter*? After all, this was the first generation of students who had really grown up with the books. My freshman student read the first book in fourth grade and the last came out after her graduation from high school. Another one of my students called the books her "rainy day friends." These books were important to them; they influenced their development during childhood and the teenage years in ways that I, as an older person, cannot begin to fathom. As a result, it seemed like the paradigmatic teaching tool to show why theology matters today.

I ultimately hoped the seminar would be one small step to address what I viewed as a flaw in theological education. Yet during the four-month approval process, I did encounter some voices of doubt. Much ink has already been spilled on the relationship of the *Harry Potter* series to Christianity, and it is no secret that many are opposed to using the books as theological tools. I'd like to explore two of these perspectives and respond to them.

One group, comprised mainly of Christian conservatives, asserts that the books blaspheme Christianity. These critiques usually focus upon the use of witchcraft in the books, asserting that the Bible is staunchly opposed to the practice on the grounds that it promotes idolatry, encouraging humans to think that they have powers that are rightly reserved for God. Hence, Paul writes in his letter to the Galatians that witchcraft is sinful – as are jealousy, anger, drunkenness, ambition, bacchanalianism and a host of other vices (Galatians 5:19-21). Because of passages like this one, Christian conservatives believe that the *Harry Potter* series endangers a believer's relationship to Christ. They see witchcraft glorified because the protagonists are witches and wizards whose powers are not denounced. They worry that too much trust is placed in the power of magic and not in the power of Christ's salvation. Finally, they claim that the use of witchcraft in the series is misleading to young people, leading them away from Christ and towards practice that their faith condemns. In short, they see the books as a kind of heretical Wiccan evangelism.

My response to this critique is twofold. First, these critics are not wrong in saying that the Bible opposes witchcraft. It does. However, the Bible also tells us to notify our religious leaders and shut up our homes for seven days if we find mildew on the walls, and how many us of hear that preached from the pulpit on Sunday morning (Leviticus 14:33-43)? Now, this could easily turn into a downward spiral where I begin to question all sorts of biblical passages, begging whether the Bible has any authority, and I do not want to do that. Instead, I'd like to take my critique in a different direction: opinions rooted in scriptural views of witchcraft assume that the books promote witchcraft in readers and therefore encourage a sinful practice. Yet there's no indication that this is the case; Harry's world, though it bears resemblance to our own, is clearly the stuff of fantasy. And while children blur these worlds or may wish to be like Hermione, Neville, or, dare I say it, Draco, there is no evidence that games or desires ultimately lead away from Christian faith; they are merely the stuff of childhood pretending and imagination. Put differently: how many Christians reenacted Snow White or Cinderella as children, wanting to be the wicked stepmother or the fairy godmother? I imagine quite a few; I was one of those children. Yet how many of us now follow religions rooted in worshipping magic mirrors or poisoned apples, or sing "Bippity-Boppity-Boo" as a Sunday morning hymn? I'd imagine few to none. It is not for naught, then, that Paul says that when we become adults we put away childish things (I Corinthians 13:11).

Moreover, these critics deal with only one particular issue in Christianity – the occult – without engaging other theological topics, like love, liberation from death, Christology, salvation, and the Doctrine of God, which are, I would argue, more essential to the Christian narrative. If that passage about mildew disappeared entirely from the Book of Leviticus, I doubt Christianity would look much different, because the basis of the faith has little to do with the treatment of fungi. But if one were to delete the passages that have to do with how Christ saved humanity from sin through His sacrifice and resurrection, well, the entire basis of the faith would be compromised. A similar argument goes for witchcraft. Christianity would pretty much still look like Christianity if the passages about witchcraft were deleted. But take away the Eucharist, and most of the doctrine and liturgy of the Church would look very different.

Likewise these critics ignore that theology is a discipline of synthesis. A constructive or systematic theology does not just look at one idea – like biblical perspectives on witchcraft. It aims to connect different doctrines in coherent and non-contradictory ways; it seeks to interpret scripture in truthful and culturally accessible language, using tools from tradition, reason, and experience. So, it is the theologian's job to look at not one doctrine in isolation but to hold all the different doctrines of the Church in tension – from creation to eschatology – and show how they interrelate. This was precisely what my class set out to do.

Thus, if one truly wants to assess how a piece of literature aligns with Christianity, one has to look at not just one tenet of Christianity but at as many of them as possible. That means thinking about ideas like resurrection, death, sacrifice, the Eucharist, love, God's identity, evil, community, sin, and salvation and asking repeatedly, "Is what the *Harry Potter* books say about X issue similar to what Christianity says?"

In short, I find arguments rooted in opposition to witchcraft to be non-starters. Whether or not the *Harry Potter* series encourages witchcraft is not an appropriate indicator of whether it contains elements of Christian theology, and if individuals really want to assess whether the books have a Christian worldview, then they need to probe the series with questions about sin, salvation, death, and resurrection. They need to look at the relationship between those ideas, and they need to assess how all of that relates to Christian belief. Looking at one slim set of biblical passages in isolation from the rest of the text is simply not enough.

Relatedly, these critics also overlook the more nuanced way that the *Harry Potter* series might illuminate Christ's message. This is not to say that the books are a Christian allegory because I do not think they are. There is no clear Christ figure in the books – Harry is far too flawed and it could be argued that he could do with some serious anger management therapy – nor is there a clear God figure, unless you consider the abstract concept of love or, as one of my students suggested, Lily Potter. Yet the books could still uphold Christian themes, even if they themselves are not strict allegory. Put differently, the question is not whether the books can substitute for Christ – nothing can substitute the direct message Christ offers through the Gospel narratives. The better question is whether the books have a message that is congruent with Christian themes. I believe that the series' take on love, community, redemption, and tolerance certainly qualifies it as such.

The other voices of opposition hold a far different standpoint from the one espoused by Christian conservatives. These critics, including commentators like Christopher Hitchens, maintain that books have no theological content whatsoever. They depict a battle of good and evil, but it is a secular battle, not a Christian one.

This critique has slightly more weight. We see minimal mention of Christianity in the series, except for two biblical quotations in the seventh book – one on the Dumbledores' tomb and one on the Potter's (*Deathly*, 326, 328; Matt. 6:2, I Cor. 15:26 respectively). Yet that latter biblical quotation happens to summarize the entire purpose of the series: "The last enemy to be destroyed is death" (*Deathly*, 328). It would seem odd, then, to assert that the books lack any theological content when their overarching thesis is undergirded by a biblical quotation. Moreover, the fact that J.K. Rowling comes from a Christian culture means that even if she isn't Christian herself – though we now know that she is – elements of Christianity may have seeped into the books because of her societal context. Finally, one would be hard pressed to read certain passages in the series – like Voldemort's rising at the end of book four – and not see Christian imagery in them. Therefore, while I can understand this reading of the books, it is my purview that the content of the books is not devoid of theological thinking but rather encourages it. And it is precisely to such analysis that this essay now turns.

THEOLOGICAL REFLECTIONS

So what do the *Harry Potter* books have to say about theology? My students and I came up with a couple of interesting points worth drawing out about the theological framework Rowling sets up in her books, and I'd like to explore one of them here: God's identity.

Traditional Christian doctrine states that God has incommunicable characteristics: God is all-knowing, all-powerful, and all-good. Sometimes the word omniscient is substituted for all-knowing; omnipotent for all-powerful; and omnibenevolent for all-good.

The idea of the Three O God who is **o**mnibenevolent, **o**mniscient, and **o**mnipotent comes from some of the earliest Christian writers, known as the Patristic writers. There are several reasons why these writers fashioned the Three O God as a cornerstone of Christian thought. First, the initial chapter of the biblical book of Genesis describes God as a Creator who fashioned the universe – everything from day and night to water and sky, stars and sun, plants, animals, and humans. For God to have created all of this, God needed to know what God was doing and needed to be powerful enough to do it.

Second, God is understood as a kind of cosmic CEO in charge of creation. Since the universe is so complicated, God needs to be able to understand and manage the organization in a positive way. If God wasn't doing that in a way that was good, then there would be a tyrant running the universe that wouldn't be worth respecting, never mind worshipping.

Finally, the Patristic writers were particularly interested in bringing Greek philosophical thought into conversation with Jewish thought. One of the ideas prominent in Greek philosophical thought was that there is a chain of being, which means that things come in varieties from good to better to best, kind of like there are Saturns, Infinitis, and Rolls Royces. From this perspective, God has to be the best – the Rolls Royce, so to speak – because if something bettered God, then that something would be more deserving of the title. Hence, for God to be God, God has to be at the extreme of greatness – maximally powerful, knowing, and good.

So, how does all of this relate to *Harry Potter*? Well, one of the first questions I put to my class last year was whether or not there is a God-figure in the *Harry Potter* books. Initially discussion circulated around Dumbledore or Harry. Dumbledore, we reasoned, certainly held a supreme amount of knowledge and always did strive to love and care for all his students. Yet, as the series progresses, it becomes harder to maintain Dumbledore's absolute goodness, power, or knowledge. At the end of book five, Dumbledore admits that he made a mistake by not telling Harry about the prophecy earlier; hence, we find that Dumbledore is not all-knowing. In book seven, we learn of his poor judgment regarding his family, so no omnibenevolence either. And as his declining health in book six evidences, there are at least physical powers greater than his. It would seem, then, that Dumbledore is almost a red herring God – one that we are lead to trust and believe in – who ultimately turns out to be a wise but flawed mortal. These realizations lead one of my students to write a paper she referred to as "Dumbledore as a God figure…but only through book three."

Now, just because Dumbledore fails to qualify as a God figure doesn't mean that the series is devoid of such a character. But where that God figure is proves to be an elusive search. Harry makes far too many mistakes to be seen as a God, and his psychological need to go-it-alone often makes the reader wish Hogwarts had a school psychologist on hand. Hermione, while smart, is certainly not all-powerful or all-knowing, and neither is Ron. Lupin has moments of selfishness in book seven that preclude him from being understood as all-good; Snape certainly doesn't fit the bill; James comes off as too self-absorbed to be all-knowing; McGonagall, though sturdy, can be physically dominated and is prone to misunderstanding Harry, while Sirius is a bit of a letdown across the board. There was only one human character that stood out to our class as a potential God figure: Lily Potter. Lily's sacrifice is certainly all-good, the protective charm she places on Harry makes her seem both all-knowing and all-powerful, and her elusive character causes Harry to identify with her the way humans often identify with God – as simultaneously loving but distant.

While our class did conclude that Lily was the closest human equivalent to a God-figure in the book, we were ultimately not convinced that she was representative of the Divine. Most prominently, Lily does not seem to have the capability to solve the overarching problem in the books – evil. While her protective charm does keep Harry from death at Voldemort's hands, it does so only for a time. Morover, she does not actually defeat Voldemort. As a result, we concluded that while she may have Godlike characteristics, she was not meant to be interpreted as Divine.

Ultimately, our class decided that if there is anything akin to a God-figure in the books, it did not appear in the guise of human flesh. We found that the one thing with the power to defeat Voldemort's evil, the goodness to want to, and the knowing to guide the operation was Love. It is Love that ultimately motivates Lily and Harry's sacrificial actions, Love that keeps Hermione and Ron at Harry's side, Love that prompts Neville's nobility in book seven, and Love that saves the wizarding world at the end of the series. In fact, Rowling makes a point of driving home again and again the importance of Love as a binding power, a power greater than all others that has the capacity to save. Hence, even in the first book, Dumbledore impresses the importance of Love on Harry, saying, "Your mother died to save you. If there is one thing Voldemort cannot understand, it is love. He didn't realize that love as powerful as your mother's for you leaves its own mark. Not a scar, no not a visible sign…to have been loved so deeply, even though the person who loved us is gone, will give us some protection forever. It is in your very skin. Quirrell, full of hatred, greed, and ambition, sharing his soul with Voldemort, could not touch you for this reason. It was agony to touch a person marked by something so good" (*Stone*, 299).

So, what does having Love as a God-figure say about Rowling's theological system? Two things come to mind. First, it's a very Christian interpretation of the Divine. It says in the Bible that "God is love, and those who live in love live in God and God lives in them" (1 John 4:7-8). For Rowling to represent Love as the Divine merely reinforces a point that Christianity itself drives home. The power, goodness, and knowledge that she attributes to Love further reinforces this.

But perhaps more interestingly, Rowling's choice to figure the Divine as a non-human abstraction makes it representative of human experience. As humans, we know Love exists because we feel its effects, not because we've ever seen it. Likewise with God. Additionally, for many people, God is hard to find, and once found, hard to maintain a relationship with. We often wish God had an address or a phone number; we wish God was straightforward, delivering answers to prayers in a timely and organized way. But God is none of those things – God surprises, intrigues, allures, and sometimes disappoints. For though many people do have an intimate relationship with the Divine, many others struggle to locate God's presence in their lives and feel that comforting power in a consistent way. Similarly for Love – it can be hard to find and harder to consistently feel. But just because we can't see or touch it daily doesn't mean that it isn't always there.

Rowling's choice to depict God as Love also shows that the human experience she's choosing to represent is not that of a firm believer who never questions God's existence and is always sure of the Divine's presence. It is more like that of a seeker who really struggles to find and maintain a relationship with God, who is constantly discovering the Divine in new and surprising places. She is not representing someone with all the answers; she's representing someone with all the questions, a seeker on a journey. This is one of the reasons her books appeal to such a wide audience and part of what makes them such a powerful teaching tool. Very few of us, if any, have all the answers when it comes to faith. For most of us, faith is like climbing a mountain – there are turns and switchbacks. Sometimes we encounter a cliff so steep we wonder if we'll be able to climb it. But occasionally, between the clouds, we can see the peak, and that keeps us moving. So, by choosing a God-figure that reveals itself gradually, that appears slowly over time, Rowling makes an effort to show that God is both a very real presence and a very challenging one. In this way, she presents a depiction of the Divine that is both true to Christianity and in line with human experience.

CONCLUSION

What I offered in the above section was one example of how our class discussed a theological topic and its relationship to the *Harry Potter* series. Though it would take too long to go into all the topics we discussed, I would like to offer some closing remarks that might contain broader theological reflections.

My overarching sense is that it would be inappropriate to discount the books outright as being non-Christian or heretical. The series does contain a myriad of Christian ideas: salvific figures like Dumbledore and Harry resemble Christ in their efforts to befriend the underdog and liberate the oppressed, even if they themselves are not allegorically representative of God; apocalyptic imagery is present in the scars on Harry's forehead and hand as well as the Dark Mark – which might be likened to the Mark of the Beast; there is a consistent theme of love conquering death, as well as an emphasis on the power of self-sacrifice. J.K. Rowling also takes some Christian concepts and plays with them in pretty unconventional ways that nonetheless belie a Christian perspective: the evil Voldemort perverts Eucharistic imagery when he regains his body by forcibly taking flesh and blood from Wormtail and Harry. He corrupts ideas of self-sacrifice when he makes Horcruxes – translated to "horrible cross" from the Latin – that destine him to immortality not by saving others but by killing them.

But if Rowling gives some Christian ideals prominence, it would be unjust to call her an apologist for the faith. Rowling herself has said that she never intended the books to be allegorical, and this seems appropriate. Given that she wrote the books in response to the death of her mother, Rowling wasn't writing from a place where she had all the answers. She was writing from a seeker's perspective, as someone trying to understand who God was, given the reality of evil and death. One way this gets played out is in the way she depicts God. She hasn't created a simple God-figure; she's created a powerful but abstract one. In this way, she departs from other allegorical writers who tend to place God in a body, which allows the reader to see God in a concrete, straightforward way.

Though Rowling's books do not perfectly align with Christian doctrine, that doesn't mean that they aren't excellent teaching tools. In fact, the spiritual themes of her series can provide both solidarity and a guide for readers. In the wake of atrocities ranging from the Holocaust to Cambodian genocides, school shootings, planes crashing into skyscrapers, and global financial disasters, many are asking themselves precisely the question J.K. Rowling did: Who *is* God given the reality of evil and death? Her writings also reflect the reality of our post-modern age, where faith is more of a choice than a cultural expectation. And in a society awash with religious options ranging Mahayana Buddhism to Sufi Islam, from Hassidic Judaism to Joel Osteen's megachurch empire faith, many find themselves seeking to understand their spiritual beliefs rather than professing commitment to them.

It is no small wonder, then, that Rowling's writings appeal to so many because when reading *Harry Potter*, they find the voice of a seeker like themselves. But they also find a forum to ask the questions central to Christian faith. By looking at Harry's walk to his own death, the seeker – and the student – can ask what self-sacrifice accomplishes; by considering Dumbledore's continued mantra that love conquers death, they can assess the truth of that claim; looking at the choices the characters make throughout the series highlights the privilege and danger of free will. In the end, it may be that Rowling's books are a more appropriate way to teach theology because instead of indoctrinating students, they force them to question the assumptions of Christianity and to establish whether those assumptions are true for them.

So while the books are not an apologetic, they are good for the Church because they bring about Christian questions in a language that's relevant to today's global citizens. With church attendance dwindling, I am not the first to say that the Church is in danger of becoming irrelevant. I have seen this first-hand: by and large my students could quote more passages from *Harry Potter* than they could from Scripture. I do not mean this to say that my students somehow consider the series holy. Rather, the language of a seeker was relevant to them; the assumed language of the Church was not. Many of them have been offended by Christianity's too often closed-door policy to curiosity and its adherence to tradition at the expense of innovation. And that is deeply unfortunate. Because while I am certain that *Harry Potter* drew them to the class, I like to believe that theology kept them there, that questions like "What happens when we die?" and "How are we to love?" are as relevant for them as they were for those who were inspired to write the scriptural accounts. It is a sad day, then, when the Church shies away from allowing those questions to be asked and from guiding seekers to the heart of their own beliefs.

On a sunny but cold March afternoon, I met one of my students for lunch in New Haven. We were discussing her paper, which was on Hermione as an exemplar of liberation theology. She was a strong student who took theological concepts to heart, and she'd been working on this paper for weeks, periodically e-mailing me about sin, grace, and redemption. This was our final meeting. When we were done, she put her draft away, and said, "So tell me, do you really believe in Jesus' resurrection?"

I looked at her, at her deep, thoughtful eyes and her earnest curiosity. It was a valid question, one any student might ask their teacher. "I do," I said. "But a much more interesting question is: do you?"

Part III

Conversations on Imagination

Chapter Five

When Harry Met Faërie[1]
*Rowling's Hogwarts, Tolkien's Fairy Stories, and the
Question of Readership*

Amy H. Sturgis

I. FOR WHOM DOES THE HOGWARTS BELL TOLL?

J.K. Rowling's *Harry Potter* novels have redefined commercial literary success, and yet, oddly enough, no clear consensus exists about who is the proper audience for the books. Rowling has drawn surprise and even criticism for the dark gravity of her subjects and fierce action of her plots, leading some to suggest that the so-called children's series is unsuitable for the youngsters to whom it is marketed by publishers and booksellers. This conviction at times even translates into formal written complaints and legal actions lodged against elementary schools and libraries. In fact, the *Harry Potter* novels have continually topped the American Library Association's "Most Challenged Books List," and the series as a whole ranked as the seventh most challenged book of the decade 1990-2000, no small feat since the first volume, *Harry Potter and the Sorcerer's Stone*, did not debut until 1998 ("Harry Potter Tops Challenged Books" 67 and "The 100 Most Frequently Challenged Books of 1990-2000").

Although religious convictions lead some individuals to denounce *Harry Potter* and the tradition of fantasy to which he belongs,[2] other adults who embrace such literature still worry about Rowling's work in particular, fearing its themes might prove too much for young readers. In their article "Controversial Content in Children's Literature: Is *Harry Potter* Harmful to Children?," Deborah J. Taub and Heather L. Servaty survey the complaints raised against the *Harry Potter* novels, finding that "Objections to the books stem from their controversial content – from the centrality of magic to the topic of death to scenes that some believe are too violent, intense, or scary for children" (53).

Not all concerns about the age-appropriateness of the novels come from unfriendly voices. In *The Washington Post* article "The Trouble With Harry," for example, Marguerite Kelly lauds the books for motivating youngsters to become enthusiastic readers, but also warns that the series "has scared some little children silly." Kelly does not let her own son's anxieties dampen her appreciation for *Harry Potter*, however; she simply advises fellow parents to set the books aside until they believe their children are mature enough to enjoy the tales "J.K. Rowling writes so well and so clearly" (C4).

Likewise, Deirdre Donohue in her *USA Today* article "Some Want Harry to Vanish Till Kids Are Older" notes how independent booksellers such as Diane Garrett simultaneously praise Rowling as a genius and warn parents the *Harry Potter* books are "completely inappropriate" for their small children. Garrett imagines her active discouragement of those who would buy the series for young readers as a kind of crusade (D1). One of her opponents, the article implies, is Scholastic, the U.S. publisher of the *Harry Potter* series, who advertises to elementary-aged students and claims the novels are suitable for those as young as nine years old. Interestingly enough, as late as 2003, the Scholastic website listed the first four books in the series as appropriate for readers as young as seven (http://www.scholastic.com/consumerstore 2003 and http://store.scholastic.com 2008).

To some it seems accepted wisdom now that the dark imagery and mature issues in the *Harry Potter* books make the series akin to forbidden fruit for children: frowned upon by parents and thus all the more attractive to youngsters. In her undeniably positive analysis of the novels, "Of Magicals and Muggles: Reversals and Revulsions at Hogwarts," Jann Lacoss describes the paradox of a supposed children's series dealing with subjects often closed, even prohibited, to youngsters: "The Harry Potter series incorporates several topics that are more or less taboo to children: violence, gross and disgusting items and topics, magic and witchcraft, and the concept of evil (as well as evil incarnate). Young readers find all of these rather enticing, as anything that adults consider off-limits must be worthwhile" (79-80). The reader is left to wonder, then, if the success of the *Harry Potter* franchise rests solely on a clever but risky strategy of reverse psychology, an initial gamble that children would learn that the novels are not really children's literature at all, and thus would want to read the series all the more. As explanations go, this hardly seems satisfying.

If the issues in *Harry Potter* such as death, and the means by which they are presented such as violence, are not appropriate for children, it appears likely to follow that adults, then, are the natural target for the series. Not so, some reviewers say. In the same way that critics of content object to the so-called adult subjects in *Harry Potter*, critics of genre object to the so-called childish wrappings of fantasy through which Rowling chooses to address them. William Safire, for example, asserts that "The trouble is that grown-ups are buying these books ostensibly to read to kids, but actually to read for themselves." He complains: "These are not, however, books for adults....this is not just dumbing down; it is growing down." Safire regrets that adults choose to follow the *Harry Potter* series rather than investing the same energy reading what he considers to be three-dimensional and challenging works of mature literature. His conclusion about J.K. Rowling's work is clear: "prizeworthy culture it ain't; more than a little is a waste of adult time" (A27).

Yale professor Harold Bloom is equally dismissive of adult attention to *Harry Potter.* "Why read," he asks, "if what you read will not enrich your mind or spirit or personality?" Like Safire, Bloom revisits works he views as classic, canonical texts,[3] and laments that the success of J.K. Rowling's series diverts attention from these "more difficult pleasures." Also like Safire, Bloom sees the *Harry Potter* phenomenon as a symptom of a larger malady of general intellectual inadequacy. He predicts "The cultural critics will, soon enough, introduce *Harry Potter* into their college curriculum, and *The New York Times* will go on celebrating another confirmation of the dumbing-down it leads and exemplifies" (A26).

Authors such A.S. Byatt in "Harry Potter and the Childish Adult" also bemoan what they view as the devolution of culture brought about when adults – some not even parents – choose to read stories about Hogwarts School of Witchcraft and Wizardry (A13). Outspoken Rowling critic Philip Hensher, when reading *Harry Potter and the Order of the Phoenix* for review in his column, finds himself thinking "with shame and intensity, 'Jesus, I'm reading a book about sodding pixies.'" In fact, Pensher suffers from a sensation his own previous articles consciously fed, suggesting, or perhaps hoping, that in the case of *Harry Potter*, "the feeling of mild embarrassment is, for an adult reader, never far away" (30).

Hensher's view is not relegated to the elite circles of professional cultural criticism: undergraduate writer Craig Stern pokes fun at fellow University of Southern California students whose demand for *Harry Potter* novels strains the supply of the local retailers, campus bookstore, and university library. "I'd like to take this opportunity to provide a little reality check for USC students who seem to be a little too enraptured with the series," Stern writes. "Harry Potter is for children. It is a series of children's books...." He warns that his classmates risk being "lame" when they do not realize "We are adults in a respectable institution of higher learning. It's time we stopped deluding ourselves" ("Public Reactions Overblown in Harry Potter Hysteria"). Such opinions are so widespread that Bloomsbury Publishing even produces a separate set of *Harry Potter* novels exclusively for adults with subdued cover artwork intended not to draw attention – or ridicule – from others (http://www.bloomsbury.com/harrypotter/).

Inextricable from these authors' judgments about the quality, complexity, and future longevity of J.K. Rowling's writing are suppositions about the nature and purpose of fantasy literature. Stern's parallel of "Maybe you are a grown man who likes 'The Velveteen Rabbit'" ("Public Reactions Overblown in Harry Potter Hysteria"), Hensher's reference to pixies, and even Bloom's and Safire's invocations of classic foils to compare with Rowling's series – none of which are of like genre with *Harry Potter*[3] -- all betray a certain view of fantasy, in the same way that concerns about the age-appropriateness of the books reflect a particular perspective about young readers.

At day's end, a difficult question emerges from these disparate but repeated lines of fire: if children cannot handle dark and serious issues such as death, and adults should not enjoy such childish and light pleasures as fantasy stories, who if anyone is the proper audience for the *Harry Potter* series, and why? According to J.R.R. Tolkien, the solution to this dilemma lies not in discovering a new category of readers, but rather in dismissing the false assumptions about children, adults, and the nature of fantasy that undergird the question.

II. You Are Now Entering the Perilous Realm

In his 1908 piece "The Ethics of Elfland," G.K. Chesterton reflects, "My first and last philosophy, that which I believe in with unbroken certainty, I learnt in the nursery…. The things I believed most then, the things I believe most now, are the things called fairy tales. They seem to me to be the entirely rational things" (http://www.literatureclassics.com/etexts/322/1956). Nearly four decades later, J.R.R. Tolkien built on Chesterton's "rescue" of fairy tales with an in-depth definition of and justification for the genre in his 1947 essay "On Fairy-Stories."

Dispensing with the amorphous and often misunderstood categories of fantasy and fairy tale, the exacting Tolkien concentrates on mining the genre's essential ingredients. In the process, he identifies and sets aside related but separate literature such as travelers' tales, dream-stories, and beast-fables. The works Tolkien ultimately classifies as fairy-stories meet several key criteria: 1. they touch on or use Faërie, the "Perilous Realm," a sober magic "of a particular mood and power" (39); 2. they take the magic seriously, and do not satirize it even if the larger work is satirical in tone; 3. they involve human beings as characters and at some level speak to one or more of humanity's primal desires, such as the wish to communicate with other living things or to journey through space and time (43); and 4. they offer to the reader four valuable gifts: Fantasy, Recovery, Escape, and Consolation.

It is in his explanation of the four gifts of fairy-stories that Tolkien's most energetic defense of the genre lies. He chooses the term Fantasy to refer to "both the Sub-creative Art in itself and a quality of strangeness and wonder in the Expression, derived from Image" (68): that is, the seductive creation of an internally consistent secondary universe that, while being arrestingly strange and different from the real world, nevertheless compels belief in the reader. Tolkien is well aware of the "depreciative tone" often applied to such works of make-believe (69). Critics, he argues, assume that such fancy is irrational, when in fact only the reasonable creator can understand patterns and laws in the actual universe, construct a comparably constant framework for his own secondary world, and maintain a stark division between the two. In fact, the more carefully crafted and delicately designed the writer makes his setting, the better the Fantasy becomes. Not only does this offering delight the reader, Tolkien claims, but it reveals the author in her truest and most fundamental form, as a child of God, acting in God's image, driven to create just as she herself was created (74-75). Quality Fantasy in Tolkien's view is therefore a spiritual and intellectual achievement, and a difficult one at that. This leads him to admit that Fantasy "is, I think, not a lower but a higher form of Art, indeed the most nearly pure form, and so (when achieved) the most potent" (69).

The other three roles played by fairy-stories according to Tolkien's definition are no less complex or important. Recovery refers to the gift of childlike – though not childish, in the perjorative sense – perspective, the "regaining of a clear view" (77). By venturing into the unfamiliar, the reader can return to see the common, the trite, with fresh eyes and new attention. Such reenergized focus leads to renewed health, both in spirit and mind, according to Tolkien.

Escape, the third offering of fairy-stories, provides a temporary alternative and outlet for what Tolkien calls the "fugitive spirit" (85). That soul might be the archaic aesthete wishing to rise above or return to an era before the impersonal and automated industrialism of modernity, or the political dissident wishing to conjure an alternative regime (perhaps the first stage in what will become reaction), or merely the transcendent pilgrim wishing to meditate upon "simple and fundamental things" cut loose from the anchor of the "whims of evanescent fashion" of the time and place by which he finds himself held prisoner. Tolkien believes fairy-stories allow readers to separate themselves from the triviality of their circumstances in order to encounter, experience, and consider something otherwise lost, elusive, or as yet unborn (78, 80).

Tolkien's understanding of Consolation is twofold. In one sense, he argues, fairy-stories offer the Consolation of the fulfillment of ancient desires, whether those be communing with other creatures by speaking and understanding the languages of the animals, or defying death. But the Consolation even more essential to the essence of fairy-stories is the Happy Ending. The uplifting conclusion does not presuppose an absence of "sorrow or failure," however; in fact, Tolkien explains that "the possibility of these is necessary to the joy of deliverance" (86). Darkness might, perhaps even must, precede light, Tolkien says. Otherwise the reader would not value the "*Eucatastrophe*," the joyous turn that is the "highest function" of the genre (85). The potential for grief and tragedy in effect makes the Happy Ending all the sweeter: "it denies (in the face of much evidence, if you will) universal final defeat and in so far is *evangelium*, giving a fleeting glimpse of Joy, Joy beyond the walls of the world, poignant as grief" (86).

Not only does this joy offer an immediate Consolation to the reader for the lack of happiness in her world, but it also provides the Consolation of an answer to the fundamental question asked of any story: "Is it true?" If the writer maintains the consistency of her secondary world throughout the tale, the story is true in a narrow sense, Tolkien argues; but if she offers her readers the glimpse of real joy, she is also providing "a far-off gleam or echo of *evangelium* in the real world," a moment of communion with the divine, a taste of what is really True (88). In other words, Tolkien sees the best fairy-stories as echoes of the gospel story, evocative of the same kind of spiritual resonance and redemptive possibilities. Not only do the writers of fairy-stories recognize their humanity by mimicking their creator, Tolkien asserts, but they also recognize the divine by incorporating transcendent joy into the Happy Ending of their tales.

Tolkien's literary theory and his Roman Catholicism here cannot be divorced, but it does not require a theologian to recognize that Tolkien believes fairy-tales capable of offering sophisticated, serious, even life-changing benefits to the reader. These benefits should not to be taken lightly, in Tolkien's estimation; moreover, they should not be relegated to one particular age group. In fact, Tolkien notes that Fantasy, Recovery, Escape, and Consolation are particularly suitable as gifts for adult readers, as they are "all things of which children have, as a rule, less need than older people" (67). He calls for adults so inclined to ignore the capricious fads of popular sentiment and "read fairy-stories as a natural branch of literature – neither playing at being children, nor pretending to be choosing for children, nor being boys who would not grow up…." (67)

If fairy-stories are not naturally or exclusively appropriate for children, then why has a consensus in popular culture assumed that they are? To illustrate, Tolkien draws a comparison between "latter-day Europe" (65) – though his metaphor applies with equal usefulness to the modern United States, as well – and the future painted by H.G. Wells in his classic 1895 novel *The Time Machine.* By constructing an artificial division between youngsters and grown-ups, Tolkien argues, contemporary society has created caricatures of the two groups, casting children as the ornamental, carefree, empty-minded Eloi forever stagnant, untroubled, and unchallenged, and casting adults as the slaves to the machines, the fierce and twisted Morlocks, driven from the lovely light to toil for survival in dankness and darkness. Both views are ridiculous for a variety of reasons, most especially because they deny that both beings are the same creature at different points along a spectrum: children are adults in training, and adults are older children.

These false assumptions, these visions of idealized childhood and demonized adulthood, lead to disservices on both sides, Tolkien asserts. On the one hand, literature written specifically for children becomes at its worst "often merely silly, Piggwiggenry without even the intrigue; or patronizing; or (deadliest of all) covertly sniggering, with an eye on the other grown-ups present" (65). On the other hand, adults lose the opportunity to experience Fantasy, Recovery, Escape, and Consolation because fairy-stories, confined to the nurseries, are then erroneously "stuffed away in attics" as outgrown and unnecessary playthings of a more innocent age (65). To save fairy-stories, then, and readers as well, children must be challenged by thoughtful, quality material, and adults must be freed to read the genre without social stigma or guilt:

> If fairy-story as a kind is worth reading at all it is worthy to be written for and read by adults. They will, of course, put more in and get more out than children can. Then, as a branch of a genuine art, children may hope to get fairy-stories fit for them to read and yet within their measure; as they may hope to get suitable introductions to poetry, history, and the sciences. Though it may be better for them to read some things, especially fairy-stories, that are beyond their measure rather than short of it. Their books like their clothes should allow for growth, and their books at any rate should encourage it. (65)

III. Is Harry Potter a Hobbit?

The question then arises, where in Tolkien's schema does *Harry Potter* fit?

First, J.K. Rowling's series evokes the essence of Faërie. Though it is difficult to define, readers recognize when they encounter that "particular mood and power": at the moment Harry first sees his heart's dearest desire in the Mirror of Erised (*Sorceror's Stone*, 208), for example, or first hears murmured whispers behind the black veil in the Department of Mysteries (*Order of the Phoenix*, 774). The backdrop for such pivotal scenes also showcases a cross-section of genre tradition. The domain of witches and wizards Harry initially encounters at the age of eleven includes such classic landscapes as an enchanted castle, forbidden forest, and magical village. Moreover, in this world the inhabitants remember the past atrocities of He-Who-Must-Not-Be-Named, the Dark Lord Voldemort, and alternately fear, deny, enable, and/or resist his violent return: a "Perilous Realm," indeed.

Second, Rowling takes the magic of Hogwarts and its environment seriously. Although the Ton-Tongue Toffee or Skiving Snackboxes of troublemaking twins Fred and George Weasley may provide humor in the tales, for instance, the legitimacy of the magical charms they utilize so effectively is never questioned. (See *Goblet of Fire* and *Order of the Phoenix*, respectively.) Magic at Hogwarts is a significant and permanent force capable of offense or defense, not a temporary device later explained away by dream sequences or similar sleight-of-hand.

Third, the series involves ordinary human beings as characters, whether they be non-magical Muggles such as the Dursleys or Grangers, or magic-deprived Squibs such as Argus Filch or Arabella Figg. Even the magical witches and wizards are recognizable as humans, and the reader's point of view is echoed in the perspective of students like Harry and Hermione who were raised without magic in the so-called real world. Furthermore, episodes in the series address what Tolkien identifies as humanity's primal desires. Harry communicates with magical creatures; he even builds friendships with a half-giant, werewolf, house-elf, ghost, and centaur, among others. Through devices such as the Time-Turner and the Pensieve, characters traverse time and space. Even death, for a period, is postponed via the Sorcerer's Stone, and in *Harry Potter and the Deathly Hallows*, it is transcended for a time when Harry proves willing to sacrifice his own life; he communes not only with his deceased parents, godfather, and the father of his own godson (698-703), but also his late headmaster and mentor, Albus Dumbledore himself (707-723).

Most significantly, J.K. Rowling's work offers Tolkien's quartet of valuable gifts: Fantasy, Recovery, Escape, and Consolation. The *Harry Potter* novels meet the criteria of Fantasy by illuminating an internally consistent, believable universe beyond and parallel to the Muggle world. The magical realm follows its own dependable logic. The reader immediately gains a sense of the patterns and practices of the magical community, from its need for educating the young in the tools of the craft such as charms, potions, and transfigurations, to its complex system of transportation including the use of enchanted trains, floo powder, and portkeys, to the existence of its own bureaucracy, the Ministry of Magic, predictably rife with incompetence, pettiness, hypocrisy, and ambition, not to mention the occasional flying Ford Anglia. As Hermione repeatedly reminds her classmates who have never read *Hogwarts: A History*, no one can Apparate or Disapparate on school grounds (see *Prisoner of Azkaban* 164, *Goblet of Fire* 564, and *Order of the Phoenix* 500, for example): a rule is a rule, and within Rowling's series, the steady adherence to the laws of the magical universe seduces readers into belief.

Rowling provides Recovery for her audience, as well. Arthur Weasley's genuine delight with "eckeltricity" (*Goblet of Fire* 46) and "the fellytone" (*Order of the Phoenix* 869) make the most ordinary trappings of everyday life appear new and remarkable. Photographs that capture still images, athletes who do not fly, and letters that do not howl aloud seem dear and precious after time spent at Hogwarts: so, too, does the closeness of parents living, or at the very least remembered. And although Harry's reality quite rightly can be called dark and dangerous, it nonetheless offers Escape. Voldemort, his Death Eaters, and Slytherin House are impressive foes to be sure, but exotic ones. Although the *Harry Potter* plots unfold in the present day, Hogwarts does not wrestle with the problems of unplanned teen pregnancy or random school shootings, much less the post-9/11 threats of terrorism and war as felt in Harry's home nation, Great Britain.

Finally, and perhaps most importantly, each *Harry Potter* volume includes the joyous turn that "denies...universal final defeat," savoring a victory made all the more potent by the suffering and danger that preceded it, even while contributing to the larger meta-narrative of the series as a whole. In fact, Rowling consistently delivers her Happy Ending in a literary one-two punch, with Harry's escape from peril and frustration of Voldemort's plan followed by a second revelation once he has returned from danger. For example, the first half of the joyous turn in *Harry Potter and the Sorcerer's Stone* comes through Harry's defeat of Professor Quirrell and Lord Voldemort, initially through the skill and resourcefulness of Harry, Hermione, and Ron, and eventually due to Lily Potter's unconditional and self-sacrificing love for her son, a power that protects Harry long after his mother's death. The Happy Ending is secured when Gryffindor later wrests the House Cup from Slytherin at the Hogwarts Parting Feast thanks to the often overlooked yet significant courage of underdog Neville Longbottom.

The same pattern recurs in subsequent books in the series. The final volume, *Harry Potter and the Deathly Hallows*, provides what is perhaps Rowling's most accomplished gift of Consolation. In the first part of the one-two punch, Harry and his friends and allies definitively and completely defeat Voldemort in battle, although their victory comes at a tremendous cost. The sacrifices of many of Harry's dearest friends make the ultimate final triumph all the more meaningful and affecting. Although this success is not easy to accomplish, it is simple to understand: to quote Peeves's victory song, "We did it, we bashed them, wee Potter's the one,/ And Voldy's gone moldy, so now let's have some fun!" (746)

The second half of Rowling's climactic *Eucatastrophe* is more subtle. Harry achieves his heart's desire: a family. For him to have such a family – a safe, healthy, normal family – Harry must prove willing to make still more difficult choices. First, he chooses to overcome temptation by surrendering the Elder Wand. Recognizing that it is "more trouble than it's worth," Harry reveals that he values a stable and quiet life, a life suitable for building a family, above an opportunity for power and fame (749). Second, he chooses to admit he was wrong and recognize uncomfortable truths about those closest to him, truths to which he willingly had been blind. He embraces the fact that Dumbledore, while fallible, was nonetheless a great wizard, mentor, and friend. More to the point, Harry accepts the fact that he was mistaken in almost every way about the man he despised for seven years, Severus Snape. Harry's mature understanding is embodied in the name of his son, Albus Severus. Rowling spotlights the humbler and wiser Harry most clearly when he explains to his son that Snape "was probably the bravest man I ever knew" (758). Discovering not only that Harry's dearest wish for a family has come true, but also that he has grown into a man who is worthy of it, evokes in readers that "joy as poignant as grief."

In accomplishing these four tasks, J.K. Rowling's *Harry Potter* novels meet Tolkien's criteria for fairy-stories. This places Rowling squarely in the tradition of many of Tolkien's chief literary influences – and, of course, Tolkien himself. In fact, many parallels exist between Rowling's primary themes and those expressed in Tolkien's fiction. In his analysis of the *Harry Potter* texts, related interviews, and guides, Rowling scholar John Granger identifies four central issues in the author's series: Prejudice, Change, Choice, and Death (33). This same foursome of subjects runs throughout Tolkien's novels and short stories.

In a July 7, 2000 *Entertainment Weekly* interview, J.K. Rowling admits "bigotry is probably the thing I detest most. All forms of intolerance, the whole idea of 'that which is different from me is necessarily evil'" (http://mugglenet.com/ewinterview1.shtml). She explores Prejudice in her series through a variety of relationships and metaphors. Whether it is the elite Malfoys' distaste for the poor or non-pureblood magical folk, or the Dursleys' fear of anyone abnormal, or the wizarding community's prejudice toward giants and werewolves and Squibs, or the centaurs' disdain toward humans, or even the headless ghosts' dismissal of the nearly headless, Rowling provides a variety of examples of how bigotry hurts its victims and, in the end, the bigots themselves, as well. (See Granger's discussion of Rowling's prejudice theme in *The Hidden Key to Harry Potter* 35-44.)

Rowling worries that "Oppressed groups are not, generally speaking, people who stand firmly together – no, sadly, they kind of subdivide among themselves and fight like hell" (http://mugglenet.com/ewinterview1.shtml). Tolkien addresses this aspect of Prejudice repeatedly in his works, suggesting a hope not always untouched by skepticism. In *The Hobbit*, Bilbo Baggins watches uncomprehendingly as the Dwarves and Elves and Men only overcome their inexplicable and petty bigotry when forced to join ranks and face foes whose combined unreasoning hate is even stronger in what becomes the Battle of Five Armies. *The Lord of the Rings* seems at times to be a protracted meditation on intolerance as Tolkien pairs characters from distrustful, suspicious backgrounds together and forces them into alliance: Elf and Dwarf, Man and Hobbit, Rohirrim and Wild Men, even Shieldmaiden and Philosopher-Statesman.

In a telling twist, Tolkien launches his most poignant attack against those disdainful of Faërie itself, those prejudiced against the very essence of fairy-stories. In "Smith of Wootton Major," the narrow-minded Nokes the Cook is mocking and dismissive of his assistant Prentice, who unbeknownst to him is actually the King of Faery. When Prentice identifies a magical star, the Cook jeers at the apparent immaturity of his helper:

> 'What do you mean, young fellow?' he said, not much pleased. 'If it isn't funny, what is it?'
>
> 'It's *fay*', said Prentice. 'It comes from Fairy.'
>
> Then the Cook laughed. 'All right, all right', he said. 'It means the same; but call it that if you like. You'll grow up some day....' (8)

Yet Nokes is the one who suffers most from his prejudice. When he is confronted with the King of Faery in his splendor, his "'Take your Fairy and your nonsense somewhere else!'" (33) attitude does not allow him to see the magic right before his eyes. He is limited by his preconceptions of Faery – "'King o' Fairy! Why, he hadn't no wand.'" – and thus is able to delude himself about the nature of his weight loss and, in fact, his entire world: "'There ain't no magic in it'" (33). Nokes ends as a diminished, pitiable, empty character, untouched by the wonder of magic that transforms and illuminates the humble protagonist Smith.

Change, too, plays its role in the works of Rowling and Tolkien. The imagery of alchemy – transfiguring, transforming, turning the crude into the golden – pervades the *Harry Potter* series (See Granger 85-102). This theme seems particularly fitting in books that follow the growth and maturation of an anti-heroic boy into an undeniably heroic man: even more so, perhaps, as the action takes place in the mercurial climate of Lord Voldemort's rebirth and renewed bid for domination. With every new revelation Harry and those around him find themselves at a point of no return, heavily laden with knowledge, responsibility, and reputation, compelled to act. Harry can no more deny his destiny and return to the simplicity of innocence and obscurity than Tolkien's Frodo can return to his beloved Shire and live in contented peace after parting with the Ring.

In *The Lord of the Rings*, change also appears in the ebbs and flows of the peoples of Middle-earth. The War of the Ring is the moment for the Halflings to take center stage, but it also marks the rise of the race of Men and the waning of the power of Elves. The protagonists of one Age must purchase the next with their blood and sacrifice, and then surrender to it. Leaders such as Elrond and Galadriel embrace the strategy of the Ring's destruction despite the fact they know it means irreparable change to their diminishing world, the unmaking of so much of its magic. So, too, in *Harry Potter and the Order of the Phoenix*, for example, does Dumbledore encourage Harry's and the Order's actions, though it costs him his Headmaster position at Hogwarts, his honors, and his reputation; he later proves willing to sacrifice his life in *Harry Potter and the Half-Blood Prince*. In *Harry Potter and the Order of the Phoenix*, Mad-Eye Moody's rumination on the photograph of the first Order of the Phoenix, his laundry list of courage and death and loss, further serves to underscore the fact that actions have consequences, that taking a stand changes the individual and his or her world forever. The deaths of multiple major characters in *Harry Potter and the Deathly Hallows* reinforce this message.

Tolkien and Rowling dovetail the themes of Change and Choice. Both writers remain preoccupied with what Dumbledore calls "a choice between what is right and what is easy" (*Goblet of Fire* 724). When Gandalf's complicated history of the One Ring and all that it means overwhelms Frodo, the wizard cuts to the heart of the crisis and the *The Lord of the Rings*: "All we have to decide is what to do with the time that is given us" (50). Elrond notes that the journey to Mordor falls to Hobbits due to "neither strength nor wisdom" (262), but because Frodo decides to accept the burden willingly: "But it is a heavy burden. So heavy that none could lay it on another. I do not lay it on you. But if you take it freely, I will say that your choice is right" (264). Similarly, Dumbledore considers Harry's decision to deny a possible future in Slytherin House in favor of a more difficult, even dangerous path as "a true Gryffindor" more important than any specific talent or trait: "It is our choices, Harry, that show what we truly are far more than our abilities" (*Chamber of Secrets* 334, 333). Therefore a small hobbit or a young boy can succeed where powerful wizards fail. To use Dawn Ellen Jacobs' words in "Tolkien and Rowling: Reflections on Receptions," "Harry's loyalty to Albus Dumbledore and Hagrid marks his own inherent nature as surely as Frodo's ability to bear the ring marks his" (50).

The two authors center their secondary worlds on the foundational issue of Death. The events in Tolkien's story "Leaf by Niggle" create an extended metaphor for Life, Death, Purgatory, and Heaven, literally walking the reader from one world into the next. His Middle-earth books, *The Hobbit*, *The Lord of the Rings*, and *The Silmarillion*, juxtapose the melancholy of the deathless Elves and the vitality of the mortal Hobbits, Men, and Dwarves, defending the notion that Death is, in fact, a gift from the creator, and unceasing life is but a pale imitation of an immortal afterlife. In a letter to Milton Waldeman written perhaps in 1951, Tolkien says, "You asked for a brief sketch of my stuff that is connected with my imaginary world…. Anyway all this stuff is mainly concerned with Fall, Mortality, and the Machine" (*Letters* 143, 145). He puts a finer point on his key theme in a 1957 letter to Christopher and Faith Tolkien: "But I should say, if asked, the tale [*Lord of the Rings*] is not really about Power and Dominion: that only sets the wheels going; it is about Death and the desire for deathlessness" (*Letters* 261-262).

J.K. Rowling makes a similar statement in a July 2000 interview with *Newsweek*: "In fact, death and bereavement and what death means, I would say, is one of the central themes in all seven books" ("Harry's Hot" 56). The idea plays itself out particularly clearly in the clash between Albus Dumbledore and Lord Voldemort. Dumbledore does not fear death; in fact, he tells Harry, "to the well-organized mind, death is but the next great adventure." (*Sorcerer's Stone* 297). He implies that deathlessness ultimately is not a desirable fate when he notes that the Sorcerer's Stone provided "two things most human beings would choose above all" – unlimited wealth and life – "the trouble is, humans do have a knack of choosing precisely those things that are worst for them" (*Sorcerer's Stone* 297). Lord Voldemort, it seems, is one such human. He boasts to his Death-Eaters that he has "gone further than anybody along the path that leads to immortality. You know my goal – to conquer death" (*Goblet of Fire* 653). The two legendary wizards voice their opposing views during their battle in *Harry Potter and the Order of the Phoenix*:

> "You do not seek to kill me, Dumbledore?" called Voldemort, his scarlet eyes narrowed over the top of the shield. "Above such brutality, are you?"
>
> "We both know there are other ways of destroying a man, Tom," Dumbledore said calmly, continuing to walk toward Voldemort as though he had not a fear in the world, as though nothing had happened to interrupt his stroll up the hall. "Merely taking your life would not satisfy me, I admit –"
>
> "There is nothing worse than death, Dumbledore!" snarled Voldemort.
>
> "You are quite wrong," said Dumbledore.... "Indeed, your failure to understand that there are things much worse than death has always been your greatest weakness –" (*Order of the Phoenix* 814)

Presumably informed by his own experience of death, the late Dumbledore repeats his sentiment from beyond the grave in *Harry Potter and the Deathly Hallows* when he exhorts Harry, "Do not pity the dead, Harry. Pity the living, and, above all, those who live without love" (722).

Here Dumbledore's words clearly parallel Tolkien's own: "Death is not an Enemy! I said, or meant to say, that the 'message' was the hideous peril of confusing true 'immortality' with limitless serial longevity. Freedom from Time, and clinging to Time. The *confusion* is the work of the Enemy, and one of the chief causes of human disaster" (*Letters* 267). Rowling's Voldemort, like some of Tolkien's ancient Númenoreans, not only fails to understand and appreciate death, but also seeks to cheat it at substantial peril to himself and his realm.

Sophisticated, complex, even troubling themes such as Prejudice, Change, Choice, and especially Death, do not necessarily fit with popular understandings of light-hearted fantasy stories and the small children for whom they must be written. These themes do fit, however, with Tolkien's theory of the high art and serious purpose of fairy-stories. J.K. Rowling's approach to her writing also matches Tolkien's call for genre fiction able to satisfy other adults and challenge young readers to grow, rather than surrender to the "often merely silly" stereotypes of what nursery room tales should be.

Rowling alludes to this question by drawing a sharp contrast in her works. On the one hand is the wise and compassionate Dumbledore at the close of *Goblet of Fire*, who proves willing to share with students dark and disturbing truths that their parents and even government fear is too much for them in his "Remember Cedric Diggory" speech, a step he takes to prepare, challenge, and protect Hogwarts' young charges (*Goblet of Fire* 721-724). On the other hand is High Inquisitor Dolores Jane Umbridge, an authoritarian villain who tells condescending, soothing lies of safety to the students that, if believed, ultimately will endanger the children, leaving them unprepared and unwary even as her own self-righteous methods of control enable Voldemort's evil plans (*Order of the Phoenix* 241-246).

In interviews, Rowling is forthright about her convictions. When asked if she ever thinks "Maybe I should just tone it down" with regard to the action and issues in her *Harry Potter* novels, Rowling responds: "No. I know that sounds kind of brutal but no, I haven't. The bottom line is, I have to write the story I want to write. I never write them with a focus group of 8-year-olds in mind. I have to continue telling the story the way I want to tell it" (http://mugglenet.com/ewinterview1.shtml).

IV. Putting the So-Called Adult in So-Called Children's Literature

Tolkien's friend, colleague, and fellow Inklings author C.S. Lewis wrote the 1966 essay "On Three Ways of Writing for Children" in part to praise and expand upon Tolkien's literary theory. In it Lewis says, "I hope everyone had read Tolkien's essay on Fairy Tales, which is perhaps the most important contribution to the subject that anyone has yet made" (35). He goes on to add his agreement to Tolkien's thesis that "The whole association of fairy tale and fantasy with childhood is local and accidental" (35). This conclusion has significant implications for both camps of critics taking aim at the *Harry Potter* series. According to Tolkien and Lewis, those who worry about the age-appropriateness of the novels and those who argue that adults should not read the works both are beginning from the wrong premise by assuming that, because the books rest on fantastic premises and include school-aged protagonists, they are intended only for youngsters.

And what of Rowling's dark, mature themes that might be too much for children? Tolkien responds by saying that it is healthy for children to read some works "beyond their measure," that fiction should promote development, offer challenge, and allow youngsters to grow into its style and message. How can there be Consolation, the solace and relief of the joyous turn, without fear and danger first? Rowling concurs that ideas such as Death have their proper place in the tales: "I don't at all relish the idea of children in tears, and I don't deny it's frightening. But it's supposed to be frightening! And if you don't show how scary that is, you cannot show how incredibly brave Harry is" (http://mugglenet.com/ewinterview1.shtml).Without serious, believable peril, then, there is no serious, believable courage.

Lewis supports Tolkien and anticipates Rowling in his essay:

> A far more serious attack on the fairy tale as children's literature comes from those who do not wish children to be frightened.... that we must try to keep out of his mind the knowledge that he is born into a world of death, violence, wounds, adventure, heroism and cowardice, good and evil... [This] would indeed be to give children a false impression and feed them on escapism in the bad sense. There is something ludicrous in the idea of so educating a generation which is born to the Ogpu and the atomic bomb. Since it is so likely that they will meet cruel enemies, let them at least have heard of brave knights and heroic courage. Otherwise you are making their destiny not brighter but darker.... I think it possible that by confining your child to blameless stories of child life in which nothing at all alarming ever happens, you would fail to banish the terrors, and would succeed in banishing all that can ennoble them or make them endurable. For in the fairy tales, side by side with the terrible figures, we find the immemorial comforters and protectors, the radiant ones.... (39-40)

In other words, losing the terrible Voldemort, losing the violent Death-Eaters, losing the tragic deaths of James and Lily Potter and Sirius Black, also means losing Mrs. Weasley's hand-knitted Christmas sweaters, losing the best seats by the fire in the Gryffindor common room, losing the healing tears and heartening song of Fawkes the Phoenix, and losing the devoted protection of Albus Dumbledore. Lewis, restating Tolkien's position, finds this price too great to pay.

And what of those critics who remind adults that *Harry Potter* should be a series for the delight of youngsters, not the "dumbing-down" of grown-ups? Tolkien does admit his enjoyment of fairy-stories began when he was young:

I desired dragons with a profound desire. Of course, I in my timid body did not wish to have them in the neighborhood, intruding into my relatively safe world…. But the world that contained even the imagination of Fáfnir was richer and more beautiful, at whatever cost or peril ("On Fairy-Stories" 64).

Yet at the time Tolkien liked other literature as well or better. Only in his later years did Tolkien develop a true appreciation of the genre: "A real taste for fairy-stories was wakened by philology on the threshold of manhood, and quickened to full life by war" ("On Fairy-Stories" 64-65). Tolkien's own life experience with fairy-stories informs his argument that such fiction offers even more for the adult than the child. His entreaty to grown-up readers to brave the tide of public opinion and read fairy-stories for their own sake therefore is both an intellectual and a personal plea.

Readers should not assume that, because the *Harry Potter* series opens with a child protagonist, this means that J.K. Rowling crafted it for an equally young audience. As Paige Byam points out in "Children's Literature or Adult Classic? The *Harry Potter* Series and the British Novel Tradition," "the character of Harry is an adolescent – but so are Charlotte Brontë's Jane Eyre, and Charles Dickens's Pip and Esther Summerson when we first meet them, to name a few" (8). In fact, Rowling confesses to writing for herself, an adult, as her primary audience: "I cannot write to please other people. I can't… I want to be able to look in the mirror and think, I did it the way I meant to do it" (http://mugglenet.com/ewinterview1.shtml). If Rowling's books satisfy her own literary appetite, it certainly seems possible that they might appeal to others over the age of fourteen, as well.

Once more, Lewis unites the perspectives of Tolkien and Rowling, framing an answer to meet the most vocal *Harry Potter* detractor:

Critics who treat *adult* as a term of approval, instead of as a merely descriptive term, cannot be adult themselves. To be concerned about being grown up, to admire the grown up because it is grown up, to blush at the suspicion of being childish; these things are the marks of childhood and adolescence. And in childhood and adolescence they are, in moderation, healthy symptoms. Young things ought to want to grow. But to carry on into middle life or even into early manhood this concern about being adult is a mark of really arrested development. When I was ten, I read fairy tales in secret and would have been ashamed if I had been found doing so. Now that I am fifty I read them openly. When I became a man I put away childish things, including the fear of childishness and the desire to be very grown up. (34)

The primary obstacles to adult enjoyment of fairy-stories, Lewis finds, often are the so-called adults themselves. Lewis would say that critic Philip Hensher's humiliation at reading about pixies reveals much more about Hensher's unresolved psychological issues than any inherent problem with pixies as a topic. In essence, Lewis's prescription requires the reader, not the subject matter, to grow up.

And thus Lewis, writing from the common ground shared between Tolkien and Rowling, clearly sees Tolkien's solution to Rowling's dilemma of readership: bring the alleged adult subject matter to the child reader, and the adult reader to the alleged children's genre. Like Middle-earth, Hogwarts School of Witchcraft and Wizardry, he suggests, has room enough for all within its landscape.

Endnotes

1   This work has benefited from the comments and suggestions of Kathryn N. McDaniel, John Granger, Larry M. Hall, Kristi Lee, and Karen H. Sturgis, as well as the ideas discussed by Belmont University students in the "Harry Potter and His Predecessors" course taught by the author. Portions of this article were presented at *The Gathering of the Fellowship* in Toronto in 2003. A previous version of this work was published as "Harry Potter Is a Hobbit: Rowling, Tolkien, and the Question of Readership" in the May/June 2004 issue of *CSL: The Bulletin of The New York C.S. Lewis Society.*

2   For a thoughtful overview of objections from a Christian perspective, see Kimbra Wilder Gish, "Hunting Down Harry Potter: An Exploration of Religious Concerns about Children's Literature."

3   Bloom's examples of Lewis Carroll's *Alice* books and Kenneth Graham's *The Wind in the Willows* at first blush might seem to extol classic fantasy texts, J.R.R. Tolkien discusses each of these and explains how they fail to meet the necessary criteria for the genre: Carroll because his books are dream-stories that eventually deny the truth of their tales and frame them as illusions, and Graham because his work is a beast-fable "in which the animal form is only a mask upon a human face, a device of the satirist or the preacher" ("On Fairy-Stories" 42).

BIBLIOGRAPHY

Bloom, Harold. "Can 35 Million Book Buyers Be Wrong? Yes." *Wall Street Journal.* 11 July 2000. A26.

Byam, Paige. "Children's Literature or Adult Classic? The *Harry Potter* Series and the British Novel Tradition." *Topic: The Washington & Jefferson College Review.* Vol. 54. Fall 2004. 7-13.

Byatt, A.S. "Harry Potter and the Childish Adult." *New York Times.* 7 July 2003. A13.

Chesterton, Gilbert K. Gilbert K. Chesterton, "The Ethics of Elfland." *IV The Ethics of Elfland – Orthodoxy.* 5 September 2003. http://www. literatureclassics.com/etexts/322/1956.

Donohue, Deirdre. "Some Want Harry To Vanish Till Kids Are Older." *USA Today.* Arlington, Virginia. 15 June 2000. D1.

Gish, Kimbra Wilder. "Hunting Down Harry Potter: An Exploration of Religious Concerns about Children's Literature." *Horn Book.* May/June 2000. 262-271.

Granger, John. *The Hidden Key to Harry Potter: Understanding the Meaning, Genius, and Popularity of Joanne Rowling's Harry Potter Novels.* Port Hadlock, WA: Zossima Press, 2002.

"Harry Potter at Bloomsbury Publishing." *Bloomsbury.com.* 13 August 2008. http://www.bloomsbury.com/harrypotter/.

"Harry Potter Tops Challenged Books." *Teacher Librarian.* 28:4. April 2001. 67.

Hensher, Philip. "A Crowd-Pleaser but No Classic." *The Spectator.* 113:9125. 28 June 28 2003. 30.

Jacobs, DawnEllen. "Tolkien and Rowling: Reflections on Receptions." *Topic: The Washington & Jefferson College Review.* Vol. 54. Fall 2004. 46-54.

Kelly, Marguerite. "The Trouble with Harry." *Washington Post.* February 14, 2001. C4.

Lacoss, Jann. "Of Magicals and Muggles: Reversals and Revulsions at Hogwarts." 67-88. *The Ivory Tower and Harry Potter: Perspectives on a Literary Phenomenon.* Ed. Lana A. Whited. Columbia: University of Missouri Press, 2002.

Lewis, C.S. "On Three Ways of Writing For Children." *On Stories and Other Essays on Literature.* New York: Harcourt, 1966. 31-44.

"The 100 Most Frequently Challenged Books of 1990-2000." 2003. *American Library Association.* 20 August 2003. http://www.ala.org/bbooks/top100bannedbooks.html.

Rowling, J.K. quoted in Malcolm Jones. "Harry's Hot." *Newsweek*. 17 July 2000. 56.

___. *Harry Potter and the Chamber of Secrets*. New York: Scholastic, 1999.

___. *Harry Potter and the Deathly Hallows*. New York: Scholastic, 2007.

___. *Harry Potter and the Goblet of Fire*. New York: Scholastic, 2000.

___. *Harry Potter and the Order of the Phoenix*. New York: Scholastic, 2003.

___. *Harry Potter and the Prisoner of Azkaban*. New York: Scholastic, 1999.

___. *Harry Potter and the Sorcerer's Stone*. New York: Scholastic, 1998.

___. interviewed in *Entertainment Weekly*, September 7, 2000, as archived on *Mugglenet.com*. August 19, 2003. http://mugglenet.com/ewinterview1.shtml.

Safire, William. "Besotted With Potter." *New York Times*. 27 January 2000. A27.

The Scholastic Store Home Page. 1996-2003. 21 August 2003. http://www.scholastic.com/consumerstore.

The Scholastic Store Home Page. 1996-2008. 13 August 2008. http://store.scholastic.com/.

Stern, Craig. "Public Reactions Overblown in Harry Potter Hysteria." *Daily Trojan Online: Student Newspaper of the University of Southern California*. 18 August 2003. 22 August 2003. http://www.dailytrojan.com/article.do?issue=/V150/N01&id=06-public.01v.html.

Taub, Deborah J. and Heather L. Servaty. "Controversial Content in Children's Literature: Is *Harry Potter* Harmful to Children?" *Harry Potter's World: Multidisciplinary Perspectives*. Ed. Elizabeth A. Heilman. New York: RoutledgeFalmer, 2003. 53-72.

Tolkien, J.R.R. "From a Letter to Christopher and Faith Tolkien." 11 September 1957. Letter 202 of the *Letters of J.R.R. Tolkien*. Ed. Humphrey Carpenter. Boston: Houghton Mifflin, 2000. 261-262.

___. "From a Letter to C. Ouboter, Voorhoeve en Dietrich, Rotterdam." 10 April 1958. Letter 208 of the *Letters of J.R.R. Tolkien*. Ed. Humphrey Carpenter. Boston: Houghton Mifflin, 2000. 267.

___. *The Hobbit*. Reprint ed. Boston: Houghton Mifflin, 1997.

___. "Leaf by Niggle." *A Tolkien Miscellany*. New York: Science Fiction Book Club, 2002. 147-162.

___. *The Lord of the Rings*. Complete ed. London: HarperCollins, 1994.

___. "On Fairy-Stories." *The Tolkien Reader: Stories, Poems, and Commentaries by the Author of* The Hobbit *and* The Lord of the Rings. New York: Del Rey, 1966. 33-99.

___. *The Silmarillion.* Ed. Christopher Tolkien. 2nd ed. Boston: Houghton Mifflin, 2001.

___. "Smith of Wootton Major." *A Tolkien Miscellany.* New York: Science Fiction Book Club, 2002. 1-35.

___. "To Milton Waldeman." undated (1951?). Letter 131 of the *Letters of J.R.R. Tolkien.* Ed. Humphrey Carpenter. Boston: Houghton Mifflin, 2000. 143-161.

Wells, H.G. *The Time Machine.* 2nd ed. New York: Bantam, 1982.

Chapter Six

The Well-Ordered Mind
How Imagination Can Make us More Human

Travis Prinzi

"And how do you think people have survived? How do people remember who they are and where they're from? And how do they know what it means to be human, what makes us more than animals? How do they pass these things on to their children? Stories, that's how." ~ from *Floodland* by Marcus Sedgwick

"The moral imagination," wrote the late Russell Kirk for *Literature and Belief*, is the "ethical perception" which "aspires to the apprehending of right order in the soul and right order in the commonwealth." In other words, the imagination has the power to change ourselves and the world around us for the better. In his article "The Moral Imagination," Kirk explored this concept as it was originally introduced by 18th century British philosopher-statesman Edmund Burke, arguing that the "highest form" of the moral imagination was found "in poetry and art." In the pursuit of a rightly-ordered life, the writers and the artists are our greatest help. Kirk wrote, "The end of great books is ethical – to teach us what it means to be genuinely human."

Why is this? Why not rational arguments and straightforward propositions proven with scientific fact? Why would we not seek knowledge that we can "prove" in order to define humanity? Clyde Kilby, in the foreward to Rolland Hein's book *Christian Mythmakers,* explains the necessity of the imagination:

> We intellectualize in order to know, but paradoxically, intellectualization tends to destroy its object. The harder we grasp at the thing, the more its reality moves away.
>
> So what is to be done? Man finds himself a third characteristic called imagination, by which he can transcend statements and systems. By some magic, imagination is able to disengage our habitual discursive and system-making and send us on a journey toward gestures, pictures, images, rhythms, metaphor, symbol, and at the peak of all, myth....
>
> Myth is necessary because reality is so much larger than rationality. Not that myth is irrational, but that it easily accommodates the rational while rising above it. (x-xi)

If the definition of humanity is greater than what can be proven in a laboratory, then we need more than science and rationality to fully understand ourselves. That is where the imagination comes in.

J.K. Rowling's *Harry Potter* series, through the use of the moral imagination, teaches us what it means to be genuinely human and to live together as humans, both by demonstrating true humanity and rejecting subhumanity. What follows is an argument that J.K. Rowling's *Harry Potter* series embraces a moral imagination as defined by Burke and Kirk and rejects competing imaginations. By examining Harry's soul-purifying journey, contrasted with Voldemort's soul-destroying journey, we will see how the books encourage a rightly-ordered soul and demonstrate how that soul can encourage a rightly-ordered commonwealth.

HARRY POTTER AND MORAL IMAGINATION

J.K. Rowling quoted Plutarch at her 2008 Harvard commencement speech: "What we achieve inwardly will change outer reality." That should sound familiar, given Kirk's definition of the moral imagination: the ethical perception which aspires to the apprehending of right order in the soul and right order in the commonwealth. The Plutarch quote is simply Kirk's with a specific trajectory: "What we achieve inwardly (right order in the soul) will change outer reality (right order in the commonwealth). And what is it within us, according to Ms. Rowling, that can change the world? From the same speech:

> We do not need magic to change the world, we carry all the power we need inside ourselves already: we have the power to *imagine* better. (emphasis added)

Rowling believes that the imagination has this soul-changing and world-changing power. This should come as no surprise to us, since, more than anything else, the *Harry Potter* series is a discussion of the *soul* - a world torn apart by a dehumanized and torn-up soul (Voldemort), and that evil's defeat by a purified soul (Harry Potter).

We will take a look at the discussion of the soul in *Harry Potter* and how that leads to right order in the commonwealth, but first it would be helpful to look at two other kinds of imagination which Kirk contrasts with the moral imagination: idyllic and diabolic. Before examining in detail how it is that *Harry Potter* fits the criteria for the moral imagination, we must observe how it rejects the competing imaginations.

Rejecting the Idyllic Imagination: Harry, a True Gryffindor

Kirk defines the idyllic imagination as "the imagination which rejects old dogmas and old manners and rejoices in the notion of emancipation from duty and convention." In other words, when a culture's imagination entirely throws off the constraints of tradition, causing a historical amnesia, it moves toward this idyllic imagination. When a culture believes it finds true freedom by throwing off duty and obligation to the rest of humanity, it has embraced an idyllic imagination.

To illustrate from *Harry Potter*, consider the scene in Dumbledore's office after Harry has killed the basilisk and defeated Voldemort for a second time. Dumbledore has just told Harry to look at the name inscribed on the sword, and explained that it would take "a true Gryffindor" to pull that sword out of the Sorting Hat. Now imagine if Harry had responded by saying: "Oh, I don't care much about being a true Gryffindor. Big deal. That's so old-fashioned. I can't believe anyone expects me to care about living according to the outdated principles of some school teacher who lived over a millenium ago." *That's* an idyllic imagination.

The Wizarding World is not without its history, and its history is important. Harry's quest in *Deathly Hallows* is rooted in his own history. His return to Godric's Hollow becomes a re-enactment of his escape from death 17 years prior in that same town. This time, he consciously knows about death, and he's rattled by it. He does not derive understanding and encouragement from his visit to his parents' grave; instead he comes away wishing he himself were buried under the ground with them. Life after death is not a reality for him; it's something he cannot see, because his parents are underground, not living on.

But Harry does not move beyond old notions about death and the afterlife, as though they were outdated superstitions. Rather, he comes to terms with the tradition of belief to which he belongs: there is a "next great adventure," and dying is not to be feared. There is life after death, and there is redemption, as he learns from conversing with Dumbledore, whose repentance is evident in their final meeting. It is the tradition of courage – the willingness to sacrificially die for others – with which Harry aligns himself. He embraces his history and the power of sacrificial death while standing in Dobby's grave.

Aberforth's plea to Harry is the voice of the idyllic imagination. Harry attempts to explain his need to go on, to fight Voldemort until the end because Albus had left him that job:

"I-it's not easy, no," said Harry. "But I've got to – "

"'*Got to*'? Why '*got to*'? He's dead, isn't he?" said Aberforth. "Let it go, boy, before you follow him! Save yourself!" (*Hallows* 561, emphasis in original)

Aberforth wants Harry to run away from his duty and save himself. Harry has learned that there are things worth dying for, and that death is not the end. He has embraced not only his family history, but the courageous Gryffindor history – a "true Gryffindor," indeed. The *Harry Potter* books, then, do not embrace an idyllic imagination; Harry embraces his history and his duty, and he is willing to die for it.

Rejecting the Diabolic Imagination:
The Place of the Gothic in Harry Potter

Borrowing from T.S. Eliot's *After Strange Gods,* Kirk discusses the "diabolic imagination." Explaining that the idyllic imagination usually leads to "disillusion and boredom," he claims that a society will often turn to an imagination that not only casts away codes of ethical conduct, but "delights in the perverse and subhuman." Voldemort is the clearest example in *Harry Potter,* and "subhuman" is a fit description.

J.K. Rowling's primary motif for evil is dehumanization – a symbolic representation of evil as the rejection or distortion of what it means to be truly human.[1] The Horcrux is the starkest symbol of dehumanization in the series, and it follows a tradition of stories noted by Tolkien, who traces this motif of encapsulating one's life force in an object to preserve oneself from ancient literature like the Egyptian "The Tale of the Two Brothers" all the way through George MacDonald's, "The Giant's Heart" (Tolkien, "On Fairy-Stories"). Of course, Tolkien himself employed this device with Sauron's One Ring in *The Lord of the Rings*; and J.K. Rowling does the same with Horcruxes.

The parallel between Horcruxes and stories like "The Giant's Heart," in which a Giant hides his heart away to keep himself alive, is confirmed by the most Gothic of Rowling's *Beedle the Bard* stories – "The Warlock's Hairy Heart." A young, handsome, and well-to-do warlock sees that all his friends are foolishly falling in love and getting married, so he locks his heart away to prevent it ever happening to him. The result is that when he goes to retrieve

---

1   For a full treatment of this theme in *Harry Potter*, see Chapter Four of my book, *Harry Potter & Imagination: The Way Between Two Worlds* (Zossima Press, 2008).

his heart and returns it to his chest, the heart, and consequently he himself, are transformed into mere brute beasts, and murder ensues. Dumbledore makes the parallel clearly: "The resemblance of this action to the creation of a Horcrux has been noted by many writers" (*Beedle* 58).

If the moral imagination is about "right order in the soul," then distorted pictures of the soul are helpful in the development of great literature as mythic symbols of evil. J.K. Rowling creates grotesque and Gothic images for the purpose of portraying evil and rejecting it. Harry, in the Pensieve with Dumbledore in *Half-Blood Prince,* encounters the very Gothic Gaunts, Voldemort's Grandpa Marvolo, Uncle Morphin, and Mommy Merope. The entire scene is a picture of distorted humanity, and combines horror and the grotesque images of flowing yellow pus, spit, filth, pale faces, and dead snakes. The purpose of the encounter is to learn what *not* to be like, and to get a fuller picture of his dehumanized enemy, Voldemort. This is equally true of Harry's learning about the Horcruxes. On a very practical level, knowing about Horcruxes teaches Harry how to kill Voldemort. On a symbolic level, learning about Horcruxes prepares Harry to understand his own pure soul, and to reject the Horcrux within himself through self-sacrifice.

In short, then, it is Rowling's Gothic imagination which deals the death blow to the diabolic imagination. Furthermore, she eventually makes the perverse look not only disgusting, but utterly foolish. Voldemort, the dark, fearsome, brooding presence in the background for six books, becomes something of a cartoon villain by the end – revealed to be so foolishly prideful, that he convinced himself, standing in a room with a thousand years of hidden items from other Hogwarts students, that he was *the only person who ever found the room!* In the final Harry-Voldemort duel, Voldemort's complaints and protestations look downright silly in light of Harry's courage and his unveiling of "the flaw in the plan" to this moronic villain.

HARRY POTTER AND A CULTURE'S IMAGINATION

In 1981, Kirk assessed the literary situation thusly:

> In the franchise bookshops of the year of our Lord one thousand nine hundred eighty-one, the shelves are crowded with the prickly pears and the Dead Sea fruit of literary decadence. Yet no civilization rests forever content with literary boredom and literary violence. Once again, a conscience may speak to a conscience in the pages of books, and the parched rising generation may grope their way toward the springs of moral imagination.

Noting as a caveat that there may be some disagreement with that assessment, let me press forward by making the following proposal: *Harry Potter* is a widespread groping toward the springs of moral imagination in a time when the idyllic and diabolic imaginations are far too often to be found in and embraced by popular culture.

At the very least, the dominating motif to be found when folks choose their entertainment is the desire for a mindless escape, to "veg out" in front of a TV, or find a page-turner with exciting twists and turns, but no journey through the kinds of symbols, metaphors, and themes to be found in the best imaginative fiction. Kirk wrote,

> Comparatively few book-readers nowadays, I suspect, seek normative knowledge. They are after amusement, sometimes of a vicariously gross character, or else pursue a vague "awareness" of current affairs and intellectual currents, suitable for cocktail-party conversation.

The *Harry Potter* books are sometimes treated as just such light escapism – oh, and isn't it mildly interesting how she comments on racism through magical creatures and blood status?[2] Can I have another cocktail?

In place of this, recall Kirk's statement that "the end of great books is ethical – to teach us what it means to be genuinely human." The moral imagination of the *Harry Potter* books leads us to that end – a better picture of what it means to be human – and it uses both positive and negative examples to do so. While Harry's alchemical soul-purification gives us a positive example, Rowling's Gothic imagination gives us negative examples with stark portrayals of dehumanization.

HARRY POTTER AND MORAL IMAGINATION: IT'S ALL ABOUT SOUL

To repeat, the *Harry Potter* books are a discussion of the soul. Nevermind Rowling's statement that they are primarily "an extended argument for tolerance." On the allegorical level, they are very much that. But writers of great books craft stories at a deeper levels than the allegorical. Granger writes for *Touchstone Magazine*, reflecting on the meaning of Plato's Cave Allegory for the tradition of literature in which Rolwing writes:

---

2   This is not a rejection of the exploration of these themes, as I do that very thing in *Harry Potter & Imagination!* But the reader will notice that I start with 6 chapters on great themes of imaginative literature and 4 chapters on character development before getting to the social justice issues. In other words, the changing of "outward reality" is preceded and founded upon the "inward" change – "right order in the soul."

This story [the allegory of the cave] for shadow-landers like you and me about the nature of reality and how we know (or don't know) is pretty much the Christian consensus from Pentecost up to and into the so-called Enlightenment and Age of Empiricism we live in now. As English literature, like it or not, is a Christian show, *Beowulf* to Joyce's *Ulysses*, in which Christian writers write for a Christian audience for their greater life in Christ, novels, poems, and plays almost have to be understood in light of Plato's Cave Allegory.

Before the reader goes running from the essay because of its "Christian" content, note that Plato believed this, too. What, exactly, did he believe? Simplifying extremely, he believed that the anagogical – or spiritual – level of meaning was the foundation for all other knowledge: allegorical, moral, and literal.[3] Spiritual knowledge about reality is a more fundamental level of knowledge than what scientific facts might teach us. The current way of thinking puts the information gathered by the five physical senses – data that can be demonstrated and proven in a laboratory – as the most certain knowledge. The older way of thinking put spiritual knowledge at the most fundamental level. Or, to go back to Kirk and Burke, this level of knowing, found in the imagination, is how we understand what it is to be human – and how to be *rightly* human, to have the right ordering of the soul. Or, to put it illustratively, religious or spiritual (or, if you prefer, mythic) thinking teaches us to value life; science teaches us about the biology of life, why a life might end, and how to work to save that life. But without the mythic belief about the innate value of human life, the scientific pursuit does not happen. The two are not opposed to one another; they work together, and they both have their proper place.

The surface, moral, and allegorical meanings of the *Harry Potter* stories are there to be explored and learned from, but they are founded on the right ordering of the soul. It's the spiritual knowledge that serves as the foundation for the allegorical and moral realities that we act upon in the world.[4] How do the *Harry Potter* books promote the right ordering of the soul? Well, first we should ask at the most basic level, how does any literature do it? Recall how Clyde Kilby described the work of the imagination: a "journey toward

---

3   For in-depth treatment of these meanings, see John Granger's essay in this volume, *The Deathly Hallows Lectures* (Zossima 2008) and the forthcoming *Harry Potter's Bookshelf* (Penguin, 2009).

4   This is why, in *Harry Potter & Imagination*, I began with mythic themes from Rowling's saga, transitioned to Harry's character development in concert with Voldemort, Dumbledore, and Snape, and *then* moved on to social commentary. The ordering was not arbitrary; it was a matter of priority - the right ordering of the soul, rooted in the truth about reality, comes first.

gestures, pictures, images, rhythms, metaphor, symbol, and at the peak of all, myth." In other words – and not surprisingly – there is no scientific, formulaic answer to that question. It happens in the soul, which cannot be put under a microscope and which cannot be examined in a laboratory. Spiritual reality is perceived spiritually.

Two Themes and Two Souls: An Alchemical Journey

What, then, does the *Harry Potter* series do specifically to point readers to a rightly-ordered soul? The central themes of *Harry Potter* are self-sacrificial love and fear of death, and these two themes are fleshed out on the story line of two souls: Harry's and Voldemort's. Voldemort dehumanizes himself by caring not at all about his soul; he splits it into pieces in order to preserve his life. Harry's story is the battle between two souls, and two uses of his own body. His own soul is pure and intact, while the Voldemort piece of soul residing in his head is using his body as a Horcrux – the complete opposite of a body, as Hermione explains (*Hallows* 104).

Harry Potter goes through a transformative journey, and that journey is, as explained by John Granger, an alchemical one. The "pictures, images, rhythms, metaphors, and symbols" that Harry journeys toward are alchemical, passing through the *nigredo* (black), *albedo* (white), and *rubedo* (red) stages of alchemy, resulting in the purity of soul which allows him to overcome the evil within (Voldemort's distorted soul piece) and the evil without (Voldemort himself). In the fires of trial and difficulty, Harry is transformed and purified and made the hero who transcends his mentor, the master alchemist Albus Dumbledore, who teaches Harry that it is his ability to experience grief that proves his capacity for love and demonstrates his purity of soul.

In order to bypass the minute details of the alchemical process and get an overarching picture of Harry's soul-purifying journey, let's trace Harry's development from Sirius's death to Dobby's, and then point to his own, because much of the humanity-defining soul-discussion takes place in between Sirius's and Dobby's deaths.

The Importance of Grief

When Sirius dies, Harry is filled with rage and chases down Bellatrix Lestrange in order to exact revenge; waiting for him, however, is Voldemort. The Dark Lord, vastly more powerful than Harry, is finally forced to duel "the only one he ever feared," Dumbledore, who comes to the rescue and proves to be Voldemort's better at magic. Voldemort's only perceived way out is to possess Harry, but his stay in Harry's body does not last long; Harry's grief for Sirius and his willingness to die to be with him again demonstrates a love and a faith that terrifies Voldemort, who promptly exits Number One, Harry Drive to seek out darker quarters of residence.

Afterwards, in Dumbledore's office, the tired, old headmaster explains that Harry did not need Occlumency to defend himself against Voldemort; it was his heart – his love for Sirius – that saved him. You'll note the key element here: grief. Harry, philosopher's-stone-in-progress, is passing through the *nigredo*, or "Black," stage of alchemy. This stage is the "dark night of the soul," in which everything Harry thought defined him is torn down and taken away from him. For four books, Harry Potter was becoming a standard fairy-tale hero: orphan, who belonged to a different world and had a greater status in that world than he ever could have known, returns to that world and saves it. Harry, despite occasionally losing favor with the public (like when they thought he was Slytherin's heir, or that he cheated to get into the Triwizard Tournament) is known as "the boy who lived," and is the closest thing the Wizarding World has to an iconic hero. But all of that is ripped away from him in *Order of the Phoenix,* and he is stripped down to nothing. In a sense, just as Fawkes dies and is reborn from the ashes at book's end, so Harry must progress through the *order* of the phoenix: death, then life. He begins to learn that in this stage, but he has a ways to go, based on his anger in Dumbledore's office, and his disbelief that grief is such a great thing.

A Lesson in Love

Less than a year later, Harry engages in another argument with Dumbledore on the exact same matter – though he refrains from breaking Dumbledore's toys this time. Dumbledore explains that "the power the Dark Lord knows not" is *love*, to which Harry silently responds, "Big deal." Dumbledore's counter is that his capacity for love is "a great and remarkable thing," given all that he had been through. Not only this, but it was this ability to love which protected Harry from the lure of the Dark Arts and Voldemort's power:

> In spite of all the temptation you have endured, all the suffering, you remain pure of heart, just as pure as you were at the age of eleven, when you stared into a mirror that reflected your heart's desire, and it showed you only the way to thwart Voldemort, and not immortality or riches. (*Prince* 511)

Harry is pure of heart, but only so because of the suffering and pain through which he has gone, which has protected him from the temptation of evil because of what evil has done to him. But Harry does not leave this conversation with any particular confidence in the power of *love* or of his *pure heart*. He has learned that the choice to face Voldemort "makes all the difference in the world," but he still cannot see how purity of soul and ability to love has anything to do with it. At the end of this year, Harry will experience the loss of Dumbledore, passing through the end of the *albedo* stage (*albedo,* Albus, "white"), emerging as "Dumbledore's man, through and through." But Harry must transcend Dumbledore to be the true hero.

Fast forward, then, through many wilderness wanderings (come on – you know you wanted a fast-forward button through the wilderness the first time you read *Deathly Hallows*), to Harry's wrestling with two issues: Dumbledore's character, and the Deathly Hallows quest. He thinks he's pieced it together: Dumbledore left clues for Harry to find the three Hallows and become Master of Death – the only way he could possibly defeat Voldemort. He's clearly abandoned the lesson we just went over, if he ever believed it in the first place. Harry is not ready to believe that love is the power the Dark Lord knows not – that love can overcome death. He has pretty much come to the conclusion that the Deathly Hallows are that power, when he makes the dumb mistake of saying Voldemort's name; a few hours later, he's in the dungeon of Malfoy Manor.

Love, Defender of the Soul

Dobby to the rescue! And despite Harry's request in *Chamber of Secrets* that Dobby never try to save his life again, Dobby does just that and dies in the process. Digging Dobby's grave, without magic, Dumbledore's lesson about love collides with Harry's experience of grief, and everything comes together. Why? Because Harry has just *witnessed* the power of self-sacrificial love. Dobby saved his friends by giving up his life. In that moment, without Dobby's help, and with Voldemort speeding to Malfoy Manor, the quest to defeat Voldemort would have been over. Note the parallel, as Harry is digging Dobby's grave, to where this jet-tour through the over-arching alchemical stages started:

> His scar burned, but he was master of the pain, he felt it, yet was apart from it. He had learned control at last, learned to shut his mind to Voldemort, the very thing Dumbledore had wanted him to learn from Snape. *Just as Voldemort had not been able to possess Harry while Harry was consumed with grief for Sirius, so his thoughts could not penetrate Harry now while he mourned Dobby. Grief, it seemed, drove Voldemort out...though Dumbledore, of course, would have said that it was love.*

On Harry dug, deeper and deeper into the hard, cold earth, subsuming his grief in sweat, denying the pain in his scar. In the darkness, with nothing but the sound of his own breath and the rushing sea to keep him company, the things that had happened at the Malfoys' returned to him, the things he had heard came back to him, and *understanding blossomed in the darkness…* (*Deathly* 478-79, emphasis added)

Harry is in desperate need of *understanding*. Even after beginning to realize the power of self-sacrificial love, Harry still has this nasty problem of which he remains unaware: he's got a Voldemort soul-piece in his head. Harry's scar burning is the protestation of the evil within; his scar is where the Voldemort soul-piece is located. But Harry is now "master of the pain" and "apart from it." A distance has been created between the evil within and his own goodness, but that evil must still be revealed and killed. Harry cannot become Voldemort's vanquisher until the Voldemort within is vanquished. And that can't be done until Harry is willing to give up his own life. The transformative moment of digging Dobby's grave is key to Harry's blossoming understanding because he is finally beginning to see and to believe in love's power. In this *rubedo* or Red Stage book of the series, Harry finally dies to self, kills the Voldemort within, and is raised to life, the true Master of Death because he has embraced it in faith with open arms, trusting in the power of love to overcome it.

What did Harry learn about reality? The soul is protected by love, whether or not one dies. Only self-sacrificial love can conquer death.

Voldemort's Soul

Voldemort, on the other hand, does the exact opposite of Harry. This is a story about the way two souls approach death, and Voldemort splits his into pieces in order to run from death. Harry dies on behalf of others out of love and saves his own soul. Voldemort murders others for the preservation of his own life at the expense of his soul.

Eugene Peterson writes this about the soul:

When we say "soul" we are calling attention to the God-origins, God-intentions, God-operations that make us what we are. It is the most personal and most comprehensive term for what we are – man, woman, and child…. "Soul" is a word reverberating with relationships: God-relationships, human-relationships, earth-relationships…. "Soul" gets beneath the fragmented surface appearances and experiences and affirms an at-homeness, an affinity with whoever and whatever is at hand. (37)

Voldemort does not care about relationships, so he does not care about his soul. Dumbledore is adamant that Harry must trust his friends, Ron and Hermione especially. He is also adamant that the pain he feels after Sirius's death is a *good* thing; and Harry remembers this while considering the grief he feels at Dobby's death. "Dumbledore would have called it love." In place of Harry's ability to love and grieve – the true characteristics of the soul – Voldemort isolates himself, refuses friendship, and does not risk any relationship. He could not even experience Harry's grief and love for Sirius while possessing him. To be human is to be in relationship, in community – hence the moral imagination being about right order in both the soul and the commonwealth. Voldemort has destroyed his own humanity.

We've already discussed above the Gothic representation of distorted humanity found in the Horcruxes. We find the same in Rowling's other uses of supernatural horror and Gothic themes. Consider one example: the cursed necklace touched by Katie Bell in *Half-Blood Prince.*

> Then, six feet above the ground, Katie let out a terrible scream (*Prince* 249).

"Six feet above the ground." The necklace was cursed and meant to kill; but everything about the Dark Arts is a distortion of death, and the curse on the opal necklace causes its victim to die (Katie Bell avoided death by barely touching it) by first levitating "six feet above ground" and screaming. It's a symbol of peaceless, restless death – the body is not silently six feet below ground, but screaming six feet above ground. Consider also that this scene serves as a foreshadowing of the pursuit of the locket Horcrux – another deadly necklace – later in the same book. Dumbledore has a reaction to the green potion – the "curse" meant to protect the locket – similar to Katie Bell's. Like with Katie, Harry couldn't tell what Dumbledore was seeing or feeling; like Katie, Dumbledore screamed. The only remedy for the potion is the water in the lake, the disturbance of which calls forth the Inferi, reanimated corpses who represent Voldemort's mockery of death. He controls the dead, because he believes himself greater than death.

One could argue that Voldemort is on his own journey through symbols, gestures, metpahors, etc.; but all the symbols associated with Voldemort are about a distortion of death. Horcruxes, death curses, and Inferi are all pictures of humanity distorted in death. Voldemort's big mistake was trying to conquer death apart from love, friendship, and sacrifice. Harry learned through suffering that love, which will always cause grief, is the only thing more powerful than death. Voldemort, from age 11, had concluded that a wizard's magic could overcome death, and he gave up the essence of his humanity – his soul – in the pursuit of deathlessness.

One of those split soul-pieces ends up in Harry's head, which shows that our hero, despite his own purity of soul, does not remain untouched by distorted humanity. In fact, Rowling deliberately places Harry's journey in the midst of Gothic imagery, and even puts him in the role of the Gothic *heroine*.

HARRY AS GOTHIC HERIONE

As of my writing of this essay, the only in-depth work published on the Gothic in *Harry Potter* is June Cummins's essay, "Hermione in the Bathroom: The Gothic, Menarche, and Female Development in the Harry Potter Series," in *The Gothic in Children's Literature*.[5] Cummins explores the way the combination of the Gothic and the grotesque work together to represent female sexual development in Gothic stories, with focus on Hermione and Moaning Myrtle in *Harry Potter*. It's an interesting article which deserves careful attention and sparks good discussion, but it would be helpful to take a step back and take a broader view of the Gothic in *Harry Potter*, which we've already begun to do over the last few pages. The Gothic imagery in Rowling's books is about more than what society thinks of female sexual development. It's about death and depravity.

But strangely, the story's hero fits into both issues in a way. Consider for a moment how you'd respond if I told you a story about a hero who has an enemy, and has been attacked by this enemy. Not only attacked, but the hero was forced into a ritual of blood which gave the enemy power. There is a mind-link between the hero and the enemy, which either can shut off if they choose. There is a scar on the forehead of the hero, symbolizing the hero's having been touched by evil. In the end, guided by a wise old man who knows more about this enemy than anyone else, information gained by the hero's mind link with the enemy helps bring about his downfall.

On first glance, you'd say I was talking about *Harry Potter*, that the enemy was Voldemort, and that the wise old man was Dumbledore. But change "hero" to "herione," and I'm talking about Mina Harker in *Dracula*, with Count Dracula as the enemy, and Van Helsing as the wise old man. Oh, there are plenty of differences, and I'm not attempting to argue that Rowling simply stole Stoker's story and moved around some names and places. But

---

5   I address Rowling's use of fear and supernatural horror in Chapter 3 of *Harry Potter & Imagination*. Forthcoming treatments of the Gothic in *Harry Potter* can be found in John Granger's *Harry Potter's Bookshelf* (Penguin, 2009) and Amy H. Sturgis's *The Gothic Imagination* (Zossima Press, 2010).

thematically, similar Gothic symbolism is there and communicates much the same thing. The scar on Mina Harker's head is referred to as the "evil eye." What an apt name for Harry's scar as well, for through it Voldemort can see into his mind, and he into Voldemort's. Furthermore, when Harry willingly sacrifices himself, in the period of time with Dumbledore at "King's Cross," the scar is gone and Harry no longer needs glasses. His "evil eye" has become good, and he has the understanding he needed. So, in many ways, Harry Potter is Mina Harker, Gothic heroine.

Cummins quotes Donna Heiland, who writes in *Gothic and Gender: An Introduction* that "the typical gothic heroine" is "fairly passive, finding her way out of one disastrous situation after another only because someone comes along to rescue her" (179). Harry admits this much about himself when Hermione is trying to organize the D.A. We can see it clearly enough. While he makes a lot of courageous choices, he's also relatively clueless, and a lot of stuff just happens to him out of which he needs to be rescued. Dumbledore rescues him in the fight against Quirrell; Fawkes in the battle against the basilisk; a spell he didn't know existed from a wand phenomenon he also didn't know existed rescued him from Voldemort in the graveyard; Dumbledore to the rescue again when Harry fell for Voldemort's implanted vision to lure him to the Ministry. Until the very last book, Harry is rescued time and time again.

Another compelling tie between Harry and the Gothic heroine is Claire Kahane's explanation of the symbolism of the Gothic heroine's journey:

> Following clues that pull her onward and inward - bloodstains, mysterious sounds - she penetrates the obscure recesses of a vast labyrinthean [sic] space and discovers a secret room sealed off by its association with death. In this dark, secret center of the Gothic structure, the boundaries of life and death themselves seem confused. Who died? Has there been a murder? Or merely a disappearance? (in Cummins 179)

Can you think of a more accurate description of the plot of *Chamber of Secrets*? Harry follows the mysterious clues: bloodstains (Ginny's messages on the wall written in blood) and mysterious sounds (the basilisk's speech as it moves through the pipes, that only Harry can hear). He finds the secret room (Chamber of Secrets) that has been "sealed off by its association with death" (young Riddle closed it 50 years prior after Moaning Myrtle was killed). In that Gothic structure (the Chamber), "the boundaries of life and death themselves seem confused" (Ginny is dying, while a soul-fragment of

Voldemort is coming back to life; Harry almost dies, and is saved by Fawkes). And of course, the question, as Harry found his way into the Chamber, is whether Ginny has been murdered, or whether it's just a "disappearance" at this point.

Harry makes his way through Gothic structures throughout the story, structures which are often interpreted as "feminine," such as caves. Consider Harry's development through *Half-Blood Prince*. Harry's first lesson with Dumbledore is a trip into the Pensieve which results in observing the distorted humanity of the Gaunts, and the stunted development of their daughter, Merope, whose sexuality is mocked, because it is directed at a Muggle. The scene, as we noted already, is filled with Cummins's combination of the Gothic and the grotesque: "large amounts of … yellow pus," which "flowed" from Bob Ogden's nose, blood, filth, pale faces, dead snakes, "muck," Merope's "flushing blotchily scarlet," spit, and other pointers to gross distortions of humanity; much of the scene takes place inside the filthy Gaunt house. Where does Harry end his journey of book 6? With a trip into a cave filled with Gothic imagery (Inferi!), in which Harry finally begins to emerge as Dumbledore's successor. Harry's development into a hero under Dumbledore is framed in Gothic feminine imagery.

REJECTING THE DISTORTED, FALLEN WORLD

What is the purpose of observing all of this? Well, whether you agree with Cummins' interpretation of female sexual imagery or not, the Gothic is about depraved and distorted humanity, which Harry must reject in order to embrace what is good and pure. Dr. Ann Blaisdell Tracy's work, *Patterns of Fear in the Gothic Novel*, argues that "the Gothic world is above all the Fallen world, the projection of a post-lapsarian nightmare of fear and alienation" (313); she wrote,

> …novels with Gothic overtones might best be identified not as those which contain some superficial trapping like a ruined monastery or the rumor of a ghost,… but as those … which contain imagery or action pertinent to the Gothic/Fallen world., i.e., wandering, delusions, temptation. (327)

Rowling has both the standard "superficial trappings" of the Gothic, as well as the deeper-level, Fallen-world characteristics of wanderings (all that wandering in tents in *Deathly Hallows* had a purpose after all), delusions (Harry's dream planted by Voldemort in *Order of the Phoenix*, for example), and temptation (the Deathly Hallows). It all works together to form Harry's journey not just toward the purity of soul, but against a fallen, distorted one.

Likewise, Rowling's use of the darker elements of Gothic literature do not detract from the moral imagination, but contribute to it significantly; for in rejecting Fallen humanity and allowing the purification of his soul, Harry embraces all that is good.

RIGHT ORDER IN THE COMMONWEALTH

But the right ordering of the soul is not about private devotion or personal satisfaction. The natural corollary is that rightly-ordered souls will dwell together in a rightly-ordered commonwealth. Rowling's books contain social commentary and criticism right alongside and intertwined with Harry's transformational journey. From a year old, Harry was a figure of social justice. Dobby laments to Harry in *Chamber of Secrets:*

> "Ah, if Harry Potter only knew!" Dobby groaned, more tears dripping onto his ragged pillowcase. "If he knew what he means to us, to the lowly, the enslaved, we dregs of the magical world! Dobby remembers how it was when He-Who-Must-Not-Be-Named was at the height of his powers, sir! ... life has improved for my kind since you triumphed over He-Who-Must-Not-Be-Named. Harry Potter survived, and the Dark Lord's power was broken, and it was a new dawn, sir, and Harry Potter shone like a beacon of hope for those of us who thought the Dark days would never end..." (176-77)

Issues of power abuse (the Ministry's actions during the war against Voldemort) and racism (pure-bloods toward half-bloods and muggleborns; wizards toward muggles; Muggles toward wizards; wizards toward house-elves, centaurs, goblins, and giants), pervade this series of books, and Harry finds himself right in the midst of them. He is one of the few people able to transcend the power structures of the Wizarding World, and to reject their injustices.

Rowling does not wrap up and solve any of the major social issues by series' end. House-elves are still enslaved. Gryffindor vs. Slytherin prejudices still remain, even "nineteen years later." But this is because Rowling is a fantastic realist – she uses fantasy to portray reality. And the reality is an issue as complex and deep-rooted as slavery does not simply get fixed with one heroic defeat of a Dark Lord. To have freed all the house-elves by the end of seven books would have been an insult to the problem of slavery. It was wise on Rowling's part not to have the social issues solved. But this does not mean they're not present, or that she's failed to point us in a direction toward social change.

In fact, there is a clue hidden in Harry's key transformative moment which we discussed earlier which brings us full circle back to the importance of a moral imagination: his digging of Dobby's grave. He deliberately dug that grave *without magic*. Recall Rowling's statement from the Harvard speech:

> We do not need magic to change the world, we carry all the power we need inside ourselves already: we have the power to imagine better.

Imagination is a key element in ethics. David Baggett argues in defense of *Harry Potter* that works of imaginative literature "teach us to empathize with the sufferings of others, enhancing our capacity for seeing the world through another's eyes" (169). Rowling does this with brilliance – sometimes quite subtle brilliance – in her stories. Consider the world into which we are placed. The Wizarding World is magical and powerful in its own way, and we're put in a position where we're inclined to think ill of witches and wizards who would use their magical powers to oppress Muggles. It's an interesting position for the reader to be placed in, because before there is a question of what wizards can and can't do to Muggles, there was the simple fact that the entire Wizarding World is in hiding because Muggles oppressed, persecuted, and tried to kill them!

In other words, Rowling has put us in the place of identification with an oppressed group. This is an invaluable imaginative exercise for Muggles like me who belong to the "majority" (in my case, middle-class white males in the United States). The person like me, who belongs to the powerful majority, suddenly finds himself emotionally identifying with the oppressed, and wrestling with their dilemmas. This is why it was so important for Harry not to become a standard fairy-tale hero. The wealthy, white, Quidditch-superstar "chosen one" had to be torn down and made to identify with the oppressed and the poor in order to truly belong to them and fight on their behalf.

The story is, for the powerless minority, a tale of immediate identification with the oppressed. How many kids know what it's like to be Harry Potter in real life? How many teens and adults know what it's like to be Severus Snape – having done so many bad things, they wonder if redemption is even possible? How many people know what it's like to be Dobby, desperate just to be free? How many people know what it's like to be the centaurs and goblins, relegated to the fringes of society or to specific functions within society, allotted land where they once lived freely, and denied the most powerful weapons available, so that they're always in a state of being potentially under threat from a greater power that thinks they're dangerous?

The *Harry Potter* stories, then, open up the possibility of the emotional engagement of social issues through close identification with magical characters. Just as we travel with Harry through his soul purification, so we wrestle with Harry as he tries to decide what to do with the unjust social structure to which he belongs.

The conversation the trio has with Griphook is a perfect illustration of the imaginative identification with another person's experience. Griphook recognized from the beginning that there was something different about Harry – "You buried the elf ... You dug the grave ... You also rescued a goblin ... You are a very odd wizard" (*Deathly* 486). Harry is odd, because he is not bound by the prejudices of the rest of the Wizarding World. And yet, Harry doesn't understand the power of the social dynamics involved in the long, oppressive and conflicted history of wizards versus goblins. An argument breaks out between Ron and Griphook about the right to carry wands, which has been denied goblins. Harry attempts to intervene with race-transcending (color blind?) language:

> "It doesn't matter," said Harry, noting Griphook's rising color. "This isn't about wizards versus goblins or any other sort of magical creature –"
>
> Griphook gave a nasty laugh.
>
> "But it is, it is precisely that! As the Dark Lord becomes ever more powerful, your race is set still more firmly above mine! Gringotts falls under Wizarding rule, house-elves are slaughtered, and who amongst the wand-carriers protests?"
>
> "We do!" said Hermione. She had sat up straight, her eyes bright. "We protest! And I'm hunted quite as much as any goblin or elf, Griphook! I'm a Mudblood!"
>
> "Don't call yourself –" Ron muttered.
>
> "Why shouldn't I?" said Hermione. "Mudblood, and proud of it! I've got no higher position under this new order than you have, Griphook! It was me they chose to torture, back at the Malfoys!" (488-89)

Harry does not hold the prejudices most of the Wizarding World holds, but he has yet to emotionally identify with, in this instance, the plight of the goblins. Hermione, who has been mistreated for years because of her blood status, is much more emotionally prepared to put herself in Griphook's place.

Once again, Rowling's Harvard commencement speech is enlightening and informative, and brings us back to Russell Kirk:

> Unlike any other creature on this planet, humans can learn and understand, without having experienced. They can think themselves into other people's places.
>
> Of course, this is a power, like my brand of fictional magic, that is morally neutral. One might use such an ability to manipulate, or control, just as much as to understand or sympathise.
>
> And many prefer not to exercise their imaginations at all. They choose to remain comfortably within the bounds of their own experience, never troubling to wonder how it would feel to have been born other than they are. They can refuse to hear screams or to peer inside cages; they can close their minds and hearts to any suffering that does not touch them personally; they can refuse to know.

The imagination can be exercised toward right ordering of the soul and commonwealth (moral imagination), or it can be exercised toward freedom from restraint and duty (idyllic imagination), or even the celebration of evil (diabolic imagination). J.K. Rowling knows that great imaginative literature can and does shape readers and give them the opportunity to imaginatively "think themselves into other people's places." Her *Harry Potter* series does just that.

Concluding Thoughts

That Rowling's series is going to have an effect on society seems incontestable. Many *Harry Potter* fans have already begun serious and widespread endeavors to transform society based on what they've learned from the tales of the boy wizard. The Harry Potter Alliance has rallied *Potter* fans to join in a variety of causes, such as stopping the genocide in Darfur and donating to the fight against AIDS; but it does not do this apart from focusing on personal moral transformation, sponsoring re-reads of the *Harry Potter* series with a view toward personal reflection, and exercises for "breaking out of the Muggle mindset." Their "No New Stuff" campaign challenged people to think about spending and economic wisdom in troubled financial times. Emerson Spartz of Mugglenet fame has created a website called GivesMeHope.com, which is geared toward changing lives through short, inspirational stories; he has decided to give all the money from Mugglenet's most recent book, *Harry Potter Should Have Died*, to this cause (http://www.mugglenet.com/app/news/full_story/2434).

Not all readers will agree with the politics or efforts of these groups. Undoubtedly, Russell Kirk himself would not have approved of many of their political goals. But it can hardly be said that *Harry Potter* is "just a kids' tale," a successful marketing scheme that will fade quickly. It's already inspiring attempts to change the world, attempts which spring from the moral imagination of Rowling's novels.

Readers are bound to disagree about moral issues for many reasons, and therefore it's likely we'll continue to see disagreements about what Rowling meant or how her books are relevant to society. If Kirk's assessment of the general depravity of literature at the current time is even close to accurate, then there's a lot of confusion to deal with; such is the condition of a fallen humanity. But I maintain that the *Harry Potter* series represents a widespread move "toward the springs of moral imagination." Samuel Taylor Coleridge wrote as his first introductory aphorism in *Aids to Reflection:*

> In Philosophy equally as in Poetry, it is the highest and most useful prerogative of genius to produce the strongest impressions of novelty, while it rescues admitted truths from the neglect caused by the very circumstance of their universal admission. Extremes meet. Truths, of all others the most awful and interesting, are too often considered as so true, that they lose all power of truth, and lie bed-ridden in the dormitory of the soul, side by side with the most despised and exploded errors.

Rowling has achieved just such a novelty – one that awakens old truth with a new story which brings about, as Tolkien would say, "the imaginative satisfaction of ancient desires" ("On Fairy-Stories").

BIBLIOGRAPHY

Baggett, David. "Magic, Muggles, and Moral Imagination" in *Harry Potter and Philosophy: If Aristotle Ran Hogwarts*. Ed. by Baggett and Shawn E. Klein. Chicago: Carus Publishing Company, 2004.

Cummins, June. "Hermione in the Bathroom" in *The Gothic in Children's Literature: Haunting the Borders*. Ed. by Anna Jackson, Karen Coates, and Roderick McGillis. New York: Taylor and Francis Group, 2008.

Granger, John. "Book Binders" in *Touchstone Magazine*. December, 2008. http://www.touchstonemag.com/archives/article.php?id=21-10-028-f.

Kilby, Clyde, "What is Myth?" in Rolland Hein, *Christian Mythmakers*. Chicago: Cornerstone Press Chicago, 1998. p. ix-xv.

Kirk, Russell. "The Moral Imagination." *Literature and Belief Vol. 1* (1981), 37–49. Also published in Reclaiming a Patrimony (Washington, DC: The Heritage Foundation, 1982), 45–58. Reproduced at *The Russell Kirk Center for Cultural Renewal.* http://www.kirkcenter.org/index.php/detail/the-moral-imagination/

Peterson, Eugene. *Christ Plays in Ten Thousand Places*. Wm. B. Eerdmans Publishing Co., 2008.

Rowling, J. K. *Harry Potter and the Chamber of Secrets*. New York: Scholastic, 1999.

___. *Harry Potter and the Deathly Hallows*. New York: Scholastic, 2007.

___. *Harry Potter and the Deathly Hallows*. New York: Scholastic, 2007.

___. *Harry Potter and the Goblet of Fire*. New York: Scholastic, 2000.

___. *Harry Potter and the Half-Blood Prince*. New York: Scholastic, 2005.

___. *Harry Potter and the Order of the Phoenix*. New York: Scholastic, 2003.

___. *Harry Potter and the Sorcerer's Stone*. New York: Scholastic, 1997.

___. "The Fringe Benefits of Failure, and the Importance of Imagination." *Harvard University Gazette Online.* http://www.news.harvard.edu/gazette/2008/06.05/99-rowlingspeech.html.

Tolkien, J.R.R. "On Fairy-Stories" in *Tales from the Perilous Realm*. Boston: Houghton Mifflin Harcourt, 2008.

Tracy, Ann Blaisdell. *Patterns of Fear in the Gothic Novel, 1790-1830*. Ayer Publishing, 1980.

Part IV

Conversations on
Literary Criticism

Chapter Seven

Tom Riddle's Diary
How We Read Books

Ryan Kerr

The most infamous humans in history are often also attributed with benign interests. The Roman emperor Nero is noted for his music, and Adolf Hitler was a failed painter in his adolescence. In fiction, too, evil characters can be found to engage in seemingly harmless pastimes. We discover in *Harry Potter and the Chamber of Secrets* that Tom Riddle, better known as the youthful Lord Voldemort, began his career as a diarist. But, it becomes abundantly clear that Tom was not the Samuel Pepys of Hogwarts. Riddle's writing was not a positive creative outlet; on the contrary, Rowling's second entry in her seven-part school story reveals the duplicitous nature of Tom Riddle's diary. Harry initially sees it as an ex-student's observations, merely a young author's start at writing: he eventually experiences the diary as no less than Voldemort's own *Mein Kampf.*

Tom Riddle's diary serves an important role in both developing the plot of *Chamber of Secrets* and in furthering the series' grand mythology. In *Harry Potter and the Sorcerer's Stone* (or *Philosopher's Stone*, if you're so inclined), we are given the basic story of how the Dark Lord attempted to kill our protagonist only to fail miserably, driving himself into a semi-bodiless exile in the bargain. But even though we get Harry and Voldemort's history in short, we as readers are not entitled to any intimate knowledge of that evil wizard you love to hate.

Finally, at the end of book two, we are shown the tragic path that Tom Riddle followed in his life to become the ultimate evil. Being born of a witch mother who died when he was born, and a human father who didn't want him yet provided his namesake, Tom Marvolo Riddle rearranged (or re-authored) the letters of his name to come up with a self-fashioned title: Lord Voldemort. We are given bits and pieces of his story throughout the next few books, with book six providing the most thorough tableau. However, book two is still where we first enter into a discussion about and exploration of evil in its purest form.

Tom Riddle's diary serves another purpose beyond simply providing a back story for the villain. The way in which Voldemort's teenage self is able to control Ginny Weasley and commit heinous acts fifty years later is of utmost importance for an understanding of how texts in general operate. There are many authors throughout the *Harry Potter* series: from textbook authors such as Newt Scamander and Miranda Goshawk, to phony autobiographers such as Gilderoy Lockhart and malicious muckrakers like Rita Skeeter. However, just as Tom Riddle was the best student in his years at Hogwarts, and Voldemort was the most powerful dark wizard in living memory, the author Tom Riddle demonstrates more than any other the power that accompanies the written word. And just as importantly from a critical perspective, Voldemort shows how a single text can exemplify aspects of several paradigms at the same time. It is not surprising that the multivalent Voldemort, who has myriad identities throughout the wizarding world (Tom, Voldemort, Dark Lord, He-Who-Must-Not-Be-Named, etc.), would be able to create a text that so deftly challenges the mutually exclusive ethos often attributed to literary criticism. His text further shows the necessity of approaching powerful texts from many perspectives if the control those texts exert is to be understood and dealt with.

Not So Dear Diary

One day during his second year of school at Hogwarts, Harry Potter comes across a fifty-year-old diary with the name of "T.M. Riddle" on the first page. After finding it ejected from the toilet, Harry is perplexed to find that, as far as he could tell, nobody ever wrote a word in the diary. But as we later find out, the diary acts as a sort of "interactive" journal. As soon as Harry writes in the blank journal, his own ink is rearranged to new words in order for the author (Tom Riddle) to communicate with him. The diary, acting on behalf of the author, then shows Harry exactly what happened fifty years prior.

We find out at the end of the book that Tom Riddle (now revealed as the early Voldemort) had preserved a part of himself in his diary so as to ensnare some future pupil and continue his mission to eradicate so-called Mudbloods. "I decided to leave behind a diary, preserving my sixteen-year-old self in its pages, so that one day, with luck, I would be able to lead another in my footsteps, and finish Salazar Slytherin's noble work" (312). However, at a crucial moment, Harry plunges a basilisk tooth through the diary, thus killing Tom Riddle's memory.

AUTHOR-A KEDAVRA

There are many ways to look at the significance that exists for Tom Riddle as an author, each centering on what it means to have a fifty-year-old diary able to nearly commit murder. In many early understandings of literary criticism, textual interpretation was a matter of figuring out what the author intended or determining how the author's life influenced the text. This would include biographical readings of *Peter Pan* that see Peter, the never-aging child, as a symbol of J. M. Barrie's dead brother. This type of textual analysis works on a certain level for Tom Riddle's diary. As quoted above, Tom "preserved" his sixteen-year-old self in the pages of the diary. One could say Daniel Defoe preserved his own self in the text of *Robinson Crusoe* as the authorial voice, and that we continually come back to his self when reading; in Tom Riddle's case, this is even more literal than that. When you read Tom Riddle, Tom Riddle is there in no metaphorical way: "Tom Riddle had been at Hogwarts fifty years ago, yet here he stood, a weird, misty light shining about him, not a day older than sixteen" (307). When asked if he is a ghost, Tom merely replies that he is a memory preserved for fifty years (308).

Thus, in this critical paradigm, Tom Riddle simply recorded his thoughts and values (his self) into the diary to live on as his legacy. Understanding the diary helps one understand the young Voldemort. Approaching Riddle's diary in this way is not without value: understanding Voldemort's past is such an important enterprise that it consumes Dumbledore throughout Harry's sixth year of school. But is Tom Riddle's authorship really this simple? Because Rowling has given us such a fantastical metaphor for authorship, the ability to see beyond this simplistic explanation becomes easier. Roland Barthes, famed structuralist[1] critic, also dealt with the question of an author's role in the creation of a text. For Barthes, in "The Death of the Author," this old conception of the Author must be done away with. He writes,

> The Author, when believed in, is always conceived of as the past of his own book: book and author stand automatically on a single line divided into a *before* and an *after*...[the Author] is in the same relation of antecedence to his work as a father to his child (876).

---

1 Structuralism is a term that denotes various literary theories that are most concerned with the structures of language, stories, etc. Structuralist critics often look for recurring models and themes throughout many related narratives. A story is not so much important as a single artistic expression: instead, the story is important in how it fits into the storytelling tradition. Because the tradition and structure of the story are most important, structuralists like Barthes argued that the author is irrelevant and the concept of an author is "dead."

Barthes attributes this way of thinking to the classical critics. His own structuralist idea of the creator of a text is as follows:

> [T]he modern scriptor is born simultaneously with the text, is in no way equipped with a being preceding or exceeding the writing, is not the subject with the books as predicate; there is no other time than that of the enunciation and every text is eternally written *here* and *now* (876).

This structuralist break from tradition is clearly important to a deeper understanding of the diary Harry discovers in the bathroom. On one hand, the diary could be conceived in classical terms. Adolescent Tom Riddle wrote the diary and then passed it on as his legacy. But in Rowling's fantastic universe, Tom Riddle's authorship illustrates Barthes's structuralism as well. Tom Riddle, as a person, matured from the age of sixteen and followed the fifty year projection of his future. When it comes to writing the diary, though, Tom Riddle as author was in fact born simultaneously with the text: the part of Voldemort's soul that would remain with the diary was severed entirely from Voldemort on the enunciation (or creation) of the diary/Horcrux. The part of his soul that is in the diary was created as a scriptor (with no past or future) when the text was created. Thus, every time somebody reads the text, the diary and diarist are eternally written here and now: that 16-year-old memory is the same as when the diary was first enunciated, but fundamentally different than the actual sixteen-year-old wizard who eventually becomes Lord Voldemort. Their connection ceased upon enunciation (just as the Horcrux ceased connection to Voldemort's soul).

Barthes also argues that when "the Author is removed, the claim to decipher a text becomes quite futile. To give a text an Author is to impose a limit on that text, to furnish it with a final signified, to close the writing" (877). It could still be argued that since Tom Riddle is revived with the reading of the diary, the meaning is fixed: it is fixed as what Tom Riddle wanted the meaning to be when he first wrote it. But this ignores the context of reading. It is entirely possible that Riddle might have possessed another reader in much the same way as Ginny, but it is also crucial to understand that another reader would have brought a different personality and personal history to the diary. Thus, the way Tom Riddle possesses Ginny through the diary is very specific.

THE BOY WHO READ

The role of the reader of Riddle's diary is rendered quite literally through the use of ink. When Harry first finds the diary of Tom Riddle, he accidentally spills ink all over his books. But, Harry discovers, Tom Riddle's book is the only one of the bunch that is not tarnished with the ink: it is impervious to this type of damage (239). So, initially, we could say that Tom Riddle's diary is set in its meaning and cannot be changed in the modern day: this onslaught of ink (representing rewriting of the text, perhaps) is futile in the face of Tom Riddle's ultimate, and original, authorial power. The author, sixteen-year-old Tom Riddle, remains as he was when he wrote the journal and thus the meaning of his menacing memories remains constant.

However, even though the spilt ink was unable to damage the journal, other ink is needed to read Tom Riddle's diary. At first, there are ostensibly no words written in Tom Riddle's diary beyond the title page. But, resourceful as ever, Harry writes down his own name in the diary first. Then the very ink that Harry wrote with repositions itself into a message from the author. So, presumably, if Harry (or Ginny, or any other reader) never enters into dialogue with the diary, the diary will never speak.

Just as *Harry Potter and the Chamber of Secrets* demonstrates Barthes's brand of structuralism, it also is an exemplar of another related criticism: reader-response theory. As Terry Eagleton summarizes the theory, which in England is called reception theory, "Literary texts do not exist on bookshelves: they are processes of signification materialized only in the practice of reading. For literature to happen, the reader is quite as vital as the author" (64-65). Without anyone to read Tom Riddle's writing, the book literally waits in abeyance for fifty years: the literary soul of Tom Riddle the author is kept dormant because it does not live during that time. Given that the Tom Riddle of the diary knew nothing of the adult Voldemort before possessing Ginny, we can assume that Lucius Malfoy had never interacted with the book prior to Harry's second year at Hogwarts, though the journal was entrusted to Lucius (who can represent the book fetishist, collecting, but never reading, priceless collectibles). Since Tom Riddle never ages past sixteen, we can deduce that without a reader, his writing (and thus his authorial self) is never fully alive and eternally in hibernation. But once a reader comes onto the scene, the text comes alive through reception.

Tom Riddle's diary can be further understood by applying reader-response theory. It is not that Tom Riddle's text is inherently meaningful. Rather, depending on the reader, the text takes a different manifestation. When Ginny is the reader, and entering into a *literal* dialogue with the text, Tom is a caring (if underhanded) listener. Riddle tells Harry that Ginny had spent her time confiding in the diary, and Tom used that to his advantage: "'It's very *boring*, having to listen to the silly little troubles of an eleven-year-old girl…. But I was patient. I wrote back. I was sympathetic, I was kind. Ginny simply *loved* me'" (309, emphasis in original). Thus, Riddle becomes what he needs to be for Ginny as a reader. When Harry enters into a dialogue with the same book, the author eventually becomes Harry's once and future attempted-murderer, literally sending a basilisk after Harry. The various ways that readers interact with the same book supports an interpretation of Tom Riddle's diary as a reader-response theory text.

Working in the paradigm of reader-response theory, Stanley Fish demonstrates how much literary meaning resides with the recipient of a text. In "How to Recognize a Poem When You See One," Fish shares an amusing anecdote about how his students interpreted an arbitrary list of names as a religious poem, largely because Fish had framed the list as such. Because the class had had so much practice interpreting poetry, they brought those skills to bear on the list of names. The significance of this for Fish is that a poem is not some ideal entity that is necessarily conceived of as a poem by an author. Rather, a poem (and any other type of writing) is made by the reader: "The conclusion, therefore, is that all objects are made and not found, and that they are made by the interpretive strategies we set in motion" (1027). Fish is clear to differentiate this from utter subjectivity and relativism, where one can interpret anything in any way. Rather, the means by which we interpret are "social and conventional" (1027).

The place and time of the reading of Tom's diary dictates meaning, because different discourse communities make sense out of the diary in different ways. This is true even though, as one might assume, the memory of Tom Riddle is constant, and thus the text itself is unchanging. Had the diary been found at Hogwarts before Voldemort's adult reign of terror, for instance, by a student only a few years younger than Riddle, the unwitting student who found it would have been no more than a tool in reopening the Chamber of Secrets. This unlucky student would know nothing of Lord Voldemort and his future terrors, so the student would not be able to alter Tom Riddle's goal of merely opening the Chamber. But since the discourse community of Harry's second year already knew about the adult Voldemort, the reading of the text takes on a whole new meaning. The original authorial act called for Tom Riddle's memory to reopen the Chamber and continue the work of Salazar Slytherin, nothing more. The memory (quickly becoming real towards the end of the novel) betrays its change in conversation with Harry: "'Haven't I already told you,' said Riddle quietly, 'that killing Mudbloods doesn't matter to me anymore? For many months now, my new target has been – *you*'" (Rowling 312, emphasis in original). At sixteen, Voldemort could not have known about Harry: this was decades before Harry was born, and even decades before the prophecy foretelling Voldemort's vulnerability. For the text, this matters not. The interpretive community Harry belongs to knows about young Voldemort's future, and this has an influence on the fifty-year-old text. Therefore, Harry "reads" Voldemort's outdated text as a continuation of something that had not even started chronologically when the text was written: the murder of Harry Potter.

This type of anachronistic interpretation exists outside of Hogwarts. For instance, Shakespeare's *The Tempest* is considered a cornerstone text for post-colonial criticism, even though the play was written long before such a criticism existed. Readers thus imbue current meanings into older texts; so too does the community of post-Voldemort Hogwarts read Tom Riddle's text as influenced by his later self.

This is also why Barthes's idea of a scriptor, instead of the traditional Author, is important. The meaning of the diary is not set: it changes based on the reader. Therefore, the death of the Author in Riddle's case is the notion that Voldemort's original intentions do not entirely dictate the meaning of the text. Riddle-as-author changes his motives from killing "Mudbloods" to killing Harry Potter. This change is not predicated at all on the original authorial act: Voldemort, at sixteen, knew nothing of his future nemesis. But Riddle's text, which is in the here and now, can adapt to meet different reading situations; the meaning, thus, is not tied to the authorial act. The death of this author, then, is two-fold: though Tom Riddle as an author suffered his own death at the point of a basilisk tooth, his structuralist death occurred at sixteen. His death as an Author, fittingly for Barthes, was also tied to the birth of the Reader (or at least, Harry's assertion as the Reader).

IDEOLOGICAL-AR SLYTHERIN

Tom Riddle's experiment to both elongate his own life and take the lives of others also illustrates a potentially volatile aspect of written texts. This aspect can be especially pernicious precisely because of its ability to go unnoticed. When the Chamber of Secrets has been reopened, virtually everyone in the school wonders who is behind the attacks on cats, students, and ghosts. One person, as would be expected, knows precisely who has reopened the Chamber, because he knows who opened it initially. When McGonagall asks headmaster Dumbledore who could have opened the chamber, he responds mysteriously with, "The question is not *who*…The question is, *how*…" (181, emphasis in original). Later, after Harry has informed everyone about the escapades down in the Chamber (carefully omitting the details about Ginny's possession by Tom Riddle's diary), Dumbledore good-naturedly adds, "'What interests *me* most…is how Lord Voldemort managed to enchant Ginny, when my sources tell me he is currently in hiding in the forests of Albania'" (328, emphasis in original). Dumbledore knew that only Voldemort would have been able to open the Chamber of Secrets; his gap in knowledge was how the currently disembodied wizard could accomplish such a task. It turns out that texts can live on in power, even past the author's life.

What Rowling demonstrates with Voldemort's semi-posthumous influence is nothing less than the overwhelming influence ideology can have on a reader, illustrating yet another critical lens that Riddle's text exemplifies. Peter Hollindale, in "Ideology and the Children's Book," discusses how ideology is no less at play in children's texts as it is in every other. Specifically, he divides the types of ideology present in texts into three levels: "The first and most tractable [way ideology is presented] is made up of the explicit social, political or moral beliefs of the individual writer, and his wish to recommend them to children through the story" (10). The second level is more subtle, and often more powerful than surface ideology, because it is composed of the author's unquestioned assumptions. For Riddle, though, his wickedest ideologies are quite conscious, and he recommends them to his young readers by disguising his ideology of genocide in order to garner the trust of his reader (Ginny and then Harry). After he has been entrusted by Ginny, his true ideology begins to control her because he insinuated his mind into hers subtly. No writing is devoid of ideology: any author has certain ideologies that come through both explicitly and implicitly in the text. As such, the reader is often influenced by the text without even knowing it.

This is exactly what happens to Ginny. She writes into the diary and reads it, but doesn't realize at first that it is having any influence over her. But as Ginny becomes critically aware, she realizes that Tom (the author) is responsible for shaping her actions. Though in Ginny's case this shaping is quite literal and done through magical infestation, it represents any reader's reaction to the ideologies implicit in any author's reading. As Tom the ideologue himself says, "It took a very long time for stupid little Ginny to stop trusting her diary" (Rowling 311). He might as well have said it took Ginny a long time to stop trusting in a non-ideologically-driven text, and trusting that it was ideologically benign and innocent. So, even though Tom's text operates on one level repressively (by coming alive and attempting to carry out his evil deeds towards the end of the novel), it also operates heavily by ideology. After all, the description of his plan at sixteen could almost be an excerpt from *Mein Kampf*: Tom is setting down his "plan" so that future generations can carry on his ideological work even after his death. Thus, he as an author will presumably never die.

Tom Riddle also shapes Harry through his ideology by feigning objectivity. The positivist myth of objective truth causes many readers to ignore the inescapable ideology of any text. When first seeing the diary on the flooded bathroom floor, the following exchange takes place between Harry and Ron:

> Harry stepped forward to pick it up, but Ron suddenly flung out an arm to hold him back.
>
> "What?" said Harry.
>
> "Are you crazy?" said Ron. "It could be dangerous."
>
> "*Dangerous?*" said Harry, laughing. "Come off it, how could it be dangerous?"
>
> "You'd be surprised," said Ron, who was looking apprehensively at the book (Rowling 230, emphasis in original).

Harry, thus, does not account for the potential power of a text. To him, the idea that a book could have dangerous power is literally laughable. Harry's uncritical naiveté is further demonstrated when he accepts Tom Riddle's vision of the past as unbiased truth. When Harry asks the diary who opened the Chamber last time, Riddle replies, "*You don't have to take my word for it. I can take you inside my memory of the night when I caught him*" (241). Tom Riddle masquerades his intentionally misleading history as objective and somehow different than "taking his word for it." Harry is fooled into accepting what he sees as ultimate truth, even though Tom Riddle used the memory to lead to false conclusions.

The supposed objectivity of Riddle's memory, as with the supposed objectivity of photographic or filmed texts, makes the ideology more potent because it becomes invisible: instead of looking for the ideology in Riddle's text, Harry sees it as a snapshot of undeniable truth. James Curtis, in discussing photography used for documentaries, writes of "the widespread public belief in the inherent honesty and authenticity of all documentary photographs. Photographers have helped to nurture this public trust" (vii). Though Curtis is specifically discussing photography, the same inherent honesty is attributed to film. And when Harry is first being drawn into Riddle's diary/memory, "Harry saw that the little square for June thirteenth seemed to have turned into a minuscule television screen" (242). Muggle-raised Harry, familiar with photography and film, shares the "public belief in the inherent honesty" that Curtis talks about. Furthermore, in the words of Curtis, this same trust is nurtured by the "filmmaker" Riddle: he is the one who presents his magical film as objective. This belief in authenticity, though, is misguided. As Curtis puts it: "a photograph has no inherent or intrinsic message – only an assigned meaning. In our rush to place trust in the objectivity and realism of documentary photographs, we have lost sight of their historical value and, as a consequence, of their primary meaning" (ix). So, even though Riddle's memory is presented as an objective documentary, the diary is not devoid of meaning. As Harry learns only at the end, all texts come through the lens of ideology. When Tom Riddle appears for the first time outside the diary, "He was strangely blurred around the edges, as though Harry were looking at him through a misted window" (Rowling 307). Nearly too late, Harry realizes the essential nature of ideological lenses when reading a text: an author cannot get anything across objectively and transparently, but rather always through a misted lens. This lesson is fundamental for any education in critical thought.

This ideology is shown as especially powerful given that it causes loyal Harry to assume the guilt of one of his closest friends: Hagrid. This comes about because of something else Hollindale says about ideology: "ideology is not something which is transferred to children as if they were empty receptacles. It is something which they already possess, having drawn it from a mass of experiences far more powerful than literature" (17). Had Tom Riddle tried to incriminate somebody more trustworthy than Hagrid, it might not have worked. Unfortunately, Harry already would have expected Hagrid to be behind the attacks anyway. His experience with Hagrid included Hagrid's affinity for dangerous monsters. Also, as we learn in *Goblet of Fire*, the wizarding community in general is highly distrustful of giants. The guilt of an ostensible half-giant like Hagrid would sound highly plausible among the wizards sharing that ideology. This occurrence typifies the power of ideology over logic. Had the wizards of Tom Riddle's youth and Harry himself thought about it, the only monster that Salazar Slytherin, and thus his heir, would have logically used for his malice would be a breed of snake. To believe that the giant spider Hagrid had raised could have been used by Slytherin, the known parselmouth, is a logical misstep. But the prejudices and preconceived notions of the wizarding community allowed them to quite easily be led astray by Tom Riddle and his ideological rhetoric.

There is not a complete lack of ideological vigilance in the wizarding world, fortunately. Just as Ron was initially suspicious of the diary, so too should his sister have been. Mr. Weasley, upon learning of his daughter's role with the diary, chides her: "'What have I always told you? Never trust anything that can think for itself *if you can't see where it keeps its brain?*'" (329, emphasis in original). Just as Ginny should have been vigilant about a book that thinks for itself, so too should child readers be vigilant about the ideologies that allow a book to think and express itself. As Hollindale writes, "By teaching children how to develop an alert enjoyment of stories, we are also equipping them to meet linguistic malpractices of more consequential kinds" (14). What linguistic malpractice could be more consequential than causing a young girl to take over the genocidal work of an author, fifty years removed from the reading? Tom Riddle's appearance and possession of Ginny metaphorically shows the importance imbued in teaching children to be critical readers of any text, even those that purport historicity. Later in the series, when the Ministry attempts to discredit Harry and Dumbledore in *Order of the Phoenix*, those witches and wizards best equipped to survive Voldemort's rise are those with the critical capacities to comprehend the falseness of the *Daily Prophet*'s assurances that Voldemort's return is Harry's delusion. Thus, on a literal level, the importance of scrutinizing texts, first shown with Riddle's diary, is a value much needed in a world of potentially lethal rhetoric.

No Horcrux for the Physically Manifest

Though Riddle's diary shows the elusive and slippery nature of ideology, it shows how texts are also entrenched in materialism. Many aspects of a text work on invisible, abstract levels, but texts are also physical items based in manifest situations. Therefore, there is one way that Harry is able to do away with the rampant ideology that Riddle imparted into his text: to literally destroy the book itself. Riddle's diary, in the end, is a material object. In "The Work of Art in the Age of Mechanical Reproduction," Walter Benjamin writes that until relatively recently, art could not be reproduced mechanically. Until then, each work of art was unique in time and place: "the original preserved all its authority" (1234). Tom Riddle's diary, since it is imbued with part of his soul in the form of a Horcrux, is a unique artistic entity: it could not be mass produced. Also, Kate Behr points out in "'Same-as-Difference': Narrative Transformations and Intersecting Cultures in *Harry Potter*," that "intangibles in the Muggle world are made real in a wizarding context" (127). She notes how wizard money is actually still made from precious metals, and how memories "can be physically captured and stored in a pensieve for later sifting and retrieval" (127). Among these manifest intangibles she lists is Tom Riddle's diary, where "wizard memories captured in books can have a life of their own" (127). Voldemort made part of his soul physically manifest and put it into the diary. Imbuing it thusly with his authorial aura, as Benjamin would put it, young Tom Riddle made the diary more powerful than a mass-produced book could be in the age of mechanical reproduction: that physicality of his text cannot be so easily copied.

Of course, this is exactly what allows Harry to destroy the diary. Even though the author and author's ideology can never be completely subjugated (the authorial phantom of Tom Riddle cannot be defeated by Harry, the reader), the text itself is not so lucky. When thinking of a text as a transcendent thing, it is possible to imagine the ideas having a body and mind of their own. But, when it comes down to it, destroying a book will (if the following entities are not represented elsewhere in other copies of the book) destroy the author's frozen self, ideology, and everything else. Thus, Harry merely needs to stab the diary itself to cast the rest of Tom Riddle's authority out. This also destroys the physical shred of Voldemort's soul, or his aura. Fittingly for a world in which intangibles are made manifest, the diary bleeds as it dies.

Constant Vigilance

Textuality plays a large role in the wizarding world, just as it does in the world of Muggles. The iconic "writing on the wall" that starts the mania of Harry's second year sets that precedent early. Though Voldemort's youthful dabbling in journaling held great consequences for this novel specifically, the understanding of Voldemort as an author is crucial for the rest of the series. As *Deathly Hallows* sees Voldemort ultimately controlling the Ministry of Magic, it is not through direct leadership. Rather, the great wordsmith rules through linguistic hegemony: garnering obedience from those who would defy an openly Voldemort-led government through misinformation and propaganda. Just as Harry learns that Riddle's diary is not a static, benign entity, so too must the rest of he wizarding community comprehend the power of texts in order to defeat Voldemort. This comes into play when the truth of Voldemort's return must be understood, despite the official misleading rhetoric of the *Daily Prophet*. The power of critical thought is also crucial when the Death-Eater-led Ministry begins framing Muggle-born witches and wizards as thieves of magic. *Chamber of Secrets* remains the least-loved entry in the series for many *Potter* fans, yet its importance should not be discounted as rubbish. The great villain of this series uses language as a mighty weapon, and the critical understanding of how texts can work in multiple ways really begins with a soggy diary on a wet bathroom floor.

BIBLIOGRAPHY

Barthes, Roland. "The Death of the Author." *The Critical Tradition: Classic Texts and Contemporary Trends.* 3rd ed. Ed. David H. Richter. New York: Bedford/St. Martin's, 2007. 874-877.

Behr, Kate. "'Same-as-Difference:' Narrative Transformations and Intersecting Cultures in Harry Potter." *Journal of Narrative Theory* 35.1 (2005): 112-132.

Benjamin, Walter. "The Work of Art in the Age of Mechanical reproduction." *The Critical Tradition: Classic Texts and Contemporary Trends.* 3rd ed. Ed. David H. Richter. New York: Bedford/St. Martin's, 2007. 1233-1249.

Curtis, James. *Mind's Eye, Mind's Truth: FSA Photography Reconsidered.* Philadelphia: Temple UP, 1989.

Eagleton, Terry. *Literary Theory: An Introduction.* 2nd ed. Minneapolis: The U of Minnesota P, 2003.

Fish, Stanley. "How to Recognize a Poem When You See One." *The Critical Tradition: Classic Texts and Contemporary Trends.* 3rd ed. Ed. David H. Richter. New York: Bedford/St. Martin's, 2007. 1023-1030.

Hollindale, Peter. "Ideology and the Children's Book." *Signal* 55 (1988): 3-22.

Rowling, J. K. *Harry Potter and the Chamber of Secrets.* New York: Scholastic Press, 1999.

Chapter Eight

If Rowling Says Dumbledore is Gay, is He Gay?
Harry Potter and the Role of Authorial Intention

Karen Kebarle

To give a text an Author is to impose a limit on that text. . .the birth of the reader must be at the cost of the death of the Author. --Roland Barthes, "The Death of the Author" 1977.

Whoever said the author was dead sure hadn't meant Joanne Rowling.
–Rebecca Traister, 2007.

In October 2007, J.K. Rowling created something of an uproar by saying that she'd always thought of Albus Dumbledore as gay. While many fans cheered, others objected that there was no evidence of this in Rowling's novels. For example, John Mark Reynolds argued that there was no textual evidence that the much-beloved headmaster was gay, and that the text is what matters ("Dumbledore is Not Gay"). Another reader, "Elron," declared that while Rowling could say what she liked, it is readers, not authors, who determine what a book means (Letters, salon.com). These responses bring *Harry Potter* readers into a debate that has gone on among literary critics for over a hundred years: what role do an author's intentions play in deciding what a book means? One theory, intentionalism, says that the author's intentions determine meaning. In 1967, E.D. Hirsch defined intentionalism as "the sensible idea that a text means what its author meant" (Iseminger 11). Hirsch argued that though a literary text has different significances to different readers, it cannot mean something its author did not intend. Though some *Harry Potter* readers seem to believe that intentionalism was long ago discarded by serious readers of literature, in fact, critics continue to argue its pros and cons to this day. In this essay, I take on the challenge that the debate over Dumbledore's sexuality poses to intentionalism.

Here is the problem: there is no conclusive, incontestable proof in the *Harry Potter* novels that Dumbledore was gay and in love with Grindelwald, and that he embraced Grindelwald's ideas of Muggle domination due to this infatuation. Yet Rowling has suggested in several interviews that she intended both of these meanings from early on in her writing process ("Pottercast 130"). Reynolds, Elron, and others argue, in effect, that this proves the meaning of *Deathly Hallows* is different from what Rowling intended – and therefore that meaning is not determined by authorial intention. I propose three defenses against this argument. The first is that Rowling intended the text to be read two different ways by two kinds of readers. Rowling said, for example, that children would see Dumbledore's relationship with Grindelwald as a friendship, while adults would see more. The second defense is Rowling's statements of her intentions about Dumbledore may not reflect her original intentions. Rowling may have changed her mind, for example, or forgotten since publication what she intended while writing. The third defense I put forward is based on the work of intentionalist Walter Benn Michaels: Rowling may have failed to *communicate* to all of her readers that Dumbledore is gay, but this does not mean she failed to *mean* it. In this essay, I use the controversy over Dumbledore's sexuality to champion the theory that an author's intentions determine the meaning of a literary work, and to show how compelling and resilient that theory is.

WANTED: TEXTUAL EVIDENCE

Authorial intention has long been of interest to readers of the *Harry Potter* series. This was most evident before the seventh and last book was published, when Rowling was the only one who knew for sure which parts of her series were clues to what happened next and which were not, and readers had an irrepressible thirst to find out. In the *Priori Incantatem* debate, for example, readers of the first edition of *Harry Potter and the Goblet of Fire* argued about what happened when Voldemort's wand began regurgitating, in reverse order, ghosts of people he had killed. Readers debated at length what it meant that James Potter's ghost came out of Voldemort's wand first instead of Lily's when Lily had died last. According to the online *Harry Potter Lexicon*, some readers argued Rowling was "revealing some special truth about what happened to Harry's parents, but was doing so by hiding the clue in an exciting emotionally charged scene where we were likely to overlook it" ("The Wand-Order Problem"). As soon as they knew that having James's ghost emerge first was just a mistake by Rowling, and not a clue, all speculation about the wand order came to an end. In the *Priori Incantatem* debate, the only meaning readers cared about was the meaning Rowling intended.

At the same time, Rowling's readers – including me – did not always agree with her global pronouncements about her characters. When in October 2007, Rowling said that she had always seen Dumbledore as gay, a sizeable number of readers responded by saying that her intentions were irrelevant. Michael Dorf spoke for many of them when he wrote "an author of a work of fiction is, at best, first among equals in interpreting that work. Her intentions do not control the meaning of the text" ("Harry Potter and the Framer's Intent").[1] Some readers' intense reaction to Rowling's statement

---

1   Part of Dorf's article is about the U.S. Constitution. One of the places people continue

about Dumbledore came out of fear of or disapproval of homosexuality. Yet many readers who would be perfectly comfortable with a gay Dumbledore argued that he wasn't gay because of the lack of evidence in the books. Initially I took this argument as a challenge because I was sure I could prove that the text showed Dumbledore was gay and infatuated with Grindelwald. I found, however, that though there were moments in the text that could be evidence of this, none of the evidence was incontestable. As I will show below, each piece of evidence could also be read another way. The only direct reference to homosexuality in the books is when Dudley Dursley derisively asks Harry: "Who's Cedric – your boyfriend?" (*Order* 19). Furthermore, I saw that the question of Dumbledore's sexuality was a good one to use to explore the claims of intentionalism, since Dumbledore is either gay (attracted to a greater or lesser degree to people of the same sex) or not gay; he cannot be both.

Before we look for textual evidence of Dumbledore's sexuality, however, we must clarify one thing: intentionalism does not mean that all of Rowling's statements equal her intentions as she was writing. If it did, intentionalism would have been refuted long ago, since authors clearly can and do forget, change their minds, and lie. "Sam" demonstrates a common mistake when he writes on his blog:

> "Let's suppose for a moment that Rowling's intentions matter even if she doesn't write her intentions into the story. . . .What if she changed her mind tomorrow? Would Dumbledore then be straight just because she said so?" ("Is Dumbledore Gay," Philocristos).

What matters are the intentions Rowling writes into the story in the actual process of writing. Intentionalism is ultimately a philosophy of language, which holds that the meaning of words equals what the speaker intends as he or she says them, or what the author intends by them as he or she writes them. Intentionalism does not tell you how to know what the author's intentions are, however. In 1983, Steven Knapp and Walter Michaels cautioned that "nothing in the claim that authorial intention is the necessary object of interpretation tells us anything at all about what should count as evidence for determining the content of any particular intention" ("A Reply to Our Critics" 101). Readers still have to do all the work they always did to understand texts.[2] Ten years later, in his book *Literary Interest*, Steven Knapp

---

to debate intentionalism versus textualism is in American constitutional studies. They ask whether or not the intentions of the framers of the constitution determine what it means.

2   Stanley Fish restated this arguement in his 2005 essay "There is No Textualist

seems to give biographical information some weight when he writes that readers infer things "on the basis of biographical or other kinds of evidence, about the meaning an author is likely to have intended," but his careful use of "infer" and "likely" makes clear that our inferences may be incorrect. (5) We cannot use any of Rowling's statements about her novels as proof positive of her intentions when composing, nor therefore, of her meaning. These statements may or may not coincide with these intentions.

All the same, Rowling's statements about Dumbledore's sexuality may well coincide with what she intended as she wrote the words of *Deathly Hallows*. If they do, then we can ask: what words did Rowling write that mean that Dumbledore is gay? Rowling said in 2007 that "Dumbledore's feelings for Grindelwald, as revealed in the 7th book, were an infatuation rather than a straight-forward friendship" (Pottercast 130). The use of "revealed" implies that the 7th book contains evidence of this infatuation, and so I searched the text for clues. Gary Iseminger explores the idea of asking yes or no questions about possible evidence of a book's meaning ("An Intentional Demonstration" 77), and I borrow his strategy here. I will ask yes or no questions of each possible clue about Dumbledore's sexuality.

The most likely clue is from *Half-Blood Prince*. When Harry and Dumbledore go inside Dumbledore's memory of his first visit with Tom Riddle at the orphanage, the young Dumbledore "strode off along the pavement, drawing many curious glances due to the flamboyantly cut suit of plum velvet that he was wearing" (*Half-Blood* 246). Dumbledore's flair is especially unusual here because most wizards in the books are terrible at wearing Muggle clothes. Is Dumbledore's flamboyantly cut suit a sign of his general eccentricity? The girl who opens the orphanage door is startled by his "eccentric" appearance (247). Or is it a clue that he is gay? It is quite possible that it is a clue, especially since "flamboyant" is a word often associated with gay men, and purple a color often associated with homosexuality. Other readers agree; here's a comment from "Melkorsbane" in an online discussion board in 2007, after Rowling told the world that Dumbledore was gay: "You had to see this coming. Flamboyantly purple robes? Come on, that spells

Position"; he writes that he, Knapp, Michaels, and Larry Alexander "say repeatedly that intentionalism is simply the right answer to a question (what is the meaning of a text?) and not a method. Knowing that it is intention you are after gives you no leg up when you are faced with the task of interpreting a particular text. You still have to determine what the intention is, and more often than not that determination will involve disputes in which, by offering different accounts of the intention animating a text, interpreters will give different accounts of its "properties and meanings". . . .[Intentionalism] does not tell you what to do; it just tells you what you are doing" (16). Stanley Fish was a prominent Reader Response critic for many years but is now an intentionalist.

flamer in all caps" (digg.com).[3] "PsyDmama" responds: "Exactly!!! To me, when I heard that people were shocked and there was hub-bub, all I could think was 'Duh!! Didn't you people get that?' I don't know how she could have made it more plain" (digg.com). Though Melkorsbane and PsyDmama may be right, this one passage is not enough to prove that Dumbledore is gay. Dumbledore may just like making a splash by wearing such unusual clothing.

With the flamboyantly cut plum-colored suit as background, consider the following passages from *Deathly Hallows*. Are they possible clues that Dumbledore is gay and infatuated with Grindelwald? Hints? Subtle innuendos?

> 1) Dumbledore's brother Aberforth says: "Secrets and lies, that is how we grew up, and Albus…he was a natural" (*Deathly* 453).

> 2) As Rebecca Traister points out, Doge talks about his and Dumbledore's "mutual attraction" when they first meet at age 11 ("Dumbledore? Gay.").

> 3) The text refers to the young Grindelwald as Dumbledore's "handsome companion" (*Deathly* 288).

> 4) Dumbledore tells Harry that it was their obsession with the Deathly Hallows, most of all, "that drew us together" (572).

Were the secrets Dumbledore kept all about Ariana? Was the attraction between Dumbledore and Doge and Dumbledore and Grindelwald platonic? Does "companion" mean just friend here? Or are these hints? All of these passages could be subtle clues. All of them may not be.

Rita Skeeter's description of the intensity of the two teenagers' friendship could also be a clue. Consider the following:

> 1) Dumbledore sends Grindelwald letters in the dead of night, Skeeter says (291).

> 2) Bathilda Bagshot says that the two boys "got along like a cauldron on fire (291), while in the King's Cross chapter, Dumbledore says: "You have no idea how his ideas caught me, Harry, inflamed me" (572).

Is the mention of letters "in the dead of night" just Skeeter-style sensationalism? Or does the late night setting, and the references to fire

---

3   Melkorsbane thinks Dumbledore is wearing wizard robes, but he is wearing a Muggle-style suit. "Nice suit, sir," says Harry (*Prince* 246).

and flame, hint at a passion that goes beyond friendship? Was Dumbledore caught by ideas alone, or also by passion? All three of these passages could refer either to an infatuation or a friendship.

One possible clue is the way *Deathly Hallows* emphasizes Grindelwald's physical attractiveness again and again; perhaps Rowling wanted readers to experience what made him so attractive to Dumbledore. When Harry first sees the photo of Dumbledore and Grindelwald, Grindelwald, whose true identity neither Harry nor the reader knows for half the book, has "golden hair" which "fell in curls to his shoulders" (208). This focus on the beautiful hair shows us that this person is someone who is looked at, who draws the eye. He is also the "laughing boy," the "merry-faced thief" (275), the young man bathed in golden light who steals Gregorovitch's wand and then "soar[s] from the windowsill like a bird" (233). Because the young man is mysterious and appealing, Harry Potter can't stop thinking about him: "Harry's scar continued to burn and the merry, blond-haired boy swam tantalizingly in his memory" (240). The focus on the unknown youth's beautiful hair, overall attractiveness, and abundant laughter make it much easier, once we find out he's Grindelwald, to imagine him as an object of infatuation. Still, is this a deliberate clue that Dumbledore was infatuated with Grindelwald at age seventeen? It might be, but it could just illustrate Grindelwald's appeal as a friend and a leader.

Finally, consider the subtle suggestions in *Deathly Hallows* of something going on that exceeds conventionally acceptable limits. Firstly, in the photograph Harry sees of Grindelwald and Dumbledore, the two are "laughing immoderately." This phrase may well be a hint that their love goes beyond conventional limits. Secondly, Rita Skeeter writes this about the possible circumstances surrounding Ariana's death:

> Was she the inadvertent victim of some Dark rite? *Did she stumble across something she ought not to have done,* as the two young men sat practicing for their attempt at glory and domination? (293, emphasis added).

Rita Skeeter's words are very suggestive. Both of these passages hint that there was something clandestine about Dumbledore and Grindelwald's relationship, but they may merely refer to the young men's infatuation with dark magic and world domination.

One reason for all this ambiguity could be to keep younger children from being exposed to sexually suggestive language. Another could be that Rowling is sending this book out into a world in which many consider same-sex romance automatically inappropriate. Whatever the reason, if Rowling meant some of the above passages as clues that Dumbledore was gay, she must have decided not to show any physical affection between him and Grindelwald. Though we see many people in these books hug and kiss, we almost never see Grindelwald and Dumbledore touching; in fact, we rarely see them together at all. One exception is the photograph Harry glimpses in Umbridge's Ministry office, in which the two teenagers have their "arms around each other's shoulders"; when Harry finds this photo again at Bathilda's house in Godric's Hollow, we hear again that they are "arm in arm" (208, 275). The fact that Rowling mentions this twice could be a clue. Yet it might not, especially since platonic male friends stand arm in arm all the time in many cultures.

Rita Skeeter's derisive thoughts on the legendary 1945 duel in which Dumbledore defeats Grindelwald may be another clue. Skeeter writes: "After they've read my book, people may be forced to conclude that Grindelwald simply conjured a white handkerchief from the end of his wand and came quietly!" (28).[4] This passage may be a sexual innuendo that only a few readers are meant to catch. Does Rowling use Skeeter's lurid language as an opportunity to create a symbolic sex scene between the two men, or is this interpretation a projection by readers onto the text? *Deathly Hallows* does come close to saying that wands are phallic symbols; consider, for example, Hermione's statement that "some wizards just like to boast about how theirs are bigger and better than other people's" (337).[5] Skeeter's report of the duel may be a clue, or it may not, especially because Rowling generally avoids this level of sexual innuendo for the sake of her younger readers.

So there is the flamboyantly cut velvet suit, the passages that could hint at a relationship closer and more intense than friendship, the emphasis on Grindelwald's attractiveness, and some sexually suggestive phrases. Though these passages are intriguing, every one of them could easily be read as intending something else. I put the plum-colored suit first because it might incline some readers to see the other passages as deliberate clues, yet ultimately there is no incontestable evidence in the text that Dumbledore is gay and in love with Grindelwald.

Nor is there conclusive evidence that Dumbledore embraced Grindelwald's

---

4   Audience members at my talk at Portus in Dallas in July 2008 brought this quotation to my attention.

5   See also Dumbledore's comment in *The Tales of Beedle the Bard* that "No witch has ever claimed to own the Elder Wand" ("Albus Dumbledore on the Tale of the Three Brothers" 104).

sinister ideas because he fell in love. Rowling said that Dumbledore's story, like that of Bellatrix Lestrange, illustrates the novel's theme that love can lead a person "into acts of foolishness and even evil" (Pottercast 131). In March 2008, Rowling told student journalist Adeel Amini that she knew from early in the series that Dumbledore had

> flirted with the idea of racial domination, that he was going to subjugate Muggles . . . . He's an innately good man, what would make him do that? I didn't even think it through that way, it just seemed to come to me, I thought, "I know why he did it, he fell in love". . . he lost his moral compass completely when he fell in love ("In Conversation with J.K. Rowling").

This is an interesting story, but it is one *Deathly Hallows* does not tell. In the novel, Bellatrix Lestrange loses any moral compass she might have had due to her slavish love for Voldemort; she is ready to kill Tonks, her own niece, to please him. In contrast, we never see Dumbledore acting just to please Grindelwald, and he seems to lose his moral compass due to ambition, not love. Dumbledore tells Harry: "I was gifted. I was brilliant. I wanted to escape. I wanted shine. I wanted glory." He explains that after his mother's death he felt "[t]rapped and wasted." Then Grindelwald came: "You cannot imagine how his ideas caught me, Harry, inflamed me. Muggles forced into subservience. We wizards triumphant. Grindelwald and I, the glorious young leaders of the revolution" (*Deathly* 573). Dumbledore's statement that the ideas "caught" him suggests these ideas enticed him because they filled his need for action, glory, and escape.

Some passages make it clear that Dumbledore hid Grindelwald's true nature from himself, but he seems to do so due to his ambition, rather than his infatuation. In "King's Cross," Dumbledore tells Harry: "Did I know, in my heart of hearts, what Grindelwald was? I think I did, but I closed my eyes. . . . To him, though I pretended not to know it, [the resurrection stone] meant an army of Inferi!" (573-574). It is clear that Dumbledore hides from himself his suspicions about what Grindelwald might be like as a ruler. The exciting dream of being "glorious young leaders of the revolution" causes Dumbledore to ignore the darker side of Grindelwald's plans, including the army of Inferi, animated corpses. When Grindelwald gets in an argument with Dumbledore's brother, his worst side takes over: "That which I had always sensed in him, but pretended not to, now sprang into terrible being" (574). Dumbledore has been under the illusion that he and Grindelwald had a bond, but he can no longer hide Grindelwald's nature from himself. Yet nothing here suggests that Dumbledore's self deception was due to an infatuation with Grindelwald, rather than to ambition.

I concede that ambition and Grindelwald were bound together for the teenaged Dumbledore, since he dreamt of reigning side by side with his friend: "Invincible masters of death, Grindelwald and Dumbledore!" (574). There is nothing that says definitively that this dream stems from infatuation rather than friendship and admiration, however. Similarly, the complete despair Dumbledore feels in *Half-Blood Prince* when he hallucinates that he is watching Grindelwald hurt his brother and sister could be because he has ignored Grindelwald's faults due to selfish ambition plus love, or selfish ambition plus hero worship.

It therefore seems that there is no conclusive evidence in *Deathly Hallows* that Dumbledore is gay, and even less evidence that he flirted with Grindelwald's ideas of racial domination and Muggle subjugation because he fell in love. If Rowling's words in her interviews express her original intentions, then her intentions do not match with the text.

Call in the Literary Theorists

So what do we do now? We call in the literary theorists! When an author's text does not match what seem to be his or her own intentions and interpretations, readers start theorizing about what books mean, and this is what happened with Rowling's readers. When Rowling said that Dumbledore was gay, readers who felt her intentions did not match the text took one of two paths: they declared that what matters most is the reader, or they declared that what matters most is the text. These two reactions correspond roughly to two schools of literary criticism: Reader Response and formalism, also known as textualism and New Criticism. Reader Response critics say that ultimately only readers matter in determining what books mean. Formalists, or more specifically, New Critics, say that only the text matters in determining what books mean.

"Elron" is one of many who responded to Rowling's statements about Dumbledore by saying that the reader, not Rowling, is in charge. Elron writes:

> In the end, the definitive interpretation of a book, its characters, and its plot doesn't come from the author, it comes from the readers, through what they "see" and feel while imagining what was written. Through conversations with the author, we can flesh out aspects of that fantasy world, but for us, it still exists in our imaginations, not hers (Letters, Salon.com).

Elron's approach is Reader Response criticism. Reader Response and its many variations developed in the 1970s in reaction to the way New Criticism and intentionalism neglect the reader's experience. Norman Holland humorously writes that in New Criticism, the reader is merely a passive vessel for the text's meaning: "He or she will be filled up like an oil tank or a martini glass" (*The Critical I*). For Holland, in contrast, as for Elron, the reader is not the receptacle of meaning, but the creator of meaning. Louis Tyson explains that Reader Response critics believe that "readers do not passively consume the meaning presented to them by an objective literary text; rather they actively make the meaning they find in literature" (*Critical Theory Today* 154).Under Reader Response theory, there is no one correct meaning of a text because each reader makes the meaning for himself or herself.

Although Holland and other Reader Response critics did much of their writing in the 1970s and 80s, their approach still has great appeal, especially to readers like Elron who find that their own experience of a book differs wildly from that of the author. Studying the way that different readers respond to literature can be very interesting. For example, Norman Holland writes that we use texts to fill our psychological needs:

> [A]ny individual shapes the material the literary work offers him – and that includes the author – to give him what he characteristically both wishes and fears. . . . We interact with the work, making it part of our own psychic economy and making ourselves part of the literary work. ("Unity Identity Text Self" 124, 125).

Holland's ideas could help us understand certain wildly differing responses to Rowling's novels, such as why some readers revere Severus Snape and others hate him. Holland also argues that we are all doing Reader Response criticism whether we know we are or not. Whether we focus on the text, language, historical background, gender, sexuality, race, class, mythic structure, the psychology of the author, or the author's intention, what we see is inevitably a function of who we are ("The Story of a Psychoanalytic Critic").[6]

The problem with Reader Response is that, under its method, there are potentially as many meanings to a text as readers. Consider Elron's words:

---

6   Holland writes: "You cannot talk consistently about a text as though it were completely separate from yourself, because it isn't: you cannot perceive the text except through some human process of perception, either your own or someone else's, a critic analyzing the work, perhaps. Those processes of perception vary considerably from individual to individual, from interpretive community to interpretive community, and from culture to culture. One can therefore only talk about a text by acknowledging one's own role in its perception. One's own personality, beliefs, and culture color even the simplest sensory data." ("The Story of a Psychoanalytic Critic").

> In the end, the definitive interpretation of a book, its characters,
> and its plot doesn't come from the author, it comes from the readers,
> through what they "see" and feel while imagining what was written. .
> . .[It] exists in our imagination, not hers.

This statement is self-contradictory. There can be no "definitive interpretation" of a book under Elron's method, because each reader creates the work in his or her imagination. Two readers can't really disagree about the work, either, since each reader is creating his or her separate work. In fact, Elron cannot logically disagree with Rowling's interpretation of Dumbledore because Rowling has just as much right to create the novel in her imagination as any other reader.

Unlike Elron, Reader Response critics usually state that there is no such thing as a determinate meaning of a text, but their approach is still problematic. As Walter Michaels has argued, Reader Response criticism becomes all about the reader's subjectivity, rather than about the text (*The Shape of the Signifier* 11, 200).[7] It can be fascinating to see how Rowling's readers find in her novels what they care about most, but to decide whether or not I agree with their interpretation, I go back to the text.[8] Though Reader Response helps us understand why different readers see such different things in texts, under its method the text itself can become irrelevant.

Is formalism the answer, then? In contrast to Reader Response critics, formalists, especially New Critics, tend to focus all their attention on the text. They believe that a text has a definitive meaning, and that this meaning is to be found in the words on the page. In "The Authority of the Text" (1970), Monroe Beardsley wrote that "the literary text…is the determiner of its meaning. It has a will, or at least a way, of its own" (36). Though New Criticism was most popular in the 1940s and 1950s, its focus on the text still influences readers and critics today. One such reader is John Mark Reynolds, whose thought-provoking essay I mentioned in my introduction. Reynolds considers Rowling's statement that Dumbledore is gay to be "nonsense" due to the lack of textual evidence:

> There is no evidence of it in the books and the books (at this point)
> are all that matter. . . . Authorial intent is important, but not the

---

7   Michaels argues that Reader Response critics are not actually doing interpretation: "theorists who think there can be many (correct) interpretations of the same text are in fact committed to the idea that there can be no correct interpretations of the same text and, indeed, to the idea that there is no such thing as interpretation." (Shape of the Signifier 200).

8   Reader Response critics would no doubt argue that I, like everyone else, cannot help remaking the text in my own image.

only important thing. . . . Rowling chose to hide "opinion" of
Dumbledore's sexuality until the story arc was done, Dumbledore
dead, and his life written. Now her opinions no longer matter, just her
text ("Dumbledore is Not Gay").

One appeal of the idea that "just Rowling's text" matters is that all of
us have that text in front of us, whereas we can never be completely sure
what an author's intention was when writing. In "The Authority of the Text"
(1970), Monroe Beardsley points out that a critic is a "poem reader, not a
mind reader" (33). Dennis Dutton acknowledges that for many readers, "the
text itself will always speak with greater authority than any suppositions
or speculations about the author's purposes" ("Why Intentionalism Won't
Go Away"). Furthermore, sometimes literary works seem more powerful
or more complex than their authors realize. New Criticism's focus on the
text continues to appeal because we all have access to the text, and because
sometimes a text's meaning seems to go beyond what its author intended.

One problem with the idea that "just the text" matters, however, is that
words cannot act on their own. We saw that Monroe Beardsley said: "the
literary text. . .is the determiner of its meaning. It has a will, or at least a way,
of its own" (36). Beardsley argued against intentionalism when he wrote that
"texts acquire meaning through the interactions of their words without the
intervention of an authorial will" (32). A text does not have a will, however,
nor can it act or interact. Words and other elements of the text interact only
in the mind of the reader or of the author.

The intentionalist argument against formalism or textualism, however,
is that there is no such thing as "just the text." Stanley Fish writes in his 2005
article "There is No Textualist Position" that while formalists say words have
a literal meaning, a meaning independent of the author, in fact, text alone
"can never yield meaning" (4). Whenever you think you are seeing "just
the text," you are in fact seeing another intention. Fish gives the example of
approaching a red light with his father, at which time his father said: "Go
through the light." Fish writes that he assumed his father meant, "As soon
as the light turns green, drive straight ahead; don't turn either left or right"
(1). He says that formalists might argue that he "chose against the literal
meaning of 'go through the light,'" as in, drive through the red light, but that
this "just the text" meaning is actually another intention:

> "[W]ith which of two possible purposes (there could be many more)
> did my father produce these words? It is a question that the words

themselves cannot answer.... The choice is not between what my father said and what he meant, but between two specifications of what he meant. . . . . "Go through the light" has no determinate meaning.... Once the words are heard within the assumption of an intention, they acquire a meaning" (3-4).

In other words, whether we interpret people's spoken words or literary texts, we are always choosing between possible intentions. What seems to be "just what the words mean on the page" is in fact one possible intended meaning.

Fish's 2005 essay builds on the work of earlier intentionalists such as E.D. Hirsch, Steven Knapp, and Walter Michaels. Hirsch wrote in 1967 that "almost any word sequence can, under the conventions of language, legitimately represent more than one complex of meaning," and that what determines what words mean is what the author intended ("In Defense of the Author" 13). Intentionalism fell out of fashion for many years, but in the 1980s, Michaels and Knapp revised and radicalized Hirsch's ideas in their controversial essays "Against Theory" (1982) and "Against Theory 2" (1987). Their work made intentionalism a strong player once again in the debate over how we know what books mean.

While formalists argue that language conventions determine meaning, Knapp and Michaels argue that only the conventions the author is using determine the meaning. They write that if someone shouts "Fire!" it could mean that something is burning, or it could mean "discharge your weapon," or it could mean

> something that no one had ever meant before or would ever mean again. But in all three cases. . .the sentence would mean only what *its* speaker intended" ("A Reply to Richard Rorty" 142).

This passage illustrates that intentionalism is a philosophy of language. If you use "fire" to mean something no one has ever meant before or since, it will still mean what you meant, because that's what language does. Neither dictionary definitions, nor conventional meanings of words, nor the context in which we find them determine what a text means, argue Knapp, Michaels, and Stanley Fish, although all provide clues to what an author intends ("The Impossibility of Intentionless Meaning" 62; "There is No Textualist Position" 16).

Though the idea that language conventions and dictionary definitions do not determine meaning is hard to accept at first, many people would agree that understanding literary texts depends on knowing what certain words meant in an author's time and place. For example, how do American and Canadian readers of the British editions of Rowling's works know that, when Harry gets a jumper for Christmas, it's a sweater? (In American editions, "jumper" is replaced by "sweater.") The word "jumper" can mean a pullover sweater or a girl's sleeveless dress, depending on where you live. We know from the context that it is probably the first one – Harry is not startled by his present, and puts it on – but what clinches it is our knowledge of how the word was used in Britain at the time Rowling wrote her books, because this is a clue to what Rowling intended.[9] Intentionalists extend this argument to say that language is, by definition, expressed intention, and that there is no such thing as intentionless meaning.

Admittedly, the idea that there is no such thing as intentionless meaning is a challenging one. While writing this essay I emailed Walter Benn Michaels to ask whether he believed a text can ever mean something an author did not intend:

> What if an English speaking person is trying to speak French and says "librairie" when she means "library"? [In French] the word she used means "bookstore" ....she is using the word incorrectly. She means, I went to the library, but she has said, "Je suis allée à la librairie" [I went to the bookstore]. In this case, doesn't the text mean something different from what she intended? I know in your essays you argue that conventional definitions don't determine meaning...but it's hard for me to accept that they NEVER determine meaning.

Michaels responded:

> The person believes that the semantic rules [rules of words] she's using are the rules of French. In fact, she's using a different set (at least with respect to this one word) of semantic rules. The intentionalist claim is just that to understand what she has said is to understand what she meant according to the rules she was in fact using, not according to some set of rules she wasn't using (even the ones she hoped she was using). So she has indeed failed to communicate (she's trying to tell them she's going to the library but they can't have understood her) but

---

9   In "The Authority of the Text," Monroe Beardsley argues that texts can change their meaning over time, because words change their meaning. See Walter Michaels, "The Shape of the Signifier" 107-108, and Dennis Dutton, '"Why Intentionalism Won't Go Away," for a refutation of Beardsley's idea. How words are used changes over time, but the words in a text mean what they meant to the author. Michaels argues that readers look for what words meant to an author in his or her place and time because intention is what matters.

it doesn't at all follow that she has failed to mean. And, in fact, someone might very possibly figure out what she meant (figure out which rules she was in fact using) -- if, say, as she spoke she headed to the library across the street. . . . So the point is not exactly that conventions don't determine meaning. . . . it's that only the conventions you in fact are using determine the meaning. (January 26, 2009).

In this example, the girl is using the rules of French, except with "librarie," when she is using English rules. She says "librairie" [bookstore] and she means "library." Michaels argues that it is illogical and arbitrary for a listener to insist on another set of rules to those she is actually using (April 30, 2009). In other words, it is illogical to tell this girl that she *means* "I went to the bookstore" [librairie] rather than "I went to the library" [bibliothèque], or to tell someone who yells "fire" they mean "something is burning" when they meant "discharge your weapon." The conventions the person is actually using determine the meaning of her words.

Michaels argues that if you do not use conventional meanings of words, you may fail to communicate, but you do not necessarily fail to mean. Is Rowling sometimes speaking what amounts to a different language than some of her readers? Perhaps when Rowling was writing that Grindelwald was Dumbledore's "handsome companion," she intended to take advantage of two language conventions: the one that says "companion" means "friend," which she hoped was what children would understand by her words, and a more modern, less common one that says "companion" means "same-sex partner," which she hoped was what adults would understand. She quite possibly, of course, intended only "friend." If, however, "same-sex partner" is what she intended, she may have failed to communicate this meaning to all her readers, but she did not fail to mean.

Intentionalism is a theory about how to interpret texts, and we can see from the above examples that it is easier to work from the text outward. For example, we can ask what a particular person means by "go through the light" or "librarie" or "Fire!", or what Rowling meant by the words "handsome companion" or "mutual attraction." Intentionalism holds that a work means what the author intended when writing it, but it does not tell us how to find out what that intention is. It is therefore more difficult to start from an author's statements about the meaning of his or her works, such as Rowling's statement that Dumbledore was gay and infatuated with Grindelwald, and then decide whether or not that statement equals her intentions when writing. To ask if by "jumper" Rowling meant "sweater" or if by "companion" Rowling meant both "friend" and "same-sex partner" is much simpler than to ask by what part of the text Rowling means that Dumbledore flirted with Grindelwald's ideas because he was infatuated. Rowling's statement that infatuation was to blame for Dumbledore's embrace of Grindelwald's ideas does not seem to match with the text – which is where this quest began.

INTENTIONALISM AND THE QUESTION OF DUMBLEDORE'S SEXUALITY

As I have argued, there is no conclusive evidence in the text that Dumbledore was gay and infatuated with Grindelwald, and that this infatuation led him to flirt with the idea of racial domination of Muggles. Critics of intentionalism would argue that this gap between intention and text proves that intentionalism is wrong. Intentionalists don't give up that easily, however. Here are three possible intentionalist defenses for this gap between Rowling's stated intentions and her text

1)   "Adult" ontent in a kid's book: the "dual readers" defense

The first defense is the one I referred to in my discussion of "handsome companion." Rowling intended to create a text that was ambiguous: in this case, a text that could be read in two different ways. After all, Rowling says in a Leaky Cauldron podcast that adult and children will see different things in her text:

> I always imagined that Dumbledore was gay. How relevant is that to the books? Well, it's only relevant if you considered that his feelings for Grindelwald, as revealed in the 7th book, were an infatuation rather than a straight-forward friendship. That's how I think--In fact, I know that some, perhaps sensitive, adult readers had already seen that. I don't think that came as a big surprise to some adult readers. I think a child would see a friendship, and a very devoted friendship (Pottercast 130).

By saying that a child would see a friendship, Rowling suggests that she wanted to conceal the infatuation from those whom she felt were not ready to see it, such as children, and reveal it to those who were: "sensitive" adult readers. She repeated this idea in Toronto, Canada on October 23, 2007: " I think a child will see a friendship, and I think a sensitive adult may well understand that it was an infatuation" (Press Conference, CBC). Considering that some parents would not let their children read any book containing an identifiably gay character, it is perfectly possible that Rowling intended the text to be read two ways by two kinds of readers. One could also argue that this is why there is no clear evidence that Dumbledore flirted with racial domination due to his infatuation.

Yet this "dual readers" defense still leaves the question of whether there is evidence in the book, for any readers to find, that Dumbledore is gay and that he fell due to love.

2) The "no intent, no problem" defense

The second defense is that Rowling's statement that Dumbledore is gay does not reflect her original intention. Let's call it the "no problem" defense, since if her statements do not reflect her original intention, the fact that they do not match her text is no problem. Rowling may have changed her mind since writing the text, or changed her mind between planning her text out in her head and starting to write it down, or she may have forgotten her original intention after the fact. In the case of Rowling's statement that Dumbledore is gay, this defense is less persuasive, since Rowling's declaration that "that's the way I always saw Dumbledore" is so forceful (Pottercast 130).

In the case of Rowling's statement that Dumbledore flirted with Grindelwald's ideas of racial domination because of infatuation, this "no intent, no problem" defense works well. It is easy to imagine, for example, that Rowling said this about Dumbledore, and convinced herself that this was her original intention, because she identifies with him, and this gave her a way to let him off the hook. If Dumbledore's judgment was impaired by love it makes him less culpable than if he deliberately hid the truth from himself due to ambition. Many of the attendees at a conference panel on the issue of Dumbledore's sexuality (Portus, July 2008) welcomed Rowling's statement that Dumbledore's story was about the dangers of love because it makes Dumbledore easier to identify with as a character, and easier to forgive for embracing Grindelwald's tyrannical plans for wizard domination of Muggles. Of course, if Dumbledore fell due to infatuation, he is less dignified and less of a free agent, and his story is less grand; but we cannot decide what a text means based on which meaning is grander.

Another explanation of Dumbledore's fall that uses the "no problem" defense, and the one that I find most convincing, is that in the heat of writing Rowling got caught up in telling a story about ambition and selfishness, and she ended up focusing on that story. Rowling has said in interviews that two things, not just one, drew Dumbledore to Grindelwald's ideas and made him lose his moral compass: infatuation and ambition:

> Dumbledore was wrong and his judgement was entirely – was very suspect in that time. And of course it was more than being infatuated. Grindelwald appeared to be offering him a solution to this horrible dilemma. Dumbledore was not cut out, to his shame, to be a carer. He

was cut out to go out on the world stage and be a brilliant man. He
knows that about himself and he's ashamed of it (Pottercast 130).

Rowling says here that Grindelwald's ideas offered him a way to escape
being a "carer" for his sister and brother, to go out on the world stage and
win glory. She suggests in this interview that he fell both from love and from
ambition, but the text does not tell the story of his fall due to love. One
could speculate that whatever Rowling might have planned to write about
the dangers of love, when she actually sat down to write she focused on the
dangers of ambition.

The word "responsibility" occurs several times in the "King's Cross"
chapter of *Deathly Hallows*, as Dumbledore tells Harry of the pull between
his duties and his ambition: "when my mother died, and I was left the
responsibility of a damaged sister and a wayward brother, I returned to my
village in anger and bitterness. Trapped and wasted, I thought! And then,
of course, he came..." (573). Grindelwald's quest seems to offer escape and
fulfilment for Dumbledore. To find the resurrection stone would mean
bringing back his parents and "the lifting of all responsibility from my
shoulders" (574). These passages suggest that it was Dumbledore's ambition
which caused him to neglect his responsibilities.

The contrast between responsibility and selfishness is a major
preoccupation of Rowling's; selfishness and self-absorption are the origin of
Voldemort's evil, and selflessness is ultimately Harry's most heroic trait. I
speculate that when Rowling was writing Dumbledore's story she wrote it
primarily as an illustration of this theme, whatever she intended to do before,
or remembered she had done after.

3) The "failure to communicate" defense

The last intentionalist defense I will present is the "failure to
communicate" defense. This is the argument that Walter Benn Michaels
brings up in his discussion of the girl who says "librarie" [bookstore] when
she means "library." As Michaels explains, speakers and authors fail to
communicate all the time:

> Any time two people disagree over the meaning of a text, the author
> has failed to communicate her meaning to at least one of them. But
> it doesn't follow that she has failed to mean whatever she meant. And
> even if she failed to communicate to everyone (if, for example, she
> spoke French to a group of people who knew only English), she still
> would mean whatever she meant. So it can't really be the case that just
> because you failed to communicate what you intended you also failed
> to mean it (August 17, 2008).

None of Rowling's readers disagree that Hagrid is a half-giant, or that Hermione is a girl, so in these cases Rowling communicates her meaning to every reader. Some readers still think Snape is unredeemed after *Deathly Hallows*, however, which means that Rowling did not communicate the message of his redemption strongly enough to convince them. Walter Michaels suggests that you can criticize an author for failing to communicate what she means...but that does not mean that she failed to mean it (email, August 15, 2008).[10]

It is possible that this "failure to communicate" defense solves the problem of the gap between the text and Rowling's statement that she had always seen Dumbledore as gay. After all, as I have argued, there are some elements of the story, such as the way the younger Dumbledore draws curious stares as he walks to the orphanage in his "flamboyantly cut plum velvet suit," that could be attempts to communicate that Dumbledore is gay. Furthermore, there is nothing in the novel that would prove the opposite: that Dumbledore was heterosexual. Perhaps, then, Rowling failed to communicate that Dumbledore was gay, but did not fail to mean it.

A final possibility is that Rowling both failed to communicate that Dumbledore is gay and failed to mean it. In his 1993 book *Literary Interest*, Steven Knapp argues that in rare cases an author can fail to mean something he or she intends to mean. After carefully examining why Milton's *Paradise Lost* failed to be the Christian epic that Milton intended it to be,[11] he writes: "there is a sense in which a literary work can fail to have the content, and therefore fail even to have the form, that its author intended it to have" (27). If Rowling's intention was to depict Dumbledore as gay in her works, and to depict his infatuation with Grindelwald as the reason he accepted Grindelwald's ideas, for example, her work, too, may have failed to have the content she intended.

Knapp is talking about an unusual circumstance, however, in which the writer's logic is so contradictory that his work does not say what he intended it to say. Rowling's situation is not the same; her statements about her text sometimes seem to contradict her text, but her novels' depiction of Dumbledore is not internally contradictory, especially not on the massive

---

10 Stanley Fish makes a similar argument: "Failure to communicate a meaning does not mean that it was not intended; and while the success of communication will often be a contingent matter, depending on others and the world, the success of intending (assuming that you are not mentally ill and incapable of forming and intention) is certain" ("There is No Textualist Position" 6).

11 Knapp says that Milton "failed to project the world he intended to project" *(Literary Interest* 25).

scale Knapp is talking about. Even if Rowling's work did fit Knapp's scenario of logical implosion, Knapp goes on to argue that this situation does not mean the author's work says something else from what he or she intended. Knapp writes that "to supplement a poem [or other work] with information foreign to its author's intentions is not to elaborate the poem's world but to imagine a different world – indeed to imagine a different poem – whether or not one retains ingredients from the original poem's world" (*Literary Interest* 24). Knapp argues that Milton failed to present a narrative in which Adam was justly punished, but that does not mean he portrays God as unjust.[12] Knapp is saying, in a nutshell, that an author's meaning can very occasionally be less than he or she intends, but not more.

Therefore, if we are arguing that it was Rowling's intention to depict Dumbledore as gay, we could say that Rowling failed to communicate that he is gay, but we cannot conclude that he is not gay. To claim this is to make a new story rather than analyzing the one Rowling wrote. John Mark Reynolds, who wrote the essay "Dumbledore is not Gay," and whose championing of the authority of Rowling's text over her intentions started me on this intentionalist quest in the first place, comes to a similar conclusion by a different route; he wrote a second essay called "Dumbledore is not Hetero," in which he argues that Dumbledore's sexuality is absent from the text.

CONCLUSION

In this essay, I have explored how intentionalism might deal with the apparent gap between the text of *Deathly Hallows* and Rowling's assertions that Dumbledore is gay and infatuated with Grindelwald, and that this infatuation led him to embrace Grindelwald's sinister ideas. The first defense I consider is that Rowling may have intended the text to be read differently by two kinds of readers, children and "sensitive" adults. The second is that Rowling's statements about Dumbledore may very well not reflect her original intentions. Rowling may have changed her mind, or forgotten what, in the process of writing, she had intended. The third defense I put forward uses the argument of intentionalist Walter Michaels: to fail to communicate is not the same as to fail to mean. Though Rowling may have failed to *communicate* to some of her readers that Dumbledore is gay, it does not mean she failed to *mean* it. After considering these three defenses, I believe the right one is a blend of the three. Rowling made the text intentionally ambiguous, so that

---

12   Knapp writes that Milton intended to write a Christian epic, but if God cannot justly punish Adam according to the logic of free will in Milton's narrative, then the latter books on the punishment and redemption of man are incoherent. Therefore Milton failed to write an epic (LI 23).

children and some adults would see a different meaning than other adults. Her intention as she wrote was also different than her statements afterwards in that, as she wrote, she focused more on the danger of ambition and less on the danger of love. Finally, perhaps because she was working so hard to conceal her message from younger readers, she failed to communicate to many of her readers that Dumbledore was gay, but that does not mean she failed to mean it. What Rowling says in interviews does not determine the meaning of her texts, but what she intended as she wrote them does.

Ultimately, intentionalism remains a resilient contender in the debate about how we know what books mean. Understanding intentionalism and its rival theories can help us reflect on our own methods of interpretation, and can challenge us to look at the *Harry Potter* series in new ways.

BIBLIOGRAPHY

Barthes, Roland. "The Death of the Author." *Image, Music, Text* 1977.

Beardsley, Monroe, "The Authority of the Text." *The Possibility of Criticism.* Wayne State UP, 1970. in *Intention and Interpretation.* Philadelphia: Temple UP, 1992.

Cuddon, J.A. *Dictionary of Literary Terms and Literary Reference.* London, Penguin, 1999.

Dorf, Michael. "Harry Potter and the Framer's Intent." Findlaw. October 22, 2007. http://writ.news.findlaw.com/dorf/20071022.html. Accessed May 3, 2009.

Dutton, Dennis. "Why Intentionalism Won't Go Away." *Literature and the Question of Philosophy* ed. Anthony J. Cascardi. Baltimore: Johns Hopkins University Press, 1987. http://denisdutton.com/intentionalism.htm. Accessed May 4, 2009.

Elron, Letter, Salon.com, October 23, 2007, http://letters.salon.com/books/feature/2007/10/23/dumbledore/view/?show=ec. Accessed August 17, 2008.

Fish, Stanley. "There is No Textualist Position." *San Diego Law Review* 42:1, 2005. http://www.law.columbia.edu/null/Intention+Fish2?exclusive=filemgr.download&file_id=96496&showthumb=0. Accessed May 13, 2009.

Harry Potter Lexicon. "Help/About: The 'Wand Order Problem.'" http://www.hp-lexicon.org/about/exp-wandorder.html. Accessed August 19, 2008.

Hirsch, E.D. "In Defense of the Author." *Validity in Interpretation.* New Haven: Yale UP, 1967. Reprinted in Mitchell, below.

Hirsch, E.D. "Against Theory?" Critical Inquiry June 1983. Reprinted in Mitchell, below.

Holland, Norman N. "Unity Identity Text Self" in *Reader Response Criticism: From Formalism to Post-Structuralism.* Jane Tompkins, ed. Baltimore: John's Hopkins UP, 1980.

Holland, Norman N. *The Critical I.* New York: Columbia UP, 1992. http://www.clas.ufl.edu/users/nholland/criti.htm. Accessed March 1, 2009.

Holland, Norman N. "The Story of a Psychoanalytic Critic: an Intellectual Autobiography." September 21, 1999. http://www.clas.ufl.edu/users/nholland/autobiol.htm. Accessed May 9, 2009.

Iseminger, Gary. "An Intentional Demonstration?" *Intention and Interpretation.* Philadelphia: Temple UP, 1992.

Knapp, Steven, and Walter Benn Michaels. "Against Theory." Critical Inquiry 8:4 1982. http://academic.evergreen.edu/curricular/monstrouspossibility/DOCUMENTS/against%20theory%201.pdf. Reprinted in Mitchell, below.

Knapp, Steven, and Walter Benn Michaels. " Against Theory 2" *Critical Inquiry* 14:1,1987 49-68. Excerpted in Iseminger, *Intention and Interpretation.*

Knapp, Steven, and Walter Benn Michaels. "The Impossibility of Intentionless Meaning" Excerpts from "Against Theory" and "Against Theory 2." In Mitchell, below.

Knapp, Steven. *Literary Interest: The Limits of Anti-Formalism.* Cambridge: Harvard UP, 1993.

Melkorsbane. PsyDmama. Comments. Digg.com. October 31, 2007. http://digg. com/celebrity/J_K_Rowling_Reveals_Dumbledore_is_Gay?t=9978346. Accessed March 1, 2009.

Michaels, Walter Benn. Email Correspondence with K. Kebarle. August 15, 2008. August 17, 2008, January 26, 2009, April 30, 2009.

Michaels, Walter Benn. *The Shape of the Signifier.* Princeton, NJ: Princeton UP, 2004.

Mitchell, W.J.T. *Against Theory: Literary Studies and the New Pragmatism.* Chicago: U of Chicago Press, 1985.

Reynolds, John Mark "Dumbledore is Not Gay." The Scriptorium. October 23, 2007. http://www.scriptoriumdaily.com/2007/10/23/dumbledore-is-not-gay-taking-stories-more-seriously-than-the-author/. Accessed June 9, 2008, February 25, 2009.

Reynolds, John Mark. "Dumbledore is Not Hetero." The Scriptorium. October 24, 2007. http://www.scriptoriumdaily.com/2007/10/24/dumbledore-is-not-hetero-taking-stories-more-seriously-than-the-author-ii/. Accessed February 25, 2009.

Rowling, J.K. "Albus Dumbledore on the Tale of the Three Brothers." *The Tales of Beedle the Bard.* London: Children's High Level Group, 2007/2008.

___. *Harry Potter and the Deathly Hallows.* New York: Scholastic, 2007.

___. *Harry Potter and the Half-Blood Prince.* New York: Scholastic, 2005

___. *Harry Potter and the Order of the Phoenix.* New York: Scholastic, 2004.

___. *Harry Potter and the Prisoner of Azkaban.* New York: Scholastic, 2001.

Rowling. J.K. Interview, Carnegie Hall. October 19, 2007. http://www.the-leaky-cauldron.org/2007/10/20/j-k-rowling-at-carnegie-hall-reveals-dumbledore-is-gay-neville-marries-hannah-abbott-and-scores-more. Accessed June 9, 2008.

Rowling, J.K. Press Conference. Toronto, CBC. October 22, 2007. www. accio-quote.org/articles/2007/1022-torontopressconf.html. Accessed May 4, 2009.

Rowling, J.K. Interview. Pottercast 130. The Leaky Cauldron.org, December 18, 2007. http://www.the-leaky-cauldron.org/transcript/show/166?ordernum=2. Accessed May 4, 2009.

Rowling. J.K. Interview. Pottercast 131.The Leaky Cauldron.org. January 2, 2008. http://www.the-leaky-cauldron.org/2008/1/2/pottercast-131-j-k-rowling-interview-transcript. Accessed March 1, 2009.

Rowling, J.K. Interview, Adeel Amini. "In Conversation with J.K. Rowling." reposted from "The Student" 04/03/08. facebook.com "Adeel Amini's Notes." www.facebook.com.note.php?note_id=12898286487 Accessed May 4, 2009.

Traister, Rebecca. "Dumbledore? Gay. J.K. Rowling? Chatty." Salon.com October 23, 2007. http://www.salon.com/books/feature/2007/10/23/dumbledore/index.html. Accessed February 25, 2009.

Tyson, Louis. *Critical Theory Today: A User-Friendly Guide.* In J. Case Tompkins, Allen Brizee "Reader Response Criticism : 1960's-the present." Literary Theory, The OWL at Purdue, Purdue U English Department, February 14, 2008. http://owl.english.purdue.edu/owl/resource/722/06/ Accessed February 28, 2009.

Wimsatt, W.K, and Monroe Beardsley, "The Intentional Fallacy." *The Verbal Icon: Studies in the Meaning of Poetry.* Lexington: U. of Kentucky Press, 1954. http://faculty.smu.edu/nschwart/seminar/Fallacy.htm. Accessed February 25, 2009.

Part V

Conversations on Characters

Chapter Nine

Ginny Weasley, Girl Next-Doormat?

Gwendolyn Limbach

   Among the female characters in her age group, Ginny Weasley is one of the stronger girls we encounter throughout the *Harry Potter* series; however, her role as Harry's future and actual love interest limits her development. Ginny is kept in the periphery of the first four books, marginalized from the main story (read: Harry's story) until Harry begins to mature and girls become sexually interesting. Even when her actions indirectly constitute the main plot line of *Chamber of Secrets*, Ginny is never central to the story of The Boy Who Lived. Many fans have noted that Ginny's position as the first girl to be born into the Weasley family in generations must mean that she holds importance to the story. But as J.K. Rowling reveals, that importance lies in being Harry's love object, not in destabilizing Voldemort's reign of terror. Ginny has shown herself to be a powerful witch, yet that power to fight is secondary, as in many gender-role-enforcing narratives, to her destiny to marry. Throughout the series, Rowling implements various narrative tropes that reinforce her construction of Ginny as traditional wife, from having Harry save her life to beginning their erotic relationship in terms of exchange between men (Harry and Ron). When the trio embark on their extended camping trip, Harry fashions Ginny into the personification of peace time and normalcy, Hegel's "Beautiful Soul," that he can reminisce about on lonely nights away from home. As the time for open war is upon him, Harry refuses Ginny the agency to transcend this role and become the fighter that she clearly desires to be. Even when her skills in battle are evident, Harry's paternalism continually attempts to restrain Ginny; her desire to defeat the Dark Lord means little in the face of Harry's desire to restrict her in the name of "protection."[1] Ultimately, though she has shown herself to be a gifted and spirited witch, Ginny is defined by her relationship to Harry rather than on her own terms or in her own right. As with too many potentially powerful female characters before her, Ginny Weasley is forced to subjugate her agency

1   Never mind the fact that Harry never attempts to "protect" anyone else as he does Ginny.

in service of Harry's desires and his hero's journey.

RESCUE FROM THE CHAMBER OF SECRETS

In the second book of the series, Ginny finally gets her wish and attends Hogwarts, but her level of visibility increases only slightly. Throughout the book she is mentioned mostly in passing narration to foreshadow her connection to the Chamber of Secrets. Everyone in the castle is under threat from the monster in the Chamber, but none more so than Ginny. Though she is able to open the Chamber and unleash the basilisk, she is powerless over the monster. Her involvement with Tom Riddle's diary and the Chamber of Secrets reveals not only her powerlessness in the situation but also her exploitation at the hands of older men. Lucius Malfoy sneaks the diary into Ginny's schoolbooks to achieve his own ends by using Ginny's position as new student and Weasley child. The bad blood between Lucius and Arthur Weasley[2] is well known, and has also translated into a rivalry between the younger Weasley children and Draco Malfoy. When the two men meet at the beginning of *Chamber of Secrets*, they come to blows in the middle of Flourish and Blotts. Moments before their fight, Lucius slips the diary into one of Ginny's schoolbooks. While he is doing this Lucius insults Arthur for "being a disgrace to the name of wizard" for raiding the homes of suspected dark witches and wizards and, as evidenced by his contempt for Ginny's used books, his poverty. Both men are pure-bloods, but Lucius looks down upon Arthur for his lack of "proper" pure-blood pride and his lack of money. Rowling reinforces the connection between Lucius's disdain for Arthur and his exploitation of Arthur's daughter when he gives Ginny the Transfiguration book that contains Riddle's diary, saying, "'Here, girl – take your book – it's the best your father can give you – '" (Rowling, *Chamber* 63). Here Lucius explicitly connects Ginny, the diary, and Arthur to reflect his own internal connection of the three and emphasize to the reader how close they are (or will be).

Dumbledore sees the link quite easily when Lucius storms into Hogwarts after Ginny's rescue from the Chamber. The headmaster explains that, had Harry and Ron not found the diary, "'Ginny Weasley might have taken all the blame. No one would ever have been able to prove that she hadn't acted of her own free will... what might have happened then... The Weasleys are one of our most prominent pure-blood families. Imagine the effect on Arthur Weasley and his Muggle Protection Act, if his own daughter was discovered attacking Muggle-borns'" (335-336). Clearly Lucius tried to dishonor his

---

2   In Sir Thomas Mallory's *Le Morte d'Arthur* one of King Arthur's rivals was the Roman emperor Lucius, whom Arthur killed with Excalibur.

rival through manipulating his rival's daughter into opening the Chamber and instigating a third party to wreak havoc on the school, if not perpetrating those deeds herself. For Lucius, Ginny is a means to an end, a tool to be used in his plans to publicly disgrace Arthur. Too often in literature, and in real life, daughters are made to be the vessels of honor for their families and especially their fathers. In *Pride and Prejudice*, the Bennet family is disgraced when their youngest daughter Lydia elopes[3] with Wickham and lives with him out of wedlock. Lydia's reputation now threatens all her sisters' chances of ever being married and, through them, their mother's livelihood since, after Mr. Bennet's death, ownership of the family home of Longbourn passes to someone else. The belief is that girls and women are the vessels of a family's honor (and that vessel often exists between their legs), and that their personal behavior reflects upon the entire family's honor. Obviously the Weasleys do not severely punish Ginny for her involvement in the Chamber, and her role here is not made public. Yet Lucius's scheme to shame Arthur through Ginny's actions is clearly based on the assumption that the easiest and most effective way to disgrace an enemy is through his daughter.

Through Lucius Malfoy's actions, the piece of Tom Riddle's soul preserved in the diary is able to manipulate Ginny into fulfilling the diary's purpose of not only opening the Chamber of Secrets but also restoring the piece of soul to full existence. Whereas Lucius specifically chose Ginny because of who she is (rather, whose daughter she is), Riddle has little choice in whom he uses to emerge from the diary. What provides the most interesting avenue of exploration in this instance is how possession, both physically and metaphorically, functions in the narrative. In the horror genre of films in the 1970s and 1980s, writer Tammy Oler considers that for girls in these movies growing up is both a curse and a potential "source of tremendous power" (34). She contends that these films "propose a distinctly feminine source of power that must hide behind a satanic or otherworldly guise" (34). The divergences from these films in *Harry Potter*, however, are manifold. Whereas the horror films that Oler discusses focus on female protagonists like Carrie and Regan from *The Exorcist*, Ginny's story is never the center of Harry's specifically male narrative. The possessor is male and gives Ginny no tangible power other than speaking Parseltongue and releasing the basilisk. Even when she is possessed Ginny remembers nothing of what she has done (Rowling, *Chamber* 310). And when Riddle's plans are nearly complete, he tries to sacrifice Ginny on the (proverbial) altar of Salazar Slytherin to restore him to full life. Ginny is the object, the conduit if you will, of this narrative but never its subject. In stories about the supernatural possession of young

---

3   Elopement in this context does not mean the same as marriage

girls by an evil force, in both the horror films of Oler's discussion and in *Harry Potter*, the girls "are never truly agents of their own power. They are able to act only in relation to the greater forces that victimize them" (Oler 35). Before and after her ordeal with Tom Riddle, Ginny is still only Ron's sister, shy and quiet, who has a crush on famous Harry Potter.

Ginny also plays the part of the passive damsel in distress to Harry's knight in shining armor when he comes to rescue her from the Chamber. Specifically, Harry rescues Ginny from the peril that she got herself into. While trying to suss out Ginny's predicament, Harry asks Tom Riddle how Ginny "got like this"; Tom answers, "'I suppose the real reason Ginny Weasley's like this is because she opened her heart and spilled all her secrets to an invisible stranger'" (*Chamber* 309). After Dumbledore explains to the Weasleys how Voldemort has managed to enchant Ginny through the diary, Mr. Weasley admonishes his daughter for not following his "fatherly advice": "'Haven't I taught you *anything*? What have I always told you? Never trust anything that can think for itself *if you can't see where it keeps its brain*? Why didn't you show the diary to me or your mother?'" (329). Both Riddle and Arthur explicitly place the blame for Ginny's predicament on Ginny herself, through her naïveté in trusting a stranger. Like Sleeping Beauty trusting the disguised wicked witch and pricking her finger on the loom, Ginny has been hoodwinked by dark forces and brought trouble upon herself and the castle. For someone who has been kept in a passive object position for the majority of her interaction with Riddle,[4] when the time comes to deal with the consequences Ginny is expected to answer for her actions as though she were an active agent in the events.

Yet being the passive object of rescue is what Ginny has been set up to do throughout the book. When possessed by Riddle, Ginny (or rather, her body) must passively carry out his bidding; Ginny also remains silent throughout her ideal and is silenced when she does try to ask for help. It should come as no surprise that, when Harry enters the Chamber of Secrets to rescue her, Ginny is unconscious. With Ginny firmly in her object position, Harry is able to be the active agent of rescue and in effect reenact the King Arthur legend. Many people have already written about the connections between *Harry Potter* and the Arthur legend, postulating that Harry is the "prince in hiding" who becomes King Arthur of Camelot. Yet we must not forget that there is already one Arthur in the series: Mr. Weasley. We also know that Ginevra, Ginny's full name, is a derivation of Guinevere.

4   Though at first Ginny's writing in her diary may be considered an active subject position, because she has an authentic voice in writing, this is recounted only through Riddle and functions to repress and mock her voice.

That Arthur and Guinevere are married in the original legend but closely related in *Harry Potter* begs us to reconsider the tale. After shuddering at the incestual implications here, when we take into account Sir Thomas Mallory's *Le Morte d'Arthur*, the most widely read version of the King Arthur legend, we must bear in mind that Guinevere was betrothed to Arthur from a young age and married him more out of a sense of duty than feelings of true love. Also consider that in Mallory's version Lancelot saves Guinevere, who is held captive by Malagent, in Arthur's stead and then returns her to her husband. Rather than classifying Harry as King Arthur, it seems more likely that in Rowling's revision of the legend, Harry is Lancelot.

Though Harry is able to wield the sword of Godric Gryffindor by pulling it out of the Sorting Hat, this action is not the same as young Arthur pulling Excalibur from the stone.[5] Retrieving the sword is a sign of personal bravery rather than divine law that one is meant to rule. Allowing anyone the ability to have the sword gives the original legend an egalitarian twist common to many children's books. Situating Harry as a new Lancelot also allows the characters a happier tale than was their original lot. According to Rowling's revision, Lancelot is not the disgraced and treasonous knight who has an affair with King Arthur's wife; Guinevere is not betrothed to someone she does not love, and she does not betray him by loving Lancelot (nor is she vilified by the author for her infidelity); and Arthur is not betrayed by both his wife and his knight and does not die because he left the country to fight in the Crusades to escape all thought of Guinevere and Lancelot. This new vision of the King Arthur legend seems to benefit the involved parties overall, yet it still necessitates a rescue of the helpless damsel by the heroic knight. In her examination of feminist children's literature, Roberta Seelinger Trites quotes Jack Zipes stating, "Folk tales and fairy tales have always been dependent of customs, rituals, and values in the particular socialization process of a social system. They have always symbolically depicted the nature of power within a given society" (Trites 45). In other words, "the ways a culture uses folk tales reflect the culture's values" (45). Though Rowling has re-envisioned Mallory's King Arthur legend to benefit the three main parties, it is still dependent on female weakness. The author has not attempted to revise the depiction of the nature of power within English (magical) society, and as a result dominant cultural norms remain intact to the detriment of Ginny Weasley and female readers.

---

5   Or retrieving it from the Lady in the Lake, as Ron reenacts in *Deathly Hallows*.

EROTIC TRIANGLES

Rowling continues a more romantic imagining of classic themes in the modern hero's journey through the trials and tribulations of desire and young love. What is most interesting in the series about the desiring relationships of the characters, mainly Harry, is that they are composed of a mimetic or triangulated desire. In René Girard's *Deceit, Desire, and the Novel*, the author traces the structure of desiring relationships in some classic works of literature[6] based on the rivalry of two men over a common object of desire. Eve Kosofsky Sedgwick takes Girard's work further by theorizing that "in any erotic rivalry, the bond that links the two rivals is as intense and potent as the bond that links either of the rivals to the beloved: that the bonds of 'rivalry' and 'love,' differently as they are experienced, are equally powerful and in many senses equivalent" (21). Sedgwick posits that the rivalry between the two active (read: male) members of the triangle constitutes a homosocial bond that has more social primacy than heterosexual bonds between a rival and the desired. The homosocial bond is regulated by "the use of women as exchangeable, perhaps symbolic, property for the primary purpose of cementing the bonds of men with men" (25-26). To explore the specifics of how erotic triangles and homosocial desire function in Harry's narrative, we shall examine the three major instances, beginning with the Harry-Cho-Cedric triangle in *Goblet of Fire*.

Both Girard and Sedgwick cite many literary examples "in which the choice of the beloved is determined in the first place not by the qualities of the beloved, but by the beloved's already being the choice of the person who has been chosen as rival" (Sedgwick 21). In Girard's formulation, the protagonist's rival, or external mediator, is someone whom the protagonist looks up to and is out of reach of said protagonist, as Don Quixote admires the fictional character Amadis of Gaul as an idol of chivalry (Girard 2-4). Cedric is revered by many and positioned above Harry in *Prisoner of Azkaban* and *Goblet of Fire*; Harry acknowledges Cedric's higher position when he compares himself to the other Hogwarts Champion and realizes that Cedric fits the description much better than he. Cedric is almost three years older than Harry; a school prefect; Seeker and Captain of the Hufflepuff Quidditch team; the girls on the Gryffindor team find him quite attractive; and Cedric was the first person to ever catch the Snitch before Harry.[7] After Harry establishes a rivaling relationship with Cedric he then meets Cho Chang. The narrator mentions in passing that "Harry couldn't help noticing, nervous

6   The works of Cervantes, Stendhal, Flaubert, Proust, and Dostoevsky
7   Though Cedric protests that it was unfair due to the dementor's interference, even Wood admits he got the Snitch fair and square

as he was, that she was extremely pretty" (*Prisoner* 259). Already by the end of *Prisoner of Azkaban* we know more about Cedric and Harry's feelings toward him than we know about Cho. Harry may develop a crush during *Goblet of Fire*, but he never attempts to speak to Cho, or even bothers to learn more about her, until he is forced to find a date for the Yule Ball. When Harry does ask Cho to go with him, and she tells him she already has a partner, he feels like "he didn't... have any insides at all" (Rowling, *Goblet* 397). These pangs of disappointment suddenly solidify into jealousy when Harry learns Cedric is to be Cho's date: "His insides had come back again. It felt as though they had been filled with lead in their absence" (397). At this point Harry's feelings toward Cedric carry more weight, literally, than those toward Cho.

After the ball it is this same jealousy that stops Harry from taking Cedric's advice about the clue to the second task. Harry wonders whether Cedric is "trying to make Harry look like a fool, so Cho would like him [Cedric] even more by comparison" (432). Harry's jealousy of his rival for his possession of the desired object is made explicit when Harry thinks "he [doesn't] need that sort of help—not from someone who kept walking down corridors hand in hand with Cho" (435). Here Harry enacts Girard's contention that the bond between rivals is "even stronger, more heavily determinant of actions and choices, than anything in the bond between either of the lovers and the beloved" (Sedgwick 21). Harry jeopardizes his chances in accomplishing the second task rather than rely on Cedric for help; Harry's relationship with Cho, or rather lack of, has no influence on his actions in the book[8] and his desire for her is always secondary to his competition with Cedric. Throughout the tournament Harry becomes equal to Cedric, not in point standing, but in terms of maturity and skill level. By the third task they enter the maze as equals; Cedric has shifted from an external mediator to an internal one.[9] Suddenly within the maze's walls Harry is the more capable of the two: he stupefies Krum, who used the Cruciatus Curse on Cedric, and he warns Cedric of the spider about to attack him on his sprint to the Cup (*Goblet* 627, 631). The two defeat the spider together, but Harry is too injured to reach the Cup before Cedric; he thinks bitterly that "Cedric had beaten him to it, just as he'd beaten Harry to ask Cho to the ball" (633). Though rhetorically they are presented as peer rivals, Harry still views Cedric as unreachable because the latter possesses the object of their desire. When Cedric offers the Cup to Harry, Harry imagines finally transcending his rival and all that it entails: "He saw himself holding the Triwizard Cup aloft, heard the roar of

---

8   Other than asking her to the Yule Ball and, perhaps, fantasizing about warranting her admiration after winning the Triwizard Tournament.

9   For Girard, an internal mediator is one who is at the same level as the protagonist.

the crowd, *saw Cho's face shining with admiration*, more clearly than he had ever seen it before" (634, emphasis added). For Harry, beating Cedric in their competition for the Triwizard Tournament translates directly into possessing, if not the object of desire herself, at least her admiration. The vision quickly fades with Harry's internal realization that he can never outmatch Cedric when he sees the other's "stubborn" face; Harry resolves that now, at least, they may be equals and decides that they should take the Cup and triumph together.

Harry's maturation not only in age but also in awareness of danger, now tangible from Harry's encounter with Voldemort and the Death Eaters, is illustrated by Harry surviving and surpassing his rival; through Cedric's death Harry learns to face his own possible death. In Girard's study of triangulated desire, the protagonist does not transcend his mediator; however, in Rowling's work, Cedric is converted from an external mediator, to an internal one, and finally returns to an (altogether different kind of) external mediator. Rowling takes this external mediation one step further with the memory of Cedric mediating the triangle. When Dumbledore honors Cedric at the leaving feast by raising his goblet, Harry immediately glimpses Cho crying silently (721). By the time Harry sees Cho next, on their way to Hogwarts the following fall, Cedric's memory does not stand between them, at least for Harry. Cedric's power of mediation fades eventually and his death serves as a reminder and inspiration to Harry to fight against the evil forces in his world, much as Amadis inspires Don Quixote to chivalry.

With Cedric no longer his rival, Harry and Cho appear able to pursue their attraction for one another without a mediator. Though Harry's desire for Cho sprang from his connection with Cedric, the desire remains after the death of the mediator; because we are given no background to Cho's interest in Harry, we may assume there is no mediator here either.[10] In *Order of the Phoenix*, however, Rowling rhetorically evokes a new triangle, though not quite a mimetic one, through the introduction of Ginny to the Harry-Cho dynamic. Rowling established in *Chamber of Secrets* Ginny's crush on Harry, and though Ginny is currently dating someone else at this time, she tells Harry later in *Half-Blood Prince* that "'I never really gave up on you...Not really. I always hoped...'" (647). Ginny has taken Hermione's advice and begun to "go out with some other people" to relax around Harry, so we may assume that when Harry's fifth year begins Ginny still harbors her crush. In most fan essays dissecting Ginny's character, the authors point to *Order of the Phoenix*

10　Of course, we may also say that Cedric plays a part in Cho's desire for Harry, but because there is no competition between the two for Harry, Girard's version of the erotic triangle is missing.

as Ginny's "debut." In his essay entitled "Ginny Weasley: A Gryffindor and a Match for Harry," Tim Lambarski states that "Rowling finally defines Ginny's personality" in this book. While it is true that we see more of Ginny and begin to better understand her character, the reason for her newly prominent position does her character a disservice. Rather than presenting Ginny to the reader more often simply to flesh-out another character in the series, Rowling does so only to demonstrate Ginny's suitability as a love interest for Harry and foreshadow their relationship. Lambarski notes this design as well, stating, "Rowling has developed Ginny's character slowly through the books, giving her a personality that makes her a fit match for Harry." The author's sole purpose in creating and revealing Ginny's character is to set up Ginny's eventual marriage to Harry. To help accomplish this development, Rowling pairs Cho and Ginny throughout *Order of the Phoenix* to highlight Cho's incompatibility, and Ginny's compatibility, with Harry; in the process she (perhaps inadvertently) creates an erotic triangle that questions, yet ultimately reaffirms, Girard's masculinist trope.

Throughout the fifth book, whenever Cho appears in the scene Ginny is also present or appears soon after. Because we are (slightly) more familiar with Ginny than we are with Cho, and because Rowling intends to add depth to Ginny's character, Cho acts as a foil to Ginny. Their pairing is established in Harry's first meeting with Cho on the Hogwarts Express: Harry is sitting in a car with Ginny, Luna Lovegood, and Neville Longbottom, all covered in Stinksap, when Cho walks in on them. Cho quickly leaves, to Harry's embarrassment, and Ginny interrupts his thoughts, "bracingly" says "Never mind," and cleans up the Stinksap, rhetorically trying to erase Cho's presence from Harry's thoughts (Rowling, *Order* 188). In almost every instance of their pairing in the book, Ginny is portrayed in a better light than Cho. Whereas Cho is weepy all the time, nervous around Harry, and confusing to him, Ginny is portrayed as vivacious, adept at both magic and Quidditch, and easygoing. When the D.A. has its first meeting and decides what they will call their group, Cho suggests "'The Defense Association?...The D.A. for short, so nobody knows what we're talking about?'" Whereas Cho speaks in questions, Ginny makes declarative statements, changing Cho's suggestion: "'Yeah, the D.A.'s good... Only let's make it stand for Dumbledore's Army'" (302). During that meeting's practice Ginny performs the disarming spell very well, but Cho cannot even say the incantation correctly. In the rest of the meetings of the D.A. Ginny can be counted on to generally outperform Cho.

After Harry is banned from playing Quidditch, Ginny takes his place on the team as Seeker and, once again, bests Cho in competition. As Ron recounts the match to Harry he says, "'Did you see the look on Chang's face when Ginny got the Snitch right out from under her nose?'" (704). In this passage one can easily replace "Snitch" with "Harry" and the image evokes the same message: Ginny and Cho competing for Harry's affections, with Ginny ultimately triumphant. By the end of the novel, with Harry and Cho firmly separated, Rowling ends the foil with practically a trade between Cho and Ginny: Ginny has broken up with her Ravenclaw boyfriend Michael Corner after he sulked over losing the Quidditch match, and now Michael is dating Cho. Though Ginny is now dating Dean Thomas, Harry is now free from a distracting emotional entanglement with Ginny's foil and can now focus on the (future) object of his desire.

Whereas the erotic triangle between Harry, Cedric, and Cho fits within the scope of Girard's conception of the trope, the desire between Harry, Cho, and Ginny has the potential to fully turn that triangle on its head. With both Cho and Ginny in the position of rivals, Harry becomes the object of desire, unbeknownst to him. Placing Harry in an object position, a position that is rarely, if ever, occupied by a man, questions the privilege accorded to men within the power dynamics of desire. With Harry as object potentially traded between female subjects, both Ginny and Cho become agents of their own desire, actively participating in the sexual economy in which they heretofore were simply commodities. Yet because this is Harry's narrative, he sees himself only as the subject who desires, not as the object who is desired by another. Harry becomes the site of a chiasmus[11] between active and passive positions in the sexual economy. Because we never see Cho as an active participant in her desire,[12] besides perhaps moving in close to Harry under the mistletoe before their kiss, Harry is able to place her firmly in her original object position. Due to his male privilege, Harry never recognizes the desire of either Cho or Ginny and never sees himself as its object. Also in opposition to Girard's triangle is the lack of any bond between Ginny and Cho. The rivalry is not as evident as the one between Harry and Cedric, and any sort of bond between Ginny and Cho is tenuous at best. Whereas mimetic desire bonds the two male members of the triangle through not merely a rivalry but more importantly through homosociality, female rivals cannot form such a bond because, simply put, they are female. For homosocial bonds to exist, there must be a certain taboo on close relationships between men, so that

---

11   A diagonal crossing of elements, usually a "grammatical figure by which the order of words in one of two parallel clauses is inverted in the other" (OED).

12   Because Ginny is not the focus of Harry's attraction at this point he pays no attention to her erotic relationships.

any desire men feel towards one another[13] must be routed through women. Because women, to an extent, are permitted to form close bonds with one another their sociality is not always forced to be routed through men. In contrast to men, when women desire the same object, their bond conforms to the "Freudian model of women competing for a man's love," driving them apart rather than bringing them closer (Trites 92). The competition between Cho and Ginny is implied rather than outright, yet the potential for a bond analogous to that of Cedric and Harry is not fulfilled. Though a Ginny-Cho-Harry triangle could bring into question Girard's male-centric erotic triangle tropes, Rowling reaffirms the literary tradition. It appears that simply because Harry is male and the protagonist he is able to reinscribe the dominant prescriptions of gendered desire.

Once Cho and Harry's relationship is finally severed, the triangular desire shifts once again to include a new active participant, though an unexpected and, ultimately, traditional one. Although foreshadowed in *Order of the Phoenix* and *Half-Blood Prince*, Harry does not recognize his attraction to Ginny as a viable erotic object until he literally sees evidence of her value in the male transactive circulation. On the way back to Gryffindor Tower, Harry and Ron stumble upon Ginny and Dean "locked in a close embrace and kissing fiercely as though glued together" (Rowling, *Half-Blood* 286). Up to this point Harry has not actually seen Ginny sexually engaged with a boyfriend, so he has never considered her sexuality. Sedgwick contends that "erotic perceptions are entirely shaped by the structure of the male traffic in women – the use of women by men as exchangeable objects, as counters of value, for the primary purpose of cementing relationships with other men" (123). Harry does not include Ginny in this sexual economy until Dean shows him that she has already been introduced to it; Harry has continually viewed Ginny as his best friend's (non-sexual) sister, but now she has been transformed into eroticized forbidden fruit. At the same moment that Harry finally realizes his desire for Ginny, he instantly thinks of Ron: "unbidden in his mind came an image of that same deserted corridor with himself kissing Ginny instead... The monster in his chest purred... but then he saw Ron ripping open the tapestry curtain and drawing his wand on Harry, shouting things like 'betrayal of trust...supposed to be my friend'" (*Half-Blood* 289). Girard contends that "In the birth of desire, the third person is always present" (21). Thus a new erotic triangle is formed between Harry, Ginny, and Ron.

---

13 When I say "desire" here that does not necessarily translate to sexual desire but rather platonic desire.

While in Sedgwick's formulation of literary homosocial desire the triangle between the two male agents and the objectified female is an erotic one, it is not the singular expression of the triangle. Whereas the desire Harry now feels for Ginny is indeed erotic (and we may assume the same for Ginny's feelings toward Harry), the love between Harry and Ron is framed in purely platonic terms[14]; the love between Ron and Ginny is purely filial, yet the desire between all of them, in its various permutations, is the basis for the triangular relationship through much of *Half-Blood Prince* and parts of *Deathly Hallows*. As Harry ruminates on his new-found feelings for Ginny, his most immediate thought is that "*She's out of bounds.* He [Harry] would not risk his friendship with Ron for anything" (290). Now Harry's relationship with Ron is contingent on his relationship with Ginny and vice versa; unbeknownst to him, Ron has become the internal mediator in the triangle. Though Ron does not possess Ginny in the same way that Cedric possessed Cho, he is the acting patriarch for the Weasley family at Hogwarts and therefore has the power (at least in Harry's mind and in the traditional sense of family ownership of a daughter) to allow or forbid Ginny and Harry to form a sexual relationship. In his study of kinship traditions, Claude Levi-Strauss posits that "The total relationship of exchange which constitutes marriage is not established between a man and a woman, but between two groups of men, and the woman figures only as one of the objects of exchange, not as one of the partners"[15] (quoted in Sedgwick 26). While there is not a rivalry between Harry and Ron to the extent that there was one between Harry and Cedric, their bond is much stronger and more central to the narrative than either boy's bond to Ginny; "it is crucial to every aspect of social structure within the exchange-of-women framework that heavily freighted bonds between men exist, as the backbone of social form or forms" (Sedgwick 86). Hence Harry worries about losing Ron as a friend simply for desiring his sister even before he considers pursuing said desire. And he cannot pursue her without gambling his bond with Ron; Harry feels sure that if Ron discovered his desire for Ginny, Ron would at the very least hit him and at the most end their five-year friendship. Until the final Quidditch match, "the battle still raged inside his head: *Ginny or Ron?*" (*Half-Blood* 519). Though Harry acts impulsively when he sees Ginny after Gryffindor has won the Quidditch Cup and kisses her without warning, after the kiss "Harry's eyes [sought] Ron" and "[f]or a fraction of a second they looked at each other, then Ron gave a tiny jerk of the head that Harry

---

14   To the chagrin of many Ron/Harry shippers

15   While marriage is not discussed here, it is an eventuality of Ginny and Harry's romantic relationship.

understood to mean, *Well – if you must*" (534). Rather than simply accept Ginny's apparent desire for him, Harry implicitly seeks the permission of his friend and Ginny's representative patriarch before continuing any further. While obtaining Ron's approval is central to their homosocial bond, at the same time Harry's action denies Ginny's ability to decide for herself alone who she pursues a sexual relationship with. Though the "giving of a sister in marriage to cement the love of the brother for another man is central" in many narratives,[16] at the moment when Ron sees his best mate kissing his sister we have to wonder what ran through his mind (Sedgwick 124). Does he realize that his bond with Harry depends very much on his approval, or at least acceptance, of the match?

To emphasize the importance of the homosocial bond and its transaction over the body of Ginny, we shall momentarily enter the realm of pure conjecture. By denying Harry access to his sister, Ron could have effectively broken, or at least seriously damaged their friendship. Harry could ignore Ron's denial and sever the bond. Or he could acquiesce to Ron's desire. Consider the tension now created between the two boys: Harry may resent Ron for denying him Ginny, and Ron may stubbornly resent Harry for thinking of Ginny as a viable object of erotic desire. Because their homosocial desire for one another has not been cemented through the exchange of Ginny from one male to another (in effect from patriarch to husband), the desire and the bond has dissolved. Taking this into account, what choice did Ron have but to give his consent?

By using a narrative trope that reduces female characters to property traded between men without attempting to rewrite said trope, Rowling reinscribes dominant cultural traditions of the exchange of passive women between men. Rather than enabling Ginny to be an active agent of her desire for Harry, the author forces her to maintain an object position until the hero is ready to pursue her. Though Ginny has proven herself to be an active fighter and vivacious character, her appearance in the books, and her fate in the series, seem to be solely at Harry's discretion. To wit, Ginny only becomes a prominent character in the series when Harry sexually matures and gains experience through Cho Chang. Rowling has both Harry and Ginny reenact the fairy tale tropes of Heroic Knight and Damsel in Distress from the time of Ginny's first year at Hogwarts. Four years later, Ginny still must wait for her "knight" to arrive and bring her forth to the world of the living, where she may experience her surroundings as a central character in it.

---

16 Such as Tennyson's epic poem *The Princess,* See also Charles Dickens' *Our Mutual Friend* where a triangle forms between a sister, her brother, and the impoverished friend of the brother who wishes to marry the sister.

The Second War and The "Beautiful Soul" Trope

Though not quite the same trope as the damsel in distress, the Beautiful Soul paradigm also typifies another traditional and restrictive gender role, one which Ginny is forced into when her romantic relationship with Harry ends. At Dumbledore's funeral, Harry decides that he cannot continue dating Ginny because "'Voldemort uses people his enemies are close to. He's already used you as bait once, and that was just because you're my best friend's sister. Think how much danger you'll be in if we keep this up... He'll try and get to me through you'" (*Half-Blood* 646). Harry establishes the seemingly insurmountable divide between the fighter and the noncombatant; in his eyes Ginny cannot be a fighter in the same way that he is one; rather, she is a liability. When Harry leaves Ginny, literally "turn[ing] his back" on her, he reaffirms the cultural tradition of placing women outside the parameters of war and inside the home. The term "Beautiful Soul" comes from Hegel's *Phenomenology of Spirit*, in which he characterizes the "beautiful soul" as "a being defined by a mode of consciousness which allows him or her to protect 'the appearance of purity by cultivating innocence about the historical course of the world'" (Elshtain 4). Professor Jean Bethke Elshtain elaborates on Hegel's words by noting that "women in Western culture have served as collective, culturally designated 'beautiful souls'" (4). She later continues, "they [Beautiful Souls] are a necessary condition for, though not an integral part of, the world of free citizens... insulated through dense historic and social repetitions from the bruising realities of the 'actual world' (Hegel's locution), the Beautiful Soul serves as a repository of innocent convictions and self-definitions" for the Just Warrior (140). To maintain the dichotomy between his Just Warrior role and Ginny's Beautiful Soul role, Harry attempts to divorce Ginny of all associations with violence and war.

While Harry bears the mantle of the Just Warrior, he refuses to allow Ginny an equal position by his side. This is not to say, of course, that Harry disallows any woman to fight equally by his side. Hermione has time and again joined Harry to fight against Voldemort and even Professor Umbridge over the course of their friendship. Ginny, however, is no longer only Harry's friend; when their relationship shifts from platonic to erotic, Harry becomes protective and nearly paternalistic in his conduct towards Ginny. Even before his grand gesture of breaking up with Ginny "for her own protection" Harry intervenes in the first real one-on-one fight we see Ginny in during the Death Eaters' invasion of Hogwarts. As Harry chases Snape down the Astronomy Tower and through the skirmish, intent on catching the man who killed Dumbledore, he stops to curse the Death Eater who is "locked in combat" with Ginny (598). Harry's interference undermines the clear demonstration of Ginny's skill in battle,[17] making it easier for him to separate Ginny from his fight with Voldemort. Because there is such a divide in Harry's mind between the Ginny he loves and the battle he must fight against Voldemort, Harry sees Ginny solely in terms of the Beautiful Soul narrative.

Hegel's discourse of the Beautiful Soul was popularized in the late eighteenth and early nineteenth centuries when "woman as Beautiful Soul became a constitutive myth explaining, justifying, perhaps even serving as a consolation for, women's retreat from sites she once routinely occupied" (142). This "constitutive myth" seems to still hold sway in today's war narratives, for it is without any qualms that Harry leaves Ginny behind to venture into (a slightly more figurative) battle against Voldemort. Throughout his time at the Burrow before Fleur and Bill's wedding, Harry attempts to see Ginny as more than his former erotic love object as he transforms her into the Beautiful Soul he needs to define his existence as Just Warrior. What Harry needs is a Beautiful Soul figure to assuage his doubts and fears concerning the last part of his quest as well as someone to fulfill his sexual and emotional needs

Harry is unable to accept Ginny's sexuality together with her "beautiful soul" purity until she forces him to acknowledge the convergence of both on his birthday. As Harry turns 17 and wizarding culture declares him a man, Ginny commemorates the occasion by offering herself to him. Ginny commodifies herself with nearly absurd ease and places herself fully within a sexual economy. Ginny's locution is truly telling: "'I couldn't think *what to get you* ... I didn't know *what would be useful* ... So then I thought, I'd like you to *have something to remember me by*, you know, if you meet some veela when you're off doing whatever you're doing'" (*Deathly* 115-116, emphasis added). Ginny's presentation of her "gift" to Harry is framed in the language of objects and possession, transforming her own sexuality into a commodity to be given away, possibly even sold since articles of commerce are necessarily more often bought than gifted. This exchange between Ginny and Harry reaffirms cultural and social expectations of the objectification and commodification of female sexuality for the consumption of men. In an attempt to secure her position as Harry's eroticized object of desire, Ginny presents herself as such in the most bald way she knows. While she succeeds in the short term in her endeavor, their kiss is interrupted by Ron,[18] who imposes an embargo on

---

17 The Felix Felicis also undermines her manifestation of fighting skills, but since everyone from the D.A. who showed up to fight also took the potion we cannot single Ginny out in this instance.

18 I have to wonder how much of a "gift" Ginny would have given Harry had Ron not burst through the door. A girl's virginity is commonly referred to as a "gift," especially

any sexual exchange between the two. With this final push from Ron, with whom it has already been established he has a stronger bond than Ginny, and with a farewell kiss reminiscent of wives sending their husbands off to war, Harry is ready to depart on his journey to war.

As Harry, Ron, and Hermione search for the remaining Horcruxes and a way to destroy them, Harry takes comfort in his thoughts of Ginny. Though at first he worries about her safety, Harry finds solace in the idea of Ginny (along with Neville and Luna) rebelling against the man he hates most, second to Voldemort, Severus Snape. When the rest of the students return to Hogwarts, Harry imagines "Ginny, Neville, and Luna [...] sitting together... wondering where he, Ron, and Hermione were, or debating how best to undermine Snape's new regime" (227). While the Beautiful Soul is designated as a symbolic vessel of peace and nonviolence during wartime, to say that she does not defend the home when it is under threat would be to underrepresent the paradigm. For Elshtain claims that "Wartime's Beautiful Soul is no ordinary wife or mother... she becomes a civic being; she is needed by others" and that need also encompasses securing the home (9). Hogwarts has been Harry's true home since he arrived six years ago, but now it is occupied by Death Eaters and run by an enemy. In solidarity with Harry's resistance of Voldemort's regime, Ginny and the remaining members of Dumbledore's Army rebel against Snape and try to steal the sword of Gryffindor from the headmaster's office. Given the nonviolent circumstances, we cannot label this event as outright fighting but rather unarmed resistance. Because Ginny knows that Dumbledore bequeathed the sword to Harry, we may assume that had the mission succeeded the D.A. would have tried to give the sword to Harry.[19] As his exile from wizarding society and the search for Horcruxes continues, without Ron, Harry spends more and more time thinking about Ginny. Harry finds himself taking out the Marauder's Map "simply to stare at Ginny's name in the girls' dormitory, wondering whether the intensity with which he gazed at it might break into her sleep, that she would somehow know he was thinking about her, hoping that she was all right" (313). This scene evokes images of soldiers on battlefronts and in army camps, staring at pictures of or letters from their wives at home. The sexual longing is also made plain by Harry's looking at Ginny's name specifically in the girls' dormitory, when she is in bed alone. His yearning for her is also made plain when the reunited trio Apparates near the Burrow to see Xenophilius Lovegood. Staring out the window of the Lovegood home, the Burrow is just

---

within the American abstinence movement today.

19   This is pure supposition of course, and a completely unrealistic scenario. Had they stolen the sword how would they have gotten it to Harry? Or found him in the first place to tell him that they had the sword?

out of sight, but Harry believes that "Ginny [is] over there somewhere. They [are] closer to each other than they had been since Bill and Fleur's wedding, but she could have no idea he [is] gazing toward her now, thinking of her" (403). Combined with the other instances of Harry looking for Ginny on the Marauder's Map, the image created is quite voyeuristic. Trites observes that in many children's novels, visual metaphors, such as looking through a window, "emphasize the subject/object split: whoever 'sees' is automatically in the subject position... gazing at something in the object position" (33). Thus Ginny is relegated to being Harry's Beautiful Soul, and through this placement her position as object to Harry's subject position is also reified. Ginny's small rebellions against Snape's regime at Hogwarts are not relayed simply to illustrate her defiant attitude towards the new headmaster and the new direction of the curriculum, but rather to provide Harry with comforting thoughts of his Beautiful Soul at home as well as a vessel in which to place his "convictions and self-definitions" (Elshtain 140).

When Harry finally returns to Hogwarts, he fully embraces his role as Just Warrior, yet as such he refuses to allow Ginny to transcend her role as his Beautiful Soul and join the fight. As more and more Hogwarts students, both past and present, begin to enter the Room of Requirement from the Hog's Head, Ginny arrives too, but Harry has "never been less pleased to see her" (*Deathly* 582). While Harry is reluctant to involve anyone in the fight against Voldemort, he maintains this opposition, with the help of the Weasleys, to only Ginny fighting. When Molly and Bill tell her she can't fight, their given reason that she is underage, Ginny looks to Harry "beseechingly," but he simply shakes his head (605). After everyone has left to fight, the trio returns to access the Room of Hidden Things to retrieve Ravenclaw's diadem, but first Ginny must leave the Room, "just for a bit" (624). Like a parent nagging their unruly child, Harry at first tells Ginny twice that she "can come back in" when he's left, but when she shows no sign of having heard him he shouts after her "*You've got to come back in!*" (625). Harry's simple statement shifts to an imperative command. When Harry, Ron, and Hermione leave the Room of Requirement, Harry sees Ginny side by side with Tonks, the consummate Warrior Woman in these books, sending well-aimed jinxes into a crowd of Death Eaters below. Even as Ginny proves her worth and skill as a fighter, Harry ignores this information and commands her to "just keep out of the way" (627). Even at the height of battle, Harry refuses to see Ginny as a Warrior in the same way that he views anyone else as such, including himself.

Elshtain summarizes one of the main points of her argument about the roles men and women play in war thus: "war's destruction brings into being a gallery of particular male and female identities that we tend to compact into two – soldiers on the battle front, women on the home front" (171). Harry is unable, or unwilling, to place Ginny within the battle field as a soldier, either in his own mind or in reality. Some may claim that Harry is acting out of love for Ginny and simply worries for her safety. This is certainly the most superficial motivation, but the trouble here lies in the fact that Harry does not go to so much trouble to protect Ron, Hermione, or any other of his close friends when they join the fray. Harry's romantic feelings for Ginny remove her from otherwise equal standing among her and Harry's comrades. Beneath Harry's love-driven desire to protect Ginny exists a paternalistic belief that she cannot cope with the strain or the danger of war. Besides the one jinx Harry saw Ginny cast outside the Room of Requirement, he does not witness her battle anyone until she, Luna, and Hermione duel Bellatrix Lestrange in the "final showdown"; for the majority of the Battle of Hogwarts, Harry still does not consider Ginny a warrior nor does he see evidence to disprove his fear that she will not be able to fight. By whole-heartedly entering the battle, against the wishes of her family and Harry, Ginny begins to break down the divide between Beautiful Soul and Just Warrior.

But before she is allowed to truly attempt this disruption of paradigmatic dichotomy, Rowling forces her into a noncombatant role that is not quite Beautiful Soul, but still emphasizes the maternal aspects of that paradigm. After Voldemort issues his ultimatum and gives the Hogwarts fighters time to tend to their dead and injured, Harry makes his way from the castle to the Forbidden Forest, surveying the damage. Whereas Neville and Oliver Wood are carrying bodies into the Great Hall, Harry encounters Ginny comforting a wounded girl. As she tries to soothe the girl who does not want to fight anymore and tells her that "'It's going to be all right,'" Harry wants to "shout out to the night, he want[s] Ginny to know that he [is] there...to know where he [is] going" (*Deathly* 697). Situated as she is, Ginny no longer exemplifies the Beautiful Soul of Harry's imagination previously; she is not on the home front but the battle front. However, she has not become the Just Warrior but a field nurse tending to the injured. Though she has moved closer to the war in Harry's eyes, she continues to function as a source of solace (albeit to someone else), and Harry continues to voyeuristically pine for her while he maintains a safe distance from the situation. It appears that Rowling attempts to slowly transition Ginny from Beautiful Soul to Just Warrior via a more mediated and more maternal middle stage. By affirming Harry's construction of Ginny through the Beautiful Soul paradigm Rowling actually represses

Ginny's former challenge to the boundary between her position and that of the Just Warrior. In order for Harry to sacrifice himself, it seems he must retain that original vision of his "keeper of the flame of nonwarlike values" (Elshtain 144). For in what appear to be his final moments, Harry thinks "inexplicably of Ginny, and her blazing look, and the feel of her lips on his," and he does not betray fear when he faces his death with the image of Ginny, his Beautiful Soul, in mind (*Deathly* 704).

Harry survives of course, and on the other side of his almost-death he no longer needs that image of Ginny to defeat Voldemort. In this last leg of his journey, Harry needs only himself; not even Hermione or Ron are party to Harry's plan: it is left between Harry and Voldemort. Without Harry's restrictive imagining of where her place is or what trope she must conform to, Ginny is free to become a Warrior and face off against Bellatrix, accompanied by her fellow Woman Warriors Hermione and Luna. The solidarity between the three women is an equal match to Bellatrix's malevolence, yet Harry, ever paternalistically protective of Ginny, tries to intervene but is knocked aside by Molly Weasley. Harry becomes a spectator in the dual between a newly transitioned Just Warrior (Molly) and Voldemort's "best lieutenant," and he is perhaps reminded not to interfere in Ginny's battles.[20] Because there are so many fault lines, so many places where Ginny transgresses the role of Beautiful Soul, Harry forces her to conform to this paradigm where she otherwise rebels. Elshtain reminds us that the dichotomy between bellicose man and pacific female is a pervasive one in Western culture: "women are designated noncombatants because of the part they play in the reproductive process; because women have been linked symbolically to images of succoring nonviolence; [and] because men have a long history of warrioring and policing" (183). Harry expects Ginny to follow this culturally sanctioned separation of the sexes in times of war, yet when she is actually present in the narrative she refuses to do so.

After Ginny's short stint in warrioring, however, she is once again silenced. While Harry talks to the survivors of the battle, consoles the grieving, and acts every inch the part of the newly crowned king, Ginny exists, once more, in the periphery. Harry slips under the Invisibility Cloak after Luna provides a distraction, and he spots Ginny a couple tables away with her head on Molly's shoulder. Knowing that he is leaving the Great Hall to give, and receive, explanations, Harry decides not to invite Ginny along. Whereas Harry feels he owes Ron and Hermione an explanation because they "had stuck with him for so long, and [...] deserved the truth," Harry

---

20   This is an optimistic supposition at best.

believes "[t]here would be time to talk later, hours and days and maybe even years in which to talk" (*Deathly* 746, 745 respectively). At this point Ginny is still not considered in equal esteem with Ron and Hermione to warrant the same consideration in learning the truth. She has been intimately involved in many of Harry's exploits for years. Lest we forget, Ginny is the only other person who has gotten as close to Voldemort as Harry, or at least nearly there. Though Harry was a Horcrux, Ginny was possessed by Tom Riddle for the better part of her first school year. Even that close a connection between Harry and Ginny does not earn her the right to understand Harry's full story. At best she is a close second.[21] Without worrying about explaining anything to Ginny or comforting her for the deaths both of them have suffered, Harry slips easily back into his privilege, desiring nothing more than sleep and food served to him by his slave.

CONCLUSION

The *Harry Potter* series has been set up as a heteronormative tale from the beginning, and this aspect becomes especially evident in the manner through which Rowling develops, and often hinders, Ginny's character. Rather than create a heroine and love interest who is Harry's equal in all respects, the author has produced a strong character and made her conform to traditional gender roles. It is not that Rowling has not made strong female characters throughout her series (we need only look at Hermione for proof); it is that, when it comes to the protagonist's love object, she subjugates Ginny's strength and agency to help Harry fulfill a traditional hero/husband role. Whether she is in need of rescue and owes Harry her life; whether she is invisible until Harry is sexually maturing; whether she is eroticized forbidden fruit; or whether she is the supportive girlfriend and Beautiful Soul, Ginny occupies various narrative tropes solely to become Harry's love object rather than develop as a character in her own right. As Tom Riddle tried to sacrifice Ginny on the altar of Salazar Slytherin to restore himself to life, so does Rowling sacrifice her on the altar of regressive gender roles to provide Harry, first and foremost, a traditionalized happy ending.

---

21   Since Hermione and Ron are equal in the sharing of Harry's knowledge.

Bibliography

Elshtain, Jean Bethke. *Women and War*. Basic Books, Inc. New York: 1987.

Girard, Rene. *Deceit, Desire, and the Novel: Self and Other in Literary Structure*. Translator: Yvonne Freccero. Johns Hopkins Press, Baltimore, Maryland: 1965.

Lambarski, Tim . "Ginny Weasley A Gryffindor and a Match for Harry." The Harry Potter Lexicon. Jan. 2006. 23 June 2008. <http://www.hp-lexicon. info/essays/essay-ginny-weasley.html>.

Oler, Tammy. "Bloodletting." *BITCHfest: 10 Years of Cultural Criticism from the Pages of Bitch Magazine*. Lisa Jervis and Andi Zeisler, eds. Farrar, Straus, Giroux, New York: 2006.

Rowling, JK. *Harry Potter and the Chamber of Secrets*. New York: Scholastic, 1999.

___. *Harry Potter and the Deathly Hallows*. New York: Scholastic, 2007.

___. *Harry Potter and the Goblet of Fire*. New York: Scholastic, 2002.

___. *Harry Potter and the Half-Blood Prince*. New York: Scholastic, 2005

___. *Harry Potter and the Order of the Phoenix*. New York: Scholastic, 2004.

___. *Harry Potter and the Prisoner of Azkaban*. New York: Scholastic, 2001.

___. *Harry Potter and the Sorcerer's Stone*. New York: Scholastic, 1997.

Sedgwick, Eve Kosofsky. *Between Men: English Literature and Homosocial Desire*. Columbia University Press, New York: 1985.

Trites, Roberta Seelinger. *Waking Sleeping Beauty: Feminist Voices in Children's Novels*. University of Iowa Press, Iowa City: 1997

Chapter Ten

"Interpret Your Findings Correctly"[1]
Harry's Magical Self-Discovery

David Jones

Like all fantasy literature, the *Harry Potter* series deals with real-world issues by presenting them through characters, cultures and objects that are decidedly unusual. One aspect of the series that is not shared by all fantasy literature is Rowling's strong emphasis on unusual methods of sensory perception – both for enlightenment and misdirection. When we first meet Harry, he is in need of intellectual and emotional growth if he is ever going to overcome his arch-enemy, Voldemort. In order to accomplish this, he learns to use both his ordinary senses and unique magical objects to understand himself and the events around him. Harry's experiences with three magical devices in particular (the Invisibility Cloak, the Mirror of Erised, and the Pensieve) represent three kinds of self-knowledge. And these experiences are always illuminated by his reflection on the importance of one of Dumbledore's favorite themes: choice. This essay will consider Harry's three magical methods of gaining knowledge and what he learns about himself in the process. It will become clear that we, as readers, can also benefit intellectually and emotionally as a result of Harry's maturing self-discovery.

Although it has become commonplace to say that choice is a primary motif of the *Harry Potter* books, it is, nevertheless, true. Choice is a foundational theme needed to frame and critique Rowling's work. The Mirror of Erised, the Invisibility Cloak, and the Pensieve mimetically[2] represent choices to Harry and his surrounding cast of characters without offering obvious clues as to what the correct choice may be. A process of self-discovery, corresponding to each magical object, is often metaphorically represented through the sense of vision. Reflections and visions abound in the series as key elements of

---

1   This quotation is taken from Harry's first Occlumency lesson with Snape, who explains: ". . . those who have mastered Ligilimency are able, under certain conditions, to delve into the minds of their victims and interpret their finds correctly." (*Order* 531)

2   mimesis: "The Greek word for imitation. . . . A literary work that is understood to be reproducing an external reality or any aspect of it is described as mimetic."

the narrative's unfolding through these devices. Rowling takes Harry to the point of "right" action by starting him down the path of inner reflection, exposing him not just to new experiences outside what he knows, but also forcing him to question what these experiences teach him about himself and his purpose. He must engage and understand the symbolic representations of his self (and that of others) to form knowledge that leads him through the travails he faces in each book. His choices are not always gracefully executed, but his education gives him the ability to choose what is "right" over what is "easy" by teaching him to meld his ethical beliefs with the ability to infer and interpret events around him.

His Father's Cloak – The Importance of Invisibility

Chapter 12 of *Philosopher's Stone* describes Harry's first Christmas at Hogwarts. The warmth of the morning feast and the joviality of the Hogwarts faculty create a distinctly family-like atmosphere. Harry is celebrating with the Weasley siblings. George insisted that his aloof older brother, Percy, spend Christmas day with his brothers and sister instead of the other prefects. Everyone, including Harry, received a gift of a handmade sweater from Mrs. Weasley, a Christmas family tradition.

After a long day of presents, feasts, and companionship with the Weasleys (a filial relationship entirely alien to Harry's previous experience), Harry goes to his bed, perfectly primed to reflect on his own family. He feels the void created by the loss of his parents and the life he's suffered with the Dursleys. This is further emphasized by the delivery of an anonymous Christmas gift – an invisibility cloak that belonged to his father. Harry devotes his attention to the cloak and wonders who may have sent it. Harry's thoughts run thus:

> His father's ... this had been his father's. He let the material flow over his hands, smoother than silk, light as air. *Use it well*, the note had said.
>
> He had to try it now. He slipped out of bed and wrapped the cloak around himself. Looking down at his legs, he saw only moonlight and shadows. It was a very funny feeling. (150)

One can imagine that wrapping the cloak around his shoulders is a symbolic means for Harry to wrap himself in something of his parents'. He decides to use the cloak for the first time alone, choosing to exclude Ron. It is a symbolic act in which Harry claims something of his heritage as his own, not just physically, but emotionally and intellectually. And it foreshadows the theme of isolation that Harry battles with throughout the series.

The cloak had a note attached containing an imperative message, almost a warning: *"use it well."* Harry, like his father, is impulsive, often acting quickly without considering the consequences. That quality now shines through. Instead of wondering too much about his father's use of the cloak, Harry acts instinctively.

The cloak also reinforces a recurring theme for Harry's character: hiding and revealing what is hidden. One major reason the Dursleys find Harry dumped on their doorstep is that they are a place to hide, and Harry spends much of his life in the cupboard, the most secretive part of No. 4 Privet Drive. At the Dursleys', figurative invisibility is Harry's punishment for simply being Harry Potter, the son of his "abnormal" parents. At Hogwarts, literal invisibility is something Harry can control. It is a symbolic removal from universal recognition in the wizarding world. And controlling what can and cannot be seen is fundamentally important to Harry's search for knowledge in the wizarding world, as every book delivers scenes that engage the reader with multiple visual sleights of hand.

A good illustration of this is Harry's first day in Potions class. His first experience under the weight of Snape's attention is an exercise in disappointment and futility, primarily due to Snape's singling him out. Snape's questioning of Harry's knowledge has more the tenor of an interrogation than a pedagogical tool, a tone that is retained for the duration of Harry's relationship with Snape. Harry's first "I don't know" elicits this response: "Snape's lips curled into a sneer" (*Philosophers Stone* 102). It's a threatening reaction flowing from Snape's identification of Harry as a "celebrity" (101). And Harry is the center of attention; after another "I don't know", the narrator tells us: "A few people laughed; Harry caught Seamus's eye and Seamus winked. Snape, however, was not pleased" (103). As the focal point of the class and his more-than-stern teacher, Harry cannot think. After class, Harry's mind is sent "racing" while he tries to assimilate both Snape's treatment of him and the vast amount of potions information thrown his way.

A similar example is found in *Goblet of Fire* when Harry loses his composure and lashes out at Malfoy's insult of Hermione. He's already reeling from the unwanted exposure of being chosen for the Tri-wizard Tournament, and his actions do nothing more than garner Snape's unwanted attention and harm Hermione: "Harry's ears were ringing. The injustice of it made him want to curse Snape into a thousand slimy pieces" (300). Vision is an important part of this scene: "Snape's eyes [meet] Harry's" and Harry suddenly suspects that Snape "[is] going to poison [Harry]" as part of a classroom exercise (301). Harry, as the central focus of the class, leaves the dungeon with no more knowledge than when he entered. His mind is fettered by distractions and ensnared by Snape's treatment of him and his friends, a premise reinforced by placing Snape's class in the dungeon. Rowling heightens the theme even further when Dolores Umbridge ascends to the position of "High Inquisitor" and eventually Headmistress of Hogwarts in *Order of the Phoenix*. Umbridge goes to great lengths to see, know, and control *everything* at Hogwarts, even interrogating students with truth serums.

Harry is free to roam when he is invisible: "The whole of Hogwarts was open to him in this cloak" (*Philosopher's Stone* 151). The freedom is the result of choice given to Harry by invisibility. Upon entering the corridor in the cloak, his first thought is a question: "Where should he go? He stopped, his heart racing, and thought" (151). Harry can think. Here, his heart races with excitement and potential, while his mind is clear – very different from Harry's experience leaving Snape's classroom. Left to his own devices, without the attention of an oppressive figure, Harry can choose. And here, he makes a very rational choice given the goal he's shared with Ron and Hermione over the previous weeks. He decides to enter the Restricted Section of the library for information on Nicolas Flamel. His ability to choose allows him to use his cloak well, and search for knowledge, and that search follows a standard mythical trope. Knowledge can be dangerous if one doesn't know what to look for, how to look for it, or where to look. He stumbles around the Restricted Section, a little bewildered by the atmosphere, the shrieking book, and the sudden appearance of Filch who fetches Snape to the scene to investigate. Despite Harry's improved ability to think clearly, his rational decision to acquire necessary knowledge to complete his goal is frustrated by his inexperience in both the library and with objects of the magical world (other than Hermione, who would have thought a book could shriek?).

But the freedom to choose is the crux of the cloak's importance. Dumbledore comments that it is "Strange how short-sighted being invisible can make you" (156). It does not automatically convey knowledge, only a means to attain it. Indeed, if John Granger is right, what is visible versus what is invisible is the subtext for the whole series of books. Granger's central premise in *Unlocking Harry Potter* is that the ultimate story is the one that has not been *seen* by Harry, and thus, neither by the reader: Voldemort's and Dumbledore's dance of intelligence gathering and low-intensity warfare that surrounds Harry's periphery. Every book except *Half-Blood Prince* ends with Dumbledore's reappraisal of what has happened at the narrative margins of the books outside of the reader's view. Rowling even reinforces the trope of what can be seen in *Half-Blood Prince* with Dumbledore's request that Harry keep his Invisibility Cloak with him "at all times. Even within Hogwarts itself. Just in case, you understand me" (80). By this point in the series, the astute reader should find this request suggestive of the importance that knowledge will play from that moment forward.

THE MIRROR OF ERISED – DEALING WITH DESIRES

With the Mirror of Erised, Harry's search for intellectual knowledge turns into an accidental acquisition of emotional knowledge which takes several more chapters to become clear. Using the Invisibility Cloak, Harry sneaks from the library into the room containing the Mirror of Erised. The cloak is a symbol of Harry's heritage, but the Mirror presents moving, seemingly living images of people that Harry quickly realizes are his mother and father and other family members who have "green eyes like his [and] noses like his" (153). It seems no mistake by Rowling to introduce both the cloak and the mirror in the same chapter, much less that the acquisition of the cloak should lead to the discovery of the mirror. Both are means for manipulating the senses. The invisibility cloak hides Harry from the site of others and provides a kind of freedom by handing over anonymity. The mirror shuttles back to Harry what resides in himself, but he must *realize* this is the mirror's purpose.

Harry must realize what he sees in Erised is a mimetic picture designed to make him consider something else, in this case an internal conflict. Erised's magic combines both physical and intellectual phenomena, reflecting deep-seated mental projections as if they were physical realities; Harry wonders if the people he sees are present in the room with him, but invisible themselves (153), a moment indicating that, at first, Harry does not figure out the nature of what he sees. Ultimately, he does recognize that he is "looking at his family, for the first time in his life" (153), a deeply profound experience for Harry:

> The Potters smiled and waved at Harry and he stared hungrily back at them, his hands pressed flat against the glass as though he was hoping to fall right through it and reach them. He had a powerful kind of ache inside of him, half joy, half terrible sadness. (153)

Harry is primed to find his family within the mirror. He's spent the day engaged in the first real family-oriented activity he's known in his life. He has taken part in the brotherly bonding of the Weasley boys, who have adopted him as one of their own. When combined with Harry's donning of his own heritage symbolized by the cloak, his deep sense of need for a family, the torment endured under the hand of the Dursleys, and the seeming favor bestowed upon him and his parents in the wizarding world, Harry can't possibly find anything in that mirror other than his family, his entire family. They are what Harry most deeply wants: stability, connection, anonymity, and love (with love being the central theme of the series.) But Harry cannot interact with the image; he can only look at it.

Rowling, again, turns the situation to her advantage. That Harry's family exists as a projection within the Mirror of Erised, not spirits stepping through the mirror as if it were a portal, keeps the mirror's purpose subtle. Harry can only touch the glass and gaze "hungrily," a word implying an unsatisfied appetite. The mirror distorts reality by reflecting fantasy back to its subject, but only as a commentary upon that subject's inner life – not as a literal phenomena in and with which the subject can act.

According to Dumbledore, the mirror "shows us nothing more or less than the deepest, most desperate desire of our hearts," warning that "Men have wasted away before it," and that "It does not do to dwell on dreams and forget to live" (157). Harry must shove context into the discourse level of this experience, and it is in this transgressive moment that Harry must come to a profound realization about himself and his past as history, not fantasy or "dreams." He intuitively understands what he sees, but he cannot conceive of why he sees it. The only people he can recognize are his parents, and this only due to the photograph given to him as a Christmas present. He has no concrete memory of his parents, only a sense of who they were and why they were good. Thus, any real understanding of "family" in a deeper, more profound way is thwarted in this moment. And Harry can only make sense of what he has seen in the mirror after Dumbledore's tutorship.

Finding Some Space for Understanding

Dumbledore's intervention at the mirror guides Harry to understand its purpose, and Harry puts the mirror to proper use later in *Philosopher's Stone* because his internal character allows him to do so. He uses the mirror to find the Philosopher's Stone, and Dumbledore seems to have believed this to be the case. Harry *sees* himself with the Stone, but "not using it," which allows him to grasp it. We now know that Harry has made the ethical leap the mirror demands of its users in order to make sense of their visions; thus, Harry has a deeper understanding of his own self because he has found context for the transgressive discourse element to the narrative moment focused by his first encounters with the mirror. It is not his family that allows Harry to discover who he is – it is his experience in making moral distinctions.

In other words, Harry is left in the middle of a transgressive moment. Michel Foucault defines transgression in his "Preface to Transgression" as the moment when a thing's limits or boundaries are illuminated, comprehended, and crossed: "transgression incessantly crosses and recrosses a line which closes up behind it" (34). In other words, once that limit is understood and crossed, a new line is immediately established elsewhere. So, transgression's purpose is "to measure the excessive distance that it opens" and to "trace" the causes that bring boundaries into existence in the first place (35). The "distance that it opens" is a kind of negative space – an empty void into which an idea or thought can be deposited so that the moment makes sense.

Harry must look beyond the negative space of what scholars call the "discourse level" of narrative construction. The "discourse level" is the layer of a book in which the language tells what took place – we recognize it because most stories are told in past tense; whereas the details come from the "event level," or the supposed moment the events "happened" before the text was written. Thus, as a story is "told," the act of telling it opens up the distance between what happened and the audience's understanding of it. If the audience recognizes that a story is being told, and not that it is happening right now, then they can look for ways to understand the story beyond the simple surface level of who, what, where, and when. Harry must learn to infer what is happening in those parts of his story that Rowling does not allow the reader to see. Such an inference must come from within Harry, as a part of his ethical code. The Invisibility Cloak and the Mirror of Erised are designed to expose Harry to ways of gathering knowledge, but then to recognize that he must develop an internal aspect of himself (his values and ethics) before he can comprehend the wider world around him.

According to Roni Natov, the problem presented by the mirror is that "desire can be both alluring and dangerous" (320). She suggests that this scene is Rowling's version "of the great test of Odysseus, who must hear the song of the sirens but not act" (320). Without the choice to assimilate the reflection given by the mirror, along with all its revealed emotion and truth, Harry runs the risk of destroying his self by not allowing it to evolve in a manner wherein he can understand moral distinctions. The reflection is neither memory nor prediction, but a captured moment of emotional longing that has a very unstable corporeality. The mirror deconstructs Harry's psychic life. A shallow person wants to live the reflection; think of Harry's instinctive move toward the mirror to touch it. Harry must search for knowledge without losing sight of his goals:

> The *Harry Potter* stories center on what children need to find internally
> – the strength to do the right thing, to establish a moral code. As hero,
> Harry must go beyond the apparent truth of things and, ultimately,
> learn to trust what he sees and act on what is right. (323)

Natov focuses on Harry's choices during the Tri-Wizard tournament in *Goblet of Fire*. As she notes, Harry's altruism is fully realized when he decides to risk winning to save others who, under the rules of the tournament, are not his concern. This is another step for Harry's character, a journey begun when Harry used the Mirror of Erised to acquire the Philosopher's Stone.

Harry didn't want to use the stone, but only keep it from Quirrell's possession. Thus, Harry has no ambition toward personal glory and gain, unlike, say, Ron's older brother Percy who's brimming with naked ambition until the "Battle for Hogwarts" in *Deathly Hallows*. Harry never fully comprehends what he means to the wizarding world in *Philosopher's Stone* and most of *Chamber of Secrets*. Not until *Deathly Hallows* does Harry understand the full nature of his role in the Wizarding World.

The series finale of trio characters (Harry, Hermione, and Ron) wandering through the woods presents another occasion for a transgressive moment. Their characters are deconstructed, pulled away from their adolescent selves and pulled more fully into the adult world. Their decisions are no longer about fantastical quests, but about emotional stability and the ability to believe in something imperfect and without full definition – for Ron and Hermione, this imperfect something is Harry; for Harry, it is Dumbledore. Harry's rejection of the Hallows Quest described by Xenophilius Lovegood is the pivotal moment in which Harry discovers the full weight of his adulthood. That his choice comes during Dobby's burial, perhaps the most child-like character in the books – pure and unwavering in his devotions – also squarely points to the evolution from imaginative quests for mythical artifacts to straight confrontation with evil itself.

But, in *Goblet of Fire*, Rowling shifts Harry's efforts to gather and confront knowledge rather profoundly. She allows him into the head of another through Dumbledore's Pensieve.

THE PENSIEVE PERSPECTIVE #1 – THE UNREAL AS REAL

The mirror's reflections are nothing more than projections, but from *Goblet of Fire* onward, Harry is hurled into dreams and visions that are distorted and decontextualized to Harry's perceptions, though their events are quite real. At this point, contrary to Natov's explanation that the purpose of the cloak and mirror are to aid in "seeing" and "constructing a moral code," the books now seem to go out of their way to problematize Harry's perception of things. As Snape makes clear in *Order*, understanding is a matter where one must "interpret their findings correctly" (531), something Harry has been attempting throughout the series, most explicitly in the last three books of the series. *Order of the Phoenix* is the first novel in which Harry spends significant space brooding about himself and those around him. Rowling writes this transformed Harry so that almost every moment alone is spent in isolated speculation about his self and what is happening around him, and these speculations often reveal rather unpleasant things about Harry's character: hubris, the need for attention, and anger. And we see Harry forming rather well fleshed considerations of the people around him in *Half-Blood Prince*. *Deathly Hallows* is Rowling's tale of Harry's wilderness journey to fully understand himself, Dumbledore, Voldemort, and virtually every other mystery that surrounds him. He doesn't resolve every dilemma established in the series; in fact, most are left wide open. But his recognition that the dilemmas exist is one more significant move from confronting childish quest motifs to more directly adult issues – from Philosopher's Stones to inner faith.

As book 6 makes plain, the Pensieve is the most significant mimetic device conceived in the series. It is the conduit through which Harry learns explicitly about Voldemort's history, while Voldemort remains at the margins of these events. It is also the device through which Snape is redeemed in Harry's estimation just before Harry sacrifices himself to Voldemort in *Deathly Hallows*. Each mimetic device found in the novels shows not just Harry's self, but something important about those around him, as well, often the narratively marginalized Voldemort. He may be Harry's greatest enemy, but his presence in the first six books is mostly ephemeral representation (if not flatly absent) and generally involves some event or moment designed to teach Harry. Thus, reconstructing Riddle/Voldemort is a matter of reading secondary sources about the dark wizard, who has taken great pains to conceal that which would be most revealing: his personal and public histories.

This may be a good point to mention Noel Chevalier's observation that points to the discussion about the use of visibility in the books. Chevalier notes that Voldemort is little more than a sense impression through most of the series: "Voldemort is almost literally a shadow, a disembodied vestige of his former self, almost entirely out of metonymy ('You-Know-Who' and 'He Who Must Not Be Named') and memory" (399). He can only exist as a parasite who uses others to project himself incompletely into the physical world. Voldemort's presence in Harry's early life is through Harry's memory and physical sensations – through senses other than vision. Harry can feel pain and fear as a result of the sounds of his dreams, and when Voldemort returns in book 4, Harry's scar hurts almost continuously. In *Order of the Phoenix*, Harry and Voldemort seem to be sharing mental space. Voldemort is figured in the books as an apparition that can cause Harry very real harm.

In *Half-Blood Prince*, Harry only barely understands this purpose of finding out more about other people through the Pensieve. Harry expects that his private lessons with Dumbledore are going to be full illuminating: "You said, at the end of last term, you were going to tell me everything" (187). This statement comes after a "pause" before which Dumbledore states he has "decided that it is time now [to] *know* what prompted Lord Voldemort" to target Harry as a child (186-87, emphasis added). As several critics have noted, Dumbledore is precise and careful in his use of language. But what Dumbledore is offering is a conflation of knowledge with "the murky marshes of memory", and the result is the "wildest guesswork" forming his purpose in Harry's private lessons (187). Thus, the lessons engage two pragmatic objectives: discerning Voldemort's intentions and his weaknesses, and training Harry in the fine art of inferential reasoning, preparing him with knowledge for the final combat to come. What Dumbledore, and consequently Harry, does not know must be constructed as an historical interpretation of memories from various sources. Now Harry must learn that the transgressive moment will yield him only what he *infers* to be true, though solid reason might exist for such belief.

THE PENSIEVE PERSPECTIVE #2 – EMPATHY FOR OTHERS

Another way of saying this is that Harry is now ready to recognize the transgressive moment in the interpretative act as first presented to him in the Mirror of Erised. *Order of the Phoenix* shows Harry sneaking into the Pensieve in Snape's office only to view a young James Potter wantonly bullying Snape solely for the delight in doing so. Rowling's emotional metaphors mimic those of Harry's experiences in earlier sequences of knowledge acquisition; Harry's heart pumps "harder and faster than ever" and excitement "explode[s] in the pit of his stomach" (641) just like the first moments under the Invisibility Cloak. And just as before, the true nature of what Harry learns is accidental and thoroughly alters Harry's perceptions. James is mean and arrogant. His treatment of Peter Pettigrew and Snape are abhorrent, embodying everything Harry loathes in the darker corners of human nature:

> What was making Harry feel so horrified and unhappy was not being
> shouted at or having jars thrown at him – it was that he knew how
> it felt to be humiliated in the middle of a circle of onlookers, knew
> exactly how Snape felt as his father had taunted him, and that judging
> from what he had just seen, his father had been every bit as arrogant
> as Snape had always told him. (650)

This destruction of the dominating narrative of James and Sirius as
infallible heroes in Harry's worldview is a significant moment of empathy
where Harry recognizes himself within the unexpected representation of
another. Harry identifies with Snape and recognizes the moment in which
he finds himself very clearly. But he cannot manipulate the transgressive
moment – by the time we return to Hogwarts in *Half-Blood Prince*, Snape
is as much a villain in Harry's worldview as ever, despite any psychological
commonalities.

Entering the Pensieve's representation of memories as phenomena
that can be passively read and interpreted in a form that is both physically
presented, yet clearly ephemeral (every use highlights the sense of falling
through a fog into the memory), is a deconstruction of one's psychology.
The Pensieve's representation is different from the Mirror of Erised in that
it recreates memories, not desires. Instead of seeing Harry's family or Ron's
wish for glory, we see Harry sympathize first with Snape and then Riddle/
Voldemort, two of his sworn enemies. Harry's second lesson in *Half-Blood
Prince* includes Dumbledore's demonstration of magic to an eleven-year-old
Riddle that leaves the boy screaming (seemingly setting the boy's belongings
on fire), something for which "Harry could hardly blame him" (255). And
after they exit the memory, Harry's first comment is to compare himself
with Voldemort: "He believed it much quicker than I did – I mean when
you told him he was a wizard," though Dumbledore is quick to point out the
difference in that Voldemort quickly believed only because magic marked
him as "special" (258).

The scene echoes an earlier scene in *Prisoner of Azkaban* in which Harry
faces a boggart for the first time in a represented form of a dementor, a soul-
stealing guardian of the wizarding prison. The dementor literally leaves a
person demented, or destroyed psychically and spiritually so that his/her
physical existence is worthless. The dementor's kiss serves as the wizarding
world's form of capital punishment, leading to unavoidable death. The objects
in Tom's wardrobe are also "trophies," as Dumbledore refers to them (260),
the first sign of Riddle's interest in Horcruxes, the objects that store fragments
of his soul. That one steals while the other is a receptacle created by choice

continues the theme of choice and creates its own transgressive moment, one Dumbledore hopes Harry recognizes (260) as a moment in which Harry might inject his inferential reasoning and sympathies. Dumbledore primes the entrance into the Pensieve by asking Harry, "Could you possibly be feeling sorry for Voldemort?" (246).

Yet, as John Granger states of these scenes, we never come to pity Riddle/Voldemort; instead, these moments of sympathy seem to be for other reasons:

> [Voldemort] is, post-Horcruxes, simply a shattered person [...] He is himself a "deconstructed text," that no longer has an independent existence or value. Even though we learn about his painful childhood in an orphanage and about his mother's trials, Ms. Rowling never suggests there is something understandable or pitiable in the evil person Tom Riddle chooses to become in his pursuit of power.

> He is not a conceptual evil that can be parsed, broken down, and made relative [...] Rowling presents her prime villains [sic] and his henchmen as a very real wickedness, the product of human error and choice, that must be resisted at all costs, even death (208-9).

In the above scene from *Half-Blood Prince*, the discussion between Harry and Dumbledore never presumes to justify Voldemort's actions. Instead, the purpose is to evaluate Voldemort's character by looking for weaknesses: his desire to be "special," his reckless independence (a trait shared by Harry), and his penchant for "collect[ing] trophies" (259-60). All three mark Riddle as someone who seeks special recognition, separating himself from the herd even if doing so requires unfathomable crimes.

These Pensieve memories make visible what has been invisible in the earlier novels – Riddle/Voldemort – but only in an ephemeral way. Warning Harry of the guesswork ahead is Dumbledore's newest lesson about gaining knowledge. What Harry (and the reader) knows might be established according to the facts at hand, but could always possibly be wrong: "From here on in, Harry, I may be as woefully wrong as Humphrey Belcher, who believed the time was ripe for a cheese cauldron" (187). Speculation is the order of the day in *Half-Blood Prince*, one reason this book invited so much guesswork by fans and scholars alike about many of its plot points and the consequences for book 7.[2] The end of book 6 leaves us on this precipice. Dumbledore is willing to acknowledge that he could be wrong, yet he thinks he is right. Harry wants to believe Dumbledore is right; and because Harry's perspective is ours, we tend to believe Dumbledore is right, too.

ACTION BASED ON PARTIAL INFORMATION AND COMPLETE LOVE

Harry's education is more than a rote understanding of the past. He must engage with his moral self for the purpose of defining how he should proceed in the future against external threats. Synthesizing information from the fractured narrative of Riddle/Voldemort provides nothing useful without interpretation and inference – exegesis of stories to form plausible conclusions about character, motive, ability, weaknesses, strengths, etc. The end of *Half-Blood Prince* continues the theme of knowledge acquisition. In "The Cave," we are given a moment with Harry that starkly contrasts his first run-in with Snape in book 1: "His brain whirling in panic, Harry knew, instinctively, the only way left to get to water, because Voldemort had planned it so..." (*Half-Blood* 537). He desperately searches for a way to give water to his fallen mentor, and he quickly realizes that he must take water from Lake Inferi by recognizing a detail in Voldemort's thought processes. Instead of succumbing to his panic as he did in Snape's dungeon so many years before, Harry does what he does best: he acts based on a reasonable conclusion. His ability to act upon this knowledge reconfigures his student/mentor relationship with Dumbledore during the aged wizard's moment of need. Harry becomes his mentor's savior: "I am not worried, Harry. [...] I am with you" (540).

Dumbledore has inculcated in his best student a notion he values above all others: the need to learn about more than oneself, and that one could always be wrong. What differentiates Dumbledore's investigations from Voldemort's project of domination is the meticulous accumulation of information from multiple sources and perspectives. Readers can understand *Half-Blood Prince* as the classroom session that teaches Harry the value of this learning, while *Deathly Hallows* is the violent conflict in which Harry must put his abilities to serious work. Through all his doubt, the final third of the book is set up at the moment of Dobby's death. As he manually digs Dobby's grave "properly [...] Not by magic" (478), he ponders over what he has learned preceding months:

> *You gave Ron the Deluminator. You understood him....You gave him a way back....*
>
> *And you understood Wormtail too....You knew there was a bit of regret there, somewhere....*
>
> *And if you knew them...What did you know about me, Dumbledore?*
>
> *Am I meant to know, but not to seek? Did you know how hard I'd find that? Is that why you made it this difficult? So I'd have to work that out?*
> (483; emphasis in original)

Harry now understands that he must make decisions, often based on incomplete information, and often against his own natural instincts. Once he decides to pursue the Horcruxes over the Hallows, Rowling even brings her readers back to a familiar metaphor for Harry's clarity: "His heart was racing as if he had been sprinting and had just cleared an enormous obstacle" (484). His choice reveals an ability to think clearly and dispassionately.

A final moment of knowledge comes in Chapter 33 of *Deathly Hallows*, "The Prince's Tale." It answers many of the questions and doubts plaguing Harry throughout the series. He sees moments often hidden from view in earlier books, moments that are often painful, but that illuminate important and final truths to be carried to his final confrontation with Voldemort. Yet, for all the dark heartbreak revealed about Snape, the chapter is more memorable for what is absent. In *Half-Blood Prince*, Dumbledore takes note of Harry's apprehension concerning the Pensieve during their first lesson. As they are about to enter Bob Ogden's memory, Dumbledore observes, "You look worried" (187). And Harry begins to acknowledge to himself that "[h]is previous experiences with the odd device [...] though highly instructive, had also been uncomfortable" (188). Throughout the Pensieve lessons, the narrator reveals that Harry often interjects his own conclusions about what he sees, often only to have his expectations overturned. Harry is trying to understand, but he has not yet questioned his own perspective. When Dumbledore asks him if he feels sorry for Voldemort, Harry's quick "No" immediately implies that 1) he has not questioned his own assumptions, and 2) Dumbledore wants him to do so. Dumbledore's plan in *Deathly Hallows* is designed to promote this attitude in Harry. That Harry never once inserts his own commentary into his experience of Snape's memories suggests he has managed to do this. Harry emerges from the Pensieve understanding his purpose: "to walk calmly into Death's welcoming arms" (691) – an ironic and direct antithesis to the suggestions imbedded in the last volume's title.

This realization bespeaks the totality of Harry's knowledge, in contrast to the fact that Voldemort's "knowledge remained woefully incomplete" (709). Dumbledore further delineates Harry's capacity for knowledge by marking him against Voldemort:

> That which Voldemort does not value, he takes no trouble to comprehend. Of house-elves and children's tales, of love, loyalty, and innocence, Voldemort knows and understands nothing. *Nothing.* That they all have a power beyond his own, a power beyond reach of any magic, is a truth he has never grasped. (709-10; emphasis in original)

Harry, of course, has come to comprehend not only these things, but that which he himself has failed to value. His primary goal during the last two books has been to understand not only his mentor, but his enemies – both real (Voldemort) and perceived (Snape). His dispassionate acceptance of Snape's tale, and subsequent veneration of Snape in the end, indicates that this knowledge was a transformative endeavor.

Harry is the narrative filter through which readers experience the books. He is the focalized viewpoint from which the narrative voice speaks. We learn as Harry learns. As Harry understands his world, his place in it, the people surrounding him, and his relationship(s) to them, the narrative's focus, both thematically and aesthetically, shifts as Harry's understanding evolves (Behr 115-17). While focusing on the story through Harry's eyes, a reader's understanding changes as Harry's does. The images Harry is exposed to when interacting with these mimetic devices allow him to see ethics, knowledge, personal and public histories, and memories from a safer distance.

Rowling does not insert magic into her books as a mere plot device, and these magical objects are perfect examples. The Invisibility Cloak and the Mirror of Erised are designed to open Harry up as a person and prepare him for self reflection, while the Pensieve helps him incorporate events into an experience best interpreted after mastering his own self. Rowling constructs a powerful example of how we engage with ourselves and with the world around us; and she does so by acknowledging the rather messy reality of how difficult this is to accomplish. Harry overcomes his obstacles and his ultimate foe, not by sheer luck or simple determinism, but by learning how to do so.

Bibliography

Behr, Kate. "'Same-as-Difference': Narrative Transformations and Intersecting Cultures in Harry Potter." *JNT: Journal of Narrative Theory* 35.1 (Winter 2005): 113-32.

Chevalier, Noel. "The Liberty Tree and the Whomping Willow: Political Justice, Magical Science, and Harry Potter." *The Lion and the Unicorn* 29 (2005): 397-415.

Cockrell, Amanda. "Harry Potter and the Witch Hunters: A Social Context for the Attacks on *Harry Potter*." *The Journal of American Culture* 29.1 (March 2006): 24-30.

Foucault, Michel. "Preface to Transgression." *Language, Counter-memory, Practice*. Trans. Donald F. Bouchard and Sherry Simon. Ithaca, NY: Cornell University Press, 1977. 29-52.

Granger, John. *Unlocking Harry Potter: Five Keys for the Serious Reader*. Wayne, PA: Zossima Press, 2007.

Hopkins, Lisa. "Harry Potter and the Acquisition of Knowledge." *Reading Harry Potter: Critical Essays*. Ed. Giselle Liza Anatol. Contributions to the Study of Popular Culture, Number 78. Westport, CT: Praeger, 2003. 25-34.

Natov, Roni. "Harry Potter and the Extraordinariness of the Ordinary." *The Lion and the Unicorn* 25 (2001): 310-27.

Rowling, J. K. *Harry Potter and the Chamber of Secrets*. Vancouver: Raincoast Books, 1998.

___. *Harry Potter and the Deathly Hallows*. 1st American Edition. New York: Scholastic Press, 2007.

___. *Harry Potter and the Goblet of Fire*. 1st American Edition. New York: Scholastic Press, 2000.

___. *Harry Potter and the Half-Blood Prince*. London: Bloomsbury, 2005.

___. *Harry Potter and the Order of the Phoenix*. 1st American Edition. New York: Scholastic Press, 2003.

___. *Harry Potter and the Philosopher's Stone*. Vancouver: Raincoast Books, 1997.

___. *Harry Potter and the Prisoner of Azkaban*. Vancouver: Raincoast Books, 1999.

CONTRIBUTORS

(in order of the chapters)

Colin Manlove was Reader in English Literature at the University of Edinburgh till early retirement in 1993. An acknowledged expert on fantasy literature, Manlove has taught courses, given public lectures and published many books on the subject. These include *Modern Fantasy* (1975), *The Impulse of Fantasy Literature* (1983), *Science Fiction* (1986), *C.S.Lewis* (1987), *Christian Fantasy* (1992), *The Chronicles of Narnia* (1993) *Scottish Fantasy* (1994), *The Fantasy Literature of England* (1999) and *From Alice to Harry Potter: Children's Fantasy in England* (2003). Parts of this essay were originally given in a lecture at the Sectus Conference on the *Harry Potter* books in London in July 2007.'

James W. Thomas is Professor of English at Pepperdine University, where he has taught since 1981. For many years, he has done scholarly work primarily in twentieth-century American literature, publishing a number of articles and reviews, along with *Lyle Saxon: A Critical Biography*. In the last few years, Dr. Thomas has spoken at three *Harry Potter* conferences, and has been interviewed by NPR, several newspapers, and TIME magazine regarding the Potter books. He is the author of *Repotting Harry Potter: A Professor's Book-by-Book Guide for the Serious Re-Reader* (Zossima Press).

John Granger writes and speaks on the intersection of literature, philosophy, faith, and culture. He's published articles in *Touchstone*, been a Keynote Speaker at seven academic and fan conferences and at major Universities from Princeton and Pepperdine to Yale and the University of Chicago, and is the author of *Unlocking Harry Potter* (Zossima Press, 2007), *How Harry Cast His Spell* (Tyndale, 2008), *The Deathly Hallows Lectures* (Zossima Press, 2008), and *Harry Potter's Bookshelf* (Penguin, 2009).

Danielle Elizabeth Tumminio is the instructor of the Christian Theology and *Harry Potter* seminar at Yale University, a course that was profiled on CNN.com. She holds three degrees from Yale – two graduate degrees in theology and an undergraduate degree in English literature – and is currently enrolled in a Ph.D. program in practical theology at Boston University. Her doctoral work focuses on trauma theory, interreligious violence, and reconciliation. Her book *God and Harry Potter at Yale* will be published later this year (Zossima Press).

Amy H. Sturgis earned her Ph.D. in intellectual history at Vanderbilt University and teaches interdisciplinary studies at Belmont University. She is the author of four books as well as numerous book chapters and articles, and the editor of an additional four books. In 2006 she was honored with the Imperishable Flame Award for J.R.R. Tolkien/Inklings scholarship, and in 2009 she was honored with the Sofanaut Award for her regular "History of the SF Genre" segments on the StarShipSofa podcast. She is currently writing *The Gothic Imaginations of J.R.R. Tolkien, Madeleine L'Engle, and J.K. Rowling* (Zossima Press, 2010). Her website is www.amyhsturgis.com.

Travis Prinzi is the author of *Harry Potter & Imagination: The Way Between Two Worlds* (Zossima Press, 2008). His weblog, www.thehogshead.org, enjoys an international readership as it continues to explore the *Harry Potter* books and related literature. Prinzi holds an M.A in Theological Studies from Northeastern Seminary and an M.S. in Teaching and Curriculum from the University of Rochester. He has given presentations and keynote talks at five different Potter conferences in the U.S. and Canada.

Karen Kebarle is a longtime *Harry Potter* fan with a Ph.D. in English and American Literature from the University of California, Berkeley. She has given talks on *Harry Potter* at Convention Alley 2005 and 2008, Lumos 2006, Prophecy 2007, and Portus 2008. Her main interests in the Potterverse are literary technique in Rowling's series and theoretical approaches to reading *Harry Potter*. In September 2009, Karen will enter the University of Ottawa to obtain her teacher certification.

Ryan Kerr has been an avid student of children's literature and *Harry Potter* for several years. He earned his B.A. in English at Illinois State University and an M.A. in Children's Literature at Eastern Michigan University. He currently teaches English at Elgin Community College and South Suburban College.

Gwendolyn Limbach teaches English at Pace University in New York City, where she also tutors in academic writing. She holds a master's degree from Pace University. She has lectured at various conferences across the country on *Harry Potter* and feminism.

Dave Jones is a writing and literature teacher at several colleges and universities in Kentucky and Indiana. He has published research on videogames as narrative devices. He currently researches narrative and rhetoric in games, online media, and participatory cultures. He holds an M.A. in English from Morehead State University 2003 and is currently a Ph.D. student in Rhetoric and Textual Studies at Old Dominion University

INDEX

Other Zossima Press Titles

C. S. Lewis

C. S. Lewis: Views From Wake Forest
Michael Travers, editor

Contains sixteen scholarly presentations from the international C. S. Lewis convention in Wake Forest, NC. Walter Hooper shares his important essay "Editing C. S. Lewis," a chronicle of publishing decisions after Lewis' death in 1963. Other contributors include James Como and Sanford Schwartz.

"Scholars from a variety of disciplines address a wide range of issues. The happy result is a fresh and expansive view of an author who well deserves this kind of thoughtful attention." Diana Pavlac Glyer, author of *The Company They Keep: C. S. Lewis and J.R.R. Tolkien as Writers in Community.*

Why I Believe in Narnia:
33 Essays & Reviews on the Life & Work of C. S. Lewis
By James Como

Chapters range from reviews of critical books, documentaries and movies to evaluations of Lewis' books to biographical analysis. In addition to close-up looks, Como reflects on the "big picture" of the most important contributions Lewis has made, not just in literature, but as a social philosopher and reformer. An invaluable tool for appreciating the breadth and depth of Lewis' thinking.

"A valuable, wide-ranging collection of essays by one of the best informed and most astute commentators on Lewis' work and ideas." Peter Schakel, author *Imagination & the Arts in C. S. Lewis*

C. S. Lewis & Philosophy as a Way of Life
A Comprehensive Historical Examination of his Philosophical Thoughts
By Adam Barkman

C. S. Lewis, renowned Christian apologist and beloved author of childen's novels, is rarely thought of as a "philosopher" per se despite having both studied and taught philosophy for several years at Oxford. Moreover, Lewis's long journey to Christianity was essentially philosophical – passing through seven different stages. Barkman incorporates previously unexplored treasures from Lewis's unpublished philosophy lecture notes, lost philosophical essays, and hand-written annotations from copies of his philosophical books, such as Aristotle's *Ethis* and Augustine's *City of God* to help chronicle his journey. This 624 page book is an invaluable reference for C. S. Lewis scholars and fans alike.

George MacDonald

Diary of an Old Soul & The White Page Poems
George MacDonald and Betty Aberlin

In 1880, George MacDonald, the Scottish poet, novelist and preacher, published *A Book of Strife in the Form of the Diary of an Old Soul*. The first edition of this book of daily poems included a blank page opposite each page of poems. Readers were invited to write their own reflections on the "white page." MacDonald wrote: "Let your white page be ground, my print be seed, growing to golden ears, that faith and hope may feed." Betty Aberlin responded to MacDonald's invitation with daily poems of her own.

Betty Aberlin's close readings of George MacDonald's verses and her thoughtful responses to them speak clearly of her poetic gifts and spiritual intelligence. Luci Shaw, poet

George MacDonald: Literary Heritage and Heirs
Roderick McGillis

It has been 15 years since Roderick McGillis edited *For the Childlike*, a landmark collection of essays about George MacDonald's writings. This latest collection of 14 essays sets a new standard that will influence MacDonald studies for many more years. George MacDonald experts are increasingly evaluating his entire corpus within the nineteenth century context. This volume provides further evidence that MacDonald will eventually emerge from the restrictive and somewhat misleading reputation of being C. S. Lewis' spiritual "master."

This comprehensive collection represents the best of contemporary scholarship on George MacDonald. Rolland Hein, author of *George MacDonald: Victorian Mythmaker.*

In the Near Loss of Everything:
George MacDonald's Son in America
Dale Wayne Slusser

In the summer of 1887, George MacDonald's son Ronald, newly engaged to artist Louise Blandy, sailed from England to America to teach school. The next summer he returned to England to marry Louise and bring her back to America. On August 27, 1890, Louise died leaving him with an infant daughter. Ronald once described losing a beloved spouse as "the near loss of everything". Dale Wayne Slusser unfolds this poignant story with unpublished letters and photos that give readers a glimpse into the close-knit MacDonald family. Also included is Ronald's essay about his father, *George MacDonald: A Personal Note*, plus a selection from Ronald's 1922 fable, *The Laughing Elf,* about the necessity of both sorrow and joy in life.

Harry Potter

Harry Potter & Imagination:
The Way Between Two Worlds
Travis Prinzi

"What we achieve inwardly will change outer reality." Those words, written by Plutarch and quoted by J.K. Rowling her 2008 Harvard commencement speech, sum up both the importance of the *Harry Potter* series and the argument of Travis Prinzi's analysis of the best-selling books in *Harry Potter & Imagination: The Way Between Two Worlds*. Imaginative literature places a reader between two worlds: the story world and the world of daily life, and challenges this reader to imagine and to act for a better world. Starting with discussion of Harry Potter's more important themes, *Harry Potter & Imagination* takes readers on a journey through the transformative power of those themes for both the individual and for culture by placing Rowling's series in its literary, historical, and cultural contexts.

Deathly Hallows Lectures
John Granger

In *The Deathly Hallows Lectures*, John Granger reveals the finale's brilliant details, themes and meanings. Even the most ardent of *Harry Potter* fans will be surprised by and delighted with the Granger's explanations of the three dimensions of meaning in *Deathly Hallows*. Ms. Rowling has said that alchemy sets the "parameters of magic" in the series; after reading the chapter-length explanation of *Deathly Hallows* as the final stage of the alchemical Great Work, the serious reader will understand how important literary alchemy is in understanding Rowling's artistry and accomplishment.

Repotting Harry Potter:
A Professor's Book-by-Book Guide for the Serious Re-Reader
James W. Thomas

A professor of literature for over thirty years, Dr. James W. Thomas takes us on a tour through the *Potter* books in order to enjoy them in different ways upon subsequent readings. Re-readers will be pleasantly surprised at what they may have missed in the books and at what secrets Rowling has hidden for us to uncover as we revisit these stories. The professor's informal discussions focus on puns, humor, foreshadowing, literary allusions, narrative techniques, and other aspects of the *Potter* books that are hard-to-see on the hurried first or fifth reading. Dr. Thomas's light touch proves that a "serious" reading of literature can be fun.

Breinigsville, PA USA
14 September 2010
245409BV00003B/24/P